On Editing

HELEN CORNER-BRYANT

AND

KATHRYN PRICE

On Editing

How to edit your novel the professional way

First published in Great Britain in 2018 by John Murray Learning.
An Hachette UK company.
Copyright © Helen Corner-Bryant and Kathryn Price 2018
The rights of Helen Corner-Bryant and Kathryn Price to be identified as the Authors of
the Work has been asserted by them in accordance with the Copyright, Designs and Patents
Act 1988.
Database right Hodder & Stoughton (makers)

A catalogue record for this book is available from the British Library.

Paperback ISBN 978 1473 66668 9
eBook ISBN 978 1473 66669 6

1

The publisher has used its best endeavours to ensure that any website addresses referred to
in this book are correct and active at the time of going to press. However, the publisher and
the author have no responsibility for the websites and can make no guarantee that a site will
remain live or that the content will remain relevant, decent or appropriate.

The publisher has made every effort to mark as such all words which it believes to be
trademarks. The publisher should also like to make it clear that the presence of a word in
the book, whether marked or unmarked, in no way affects its legal status as a trademark.

Every reasonable effort has been made by the publisher to trace the copyright holders of
material in this book. Any errors or omissions should be notified in writing to the publisher,
who will endeavour to rectify the situation for any reprints and future editions.

Typeset by Cenveo® Publisher Services.

Printed and bound in Great Britain by CPI Group (UK) Ltd., Croydon CR0 4YY
Hachette UK's policy is to use papers that are natural, renewable and recyclable products and
made from wood grown in sustainable forests. The logging and manufacturing processes are
expected to conform to the environmental regulations of the country of origin.

Carmelite House
50 Victoria Embankment
London
EC4Y 0DZ
www.hodder.co.uk

Contents

Foreword

This book, in its original form, was *Write A Blockbuster And Get It Published* by Helen Corner and Lee Weatherly and it was published as part of the world-renowned *Teach Yourself* series.

Since this first came out, and over the decades I've run Cornerstones – a world-leading literary consultancy – we've worked with thousands of writers, and through this experience we've refined our techniques, examined how best to communicate them and delved deeper into what brings a novel to life and gives it that page-turning bestseller quality. With Lee's blessing, I reverted the rights and teamed up with my editor-in-chief and Cornerstones veteran Kathryn Price to look again at what we had. Gathering valuable insights from my US managing editor Michele Rubin, we set about writing *On Editing: How to edit your novel the professional way*.

I'm delighted to say that John Murray bought it back, and it is now their flagship creative writing title in the *Teach Yourself* series. This is a comprehensive exploration of structural editing tools and techniques: perfect for the debut author looking to raise their writing to the next level, for the published writer wanting a refresher, and for the would-be industry editor.

Editing is often seen as the boring bit. Authors find it difficult, daunting, restrictive. When you hear a writer say they enjoy self-editing as much as writing, you might wonder how this could be. How have they learned to embrace their critical voices, face their doubts head-on and know that they can edit fearlessly?

It became apparent to us that self-editing is a transformative process: not just a set of rules but also the exhilarating point where a writer's creativity and instinct meets their technique and self-discipline.

We want to give you that same confidence: the ability to trust your inner critics and let them guide you; the courage to give your creative side the freedom to fly.

We hope you'll dip into this book when you need reminding how to structure a plot that keeps its tension throughout; how to bring characters to life; or how to hone an effective query letter or synopsis. Most of all, we hope it will take your book into bestseller territory and beyond.

Acknowledgements

I'd like to sincerely thank Kathryn Price who wrote much of this while looking after two young children. She's an extraordinary colleague and mother to boot. My husband and son for bearing with me while I've been writing and editing away. Right now, I'm supposed to be at the tank museum but I have a deadline to deliver this book. I'll make it up to you both! My editors and the team – whose expertise always teaches me new things – we're all nerds here at Cornerstones and love swapping notes. Michele Rubin, whose insights are invaluable and who shares my dream to bridge the markets where possible and help authors. Lee Weatherly (award-winning writer many times in her own right) who ran Kids' Corner many moons ago. Without Lee our teaching practices would not be what they are today. And to my publisher, Jonathan Shipley: it feels like I've come home.

And finally to our authors, editors, and the inner editor in you: we love working with you.

Helen Corner-Bryant

I'd like to thank Helen, first and foremost, for bringing me on board and giving me the opportunity to share my passion for editing with a wider audience. From the moment we met, 15 years ago, Helen has supported, challenged and championed me. The world needs more bosses like her.

My husband, Mark, who shares my love of stories and is astonishingly tolerant when I ruin them for him by picking holes in them or correctly predicting what's about to happen. My lovely boys, who are just starting to learn that stories don't magically appear out of nowhere and it's actually somebody's job to make them up! And my parents, for always reading to me and teaching me that stories are about more than just the words on the page.

Finally I'd like to say a special thanks to all the Cornerstones editors (including those, like Lee, who Helen has already thanked). Your collective knowledge and expertise is awe-inspiring and together I think we make a team that really is greater than the sum of its parts.

Kathryn Price

Meet the authors

Helen Corner-Bryant, whose expertise on submission and the publishing process forms Part II of this book, spent a number of years in editorial at Penguin before setting up Cornerstones Literary Consultancy in 1998. Cornerstones is known for teaching self-editing techniques, providing feedback, scouting for agents and launching writers. In 2016, she opened Cornerstones US, creating the world's first transatlantic literary consultancy. Helen is a guest lecturer at leading universities including UCL Centre for Publishing and the Columbia Publishing Course at Oxford. She loves helping authors get a step closer towards achieving their dreams, whether that's to become a better writer, acquire an agent, get published, or hit the bestseller list.

Kathryn Price achieved a first in English Literature from UCL and then worked in literary agencies for three years before joining Cornerstones as managing editor in 2005. There she honed her passion for editing, and for teaching the skills and techniques that she breaks down in Part I of this book. She went on to become co-partner of Cornerstones and now works closely with authors at all stages of their writing journey in her role as editor-in-chief. She believes that editing should be an essential – and enjoyable – part of the writing process, helping authors to realize their creative vision in its purest, clearest form.

Michele Rubin, whose insights into the US market are featured in Part II, was a Senior Literary Agent at Writers House for 25 years where she represented, among other projects, The Estate of Martin Luther King, Jr., founding the King Legacy Imprint at Beacon Press in 2010. She left agenting in 2013 to work full-time as a freelance editor, writer, ghostwriter, and facilitator of writing workshops. In 2016 Michele took over as Managing Editor for Cornerstones US, mentoring authors across the globe aimed at the US market.

Part 1
Editing your novel

I

Getting started

When you decide to pursue your writing professionally, things get serious. But there are plenty of insider tricks you can use to keep your energy high and your creative juices flowing. By thinking carefully about genre whilst keeping your Big Idea in mind, you can clarify your vision for the novel and improve your chances of successfully targeting readers. If you start the editing process with this level of focus, the rest should follow smoothly.

So you've written a novel…

…Or maybe you're in the middle of editing one; or you're just about to begin a first draft. The chances are, if you've picked up this book, you're serious about writing and you don't need teaching how to 'be a writer'. You're thinking about taking it to the next level – hopefully, publication.

There are many reasons people write, and whilst publication/financial reward tends to be high on the list, it's not always the biggest motivation, at least initially. Though everyone's heard about authors who've hit the big time (at some point most writers allow themselves to daydream about success – and why not?!) these tend to be the exception rather than the rule. Authors write, first and foremost, because they're inspired: like most creative endeavours, it's something you're driven to do.

But the next step, *becoming good at it*, demands a mixture of imagination, talent, hard work, and craft. The craft is what this section of the book aims to teach: the ability to analyse what you've produced with an objective eye; the potential problems to watch out for, and some options for how to fix them.

This book can be used at any stage of the writing process: as a set of guidelines and tools to enable you to start writing from scratch, or as a set of principles to follow when working back through your text and redrafting. Wherever the techniques and tools are applied, you will be using publishing-level principles to produce writing you can be proud of.

Throughout the book, we illustrate some of the techniques by reference to other published works – these are all listed at the back of the book should you wish to investigate them further.

What's the Big Idea?

If you're thinking ahead to publication, you've probably done some research and submitted your book a few times already. You might be starting to realize how market-driven the industry is; the extent to which publishers need to know where what you've written might fit on their lists and, eventually, in bookshops. And the bottom line: how well it might sell. It can be hard, in these circumstances, to hold onto your original reasons for writing: your passion, your motivation, your Big Idea.

The term **high concept** is often used to describe a novel that feels genuinely fresh and ground-breaking; that publishers and readers simply can't ignore. However, it's not a quality you can force or copy, so it's best to focus on exploring an idea that's close to your heart. Sometimes studying trends can be helpful, but publishing timescales are so long that what's fashionable now might be saturated by the time your book makes it to the shelves (a year to 18 months in the future; longer if you're still looking for an agent). But if your novel is born from a genuine love for the subject and characters, this will shine through in the writing even if the subject isn't currently popular.

Writers are often asked where they get their inspiration, and generally it's a difficult question to answer, because there's no magic formula. You might be having a conversation about something stupid your dog did, and suddenly there's a picture book concept sparkling in your mind. You might be reflecting on the death of a loved one and find yourself dreaming about a parallel universe where people can't die. Great ideas come from a combination of experience, observation, and imagination, so the best idea to work on is the idea that's wholly YOURS – the one that only you could have written.

That said, you don't have to have lived through something yourself to be able to write about it – sometimes basing your fiction on fact can make the act of writing harder – but you do have to be able and willing to put yourself in someone else's place. Perhaps the real pre-requisite for writing fiction is a having a knack for watching, understanding, and unpicking the world around you: an interest in what makes people tick; what makes them extraordinary.

Knowing your genre

You may have already given this some thought. But perhaps not – just as some new authors begin without the end goal of publication in sight, so many will start out without a clear sense of *what* they're writing. The idea and the characters were what got them started; considerations like plot and genre came second.

Having a clearly defined genre can be helpful when it comes to pitching to publishers and booksellers; on the other hand, breaking the mould can result in a book that feels new and zeitgeisty. However, it's a question of making an informed choice. If your book feels like a little bit of a lot of things – commencing as romantic fiction, dipping into fantasy, concluding with a supernatural twist – this can be a sign of poor planning and lack of market understanding. And you risk missing out on tapping into a genre audience: imagine if you're a fan of romance coming to this book, only to be confounded by the direction it takes. You probably won't recommend it and might even give it a bad review.

Just as a lack of genre definition within one book can be off-putting, so an author who dabbles in **too many genres within their oeuvre** can ring alarm bells. Authors who submit a crime novel but mention that they also write comedy for children and historical fiction might appear to be casting their net wide in the hope that at least one of these projects will appeal. This can suggest a lack of faith in your writing and commitment to your chosen genre/audience. If you do get one of these books accepted, your publisher may expect you to continue writing in the same vein for a few years – that's how you build a fan base. So you – and they – need to know that you are writing what you most want to write.

The best way to decide on genre is usually to think about what you prefer to read. Research and background reading will be a pleasure rather than a chore; you'll already understand the demands and conventions of the market; you'll probably have an innate sense of how existing authors get it right and wrong. If you don't like, or know, your chosen genre, this can make it difficult to see what works and why. We've spoken with authors who've decided (for instance) to write children's fiction despite having never read a contemporary children's book. Their knowledge of the genre is based on what they read when they were young, so it's now very dated. Or, sometimes authors tell us that they don't want to muddy their own story by reading too much. That's a reasonable argument, but if you haven't read recent fiction in your genre, how can you know whether your writing is likely to appeal to its current readership?

This doesn't mean you *can't* write in a genre you're unfamiliar with, but you'll need to do a lot more research. If you're inspired by an idea that seems most at home in the sci-fi section, but you're not a sci-fi fan, you have the choice either to make your premise fit into another genre – which can be uncomfortable – or to make yourself as much of an expert as you can in that area, bearing in mind the myriad subgenres that often comprise one major genre. Resources like fanzines, journals, online enthusiasts, conventions etc can be almost as useful as published novels.

You may be reading this section with a sinking heart, realizing that you haven't given the genre much consideration. It may not matter – sometimes genre blurring can be good, and certain genres are more forgiving of crossover material than others. With the growth of online writing media, writers and readers are increasingly making their own rules. *Fifty Shades of Grey* started out as *Twilight* fanfiction, and ended up spawning a huge erotica subgenre, and, indeed, fanfiction of its own.

But let's say you decide that you need to pin down your book's genre more securely. Perhaps the main thrust is cosy crime, and there are a couple of scenes which, now you think about it, seem too gory for this market. Can you cut or amend the sections that don't fit? Or, maybe you wanted to write a gritty thriller but realize that the language and tone you've used feels too florid and sentimental. Again that's a relatively straightforward editorial process: making sure your lexicon is in line with your genre. Often, it's a question of choosing a primary genre – the strongest element in the book – and letting that guide your structure and focus, with cross-genre material playing a secondary role.

Ultimately, if the story works brilliantly then it's not going to matter if it breaks a few rules. However, knowing what those rules are means you can be clear about what you hope to achieve. Genre isn't just a tiresome set of strictures designed to make books fit into pigeon holes: it's a way of setting expectations and (sometimes) of turning those expectations on their head. It's a way of defining stories that puts your fictional world in context, so you can feed off the imaginations of the wonderful writers who've come before you. And, if you're successful, it's a way of tapping into a huge and loyal fan base to boost your sales.

'The dog ate my homework', and other excuses

Whether you're just beginning a new draft or you're already editing, it can seem like a mammoth task (and that's before you start the process of submitting, rejection, filtering feedback, rewriting and resubmission). Writing may be something you love passionately, but as soon as you start taking it seriously it can begin to feel like hard work. That's the reality of wanting to master your craft.

It sounds counter-intuitive to find reasons to avoid something that you love, but it happens a lot, even to successful published writers. The human brain is remarkably good at refusing to do as it's told. Fortunately there are habits you can get into, tricks you can use, and good working practices to help you maintain energy and focus, and give your writing the time it deserves.

Make space for yourself

Virginia Woolf wrote memorably about this need in *A Room of One's Own*. You might not require a whole room, but you do want a place where the chatter of modern life – children, laundry, partners, TVs, phones, emails – can be kept at bay.

Write

This might sound obvious, but it's amazing how many authors will say, *but I haven't written anything for a while*... Even if you only have half an hour, even if you have nothing to say, do it every day, whether you want to or not. Make it a part of your daily routine; get your family on side so that they support you and treat your writing time as sacrosanct.

Find a writing group or buddy

Writing can be lonely, and forging links with other writers can keep your inspiration and energy high. They can give you feedback (though the same rules apply as to getting feedback from family and friends – not all feedback is created equal, and for this reason it's useful if a writing group contains a mix of professional and non-professional authors); they can brainstorm ideas with you; and be your cheerleaders. Often, the very fact that someone is expecting you to have written something by this time next week will force you to do it! You can find a list of UK writers' groups at www.nawg.co.uk, check with your local library or bookshop to see if they know of one in your area, or start your own.

Set yourself goals

These don't have to be big: it might be as achievable as *write a chapter by the end of this month* or as ambitious as *finish a novel by Christmas*. It might be setting yourself a target word count for each day's writing. Don't worry if you think you're churning out garbage – that's what the editing process is for. The main thing is to take the mountain you're trying to climb and turn it into manageable hillocks.

Trick your brain

Try finishing your day's work in the middle of a scene that you're loving – you'll come back to it the next day raring to go. Or, if you've finished a scene, start a new one that you can then rejoin afresh. If you're at the editing stage, don't feel you have to start at the start – ease yourself into the revision with some new material you know you need to write. This will help you recapture the excitement you felt when you were creating the original draft.

Listen to your emotions

If you're finding a scene difficult, it might be because it's heading in the wrong direction. Maybe the character is acting in a way that isn't true to them because you need them to for the sake of plot. If something *feels* wrong, there's a good chance that it *is* wrong.

Ride your energy

Experienced authors sometimes edit as they go, but when you're still learning it's often better to maintain momentum rather than stopping too frequently to read over and change what you've written. (For this reason, it can also be counter-productive to seek feedback too early.) On the other hand, if you've been working on the same thing for a while, perhaps over several drafts, and your enthusiasm is waning, don't force it: take a break, and work on something different. If you're not feeling passionate about the idea this may come through in the writing.

Attend a writing course or workshop, or seek professional feedback

There are many writing courses, consultancies and assessment services, often of varying quality, so do some research before settling on one that feels right for the level you're at, the genre you're writing in, and the way you like to work (some services involve little or no written feedback and some provide detailed editorial notes; some involve a read-through of the entire manuscript and some don't; some automatically offer face-time and for some this costs extra). Going to conferences can also be a good way of meeting other writers, getting yourself and your writing into the public arena, and connecting with the industry.

Enter competitions

These are daunting, but a useful proving ground for both your work and your resilience. The more you submit, the more accustomed you'll get to rejection and receiving criticism, and the more you'll begin to treat it as an exercise in profession-alism rather than a personal, emotional rollercoaster. And if you're successful then you've begun the vital process of making a name for yourself.

Reach an audience

It can be disheartening to have a finished story that isn't being read. It might be that you're submitting, waiting for responses, and need a confidence boost; or you may have decided it's time to move on to something else – but you'd still like to get the story out there. Consider posting on online forums, blogging, or (if you're a children's writer for example) doing readings at schools and libraries. This will allow you to speak to your readership and give your writing a life outside your head.

The things they don't tell you

There are some aspects of the writing and editing process that you may only find out by living them for yourself, often making mistakes as you go. It can be tempting, for instance, to tell anyone and everyone about the brilliant idea you've had. **Keeping an idea secret** allows you to possess it, and it to possess you; share it with too many other people and you risk talking the story out of your system.

Similarly, **don't start writing too soon** – let an idea build until you absolutely *have* to write it. Plotting too carefully in advance can have the same effect, although for many authors it's an essential process. Find an approach that works for you, where you have a good idea of the structure in mind before you start, without planning so meticulously that there's nothing left to discover.

Many writers struggle to comprehend the length of time it can take – not just the publication process, but the act of mastering your writing and finding the right story to launch you. For every author who's had an 'overnight success' there will be literally thousands who've worked for years to become brilliant. *And some of these authors still won't be published.* Don't put pressure on yourself because you haven't made it yet. **Taking your time** will allow your writing to develop, mature, and find its true path.

This also applies to submitting: one of the most common errors we see at Cornerstones is authors sending work out to the trade before it's ready. It's natural to want to share your book – but is it definitely finished? Have you set your draft aside for a month, then come back to it? Is it absolutely the best it can be? Sending out a book too early means you might miss your one opportunity to impress an agent or editor, and needlessly exposes you to dispiriting form rejections. So **hang fire until you know you're ready**.

And finally, **don't give up your day job**. However tempting the writer's life might be, you still need an income to see you through the writing process, and even if you are lucky enough to quickly secure a deal, you may not be paid immediately, or highly. Most professional writers also have other sources of income, so don't quit until you have to because writing dead-lines and commitments demand it. Work keeps you grounded and connected with the real world, gives you a sense of success and identity that doesn't rely on your writing, and helps to remind you why you write.

For many authors, the point where you start considering publication is the first point at which you start thinking about the *process* of writing – *why* you've written, *what* you've written, and *how* you've written it. When finishing a draft, and feel-ing excited about the possibilities, it can be frustrating to be told to slow down, question your choices, and edit objectively. However, accepting the necessity of this procedure – indeed, learning to relish the challenge – is one of the most important steps in the writer's journey. If you have talent, inspiration, ded-ication, and above all a willingness to learn and develop, then there's a good chance you've got what it takes.

2

Creating (and controlling) your characters

Time to take a good look at your cast list. Have you got the right number of characters, and are they sufficiently rounded and real? Along with common problems to watch out for, this chapter contains some top techniques to help you delve deeper, using both your external description and what's below the surface of your characters to build nuance and subtext. By starting to think about your main character's core problem and goal, you'll pave the way for straightforward plotting further down the line.

My character made me do it…

Where do memorable characters come from? The Harry Potters; the Holden Caulfields; the Tyrion Lannisters? Authors often speak of characters 'springing into life' fully formed and leading the way, and in some respects that's the dream scenario: a plot that's guided by your characters' true goals and desires is unlikely to feel forced or implausible. That said, it's not always advisable to let your characters take control! Whether you're an author who likes to 'create' your characters or one who prefers to 'get to know them', most of the time you'll need to put in some solid leg-work – both into building your characters and, as the story gets going, into keeping them on track.

Getting acquainted

There are a few things you can do from the off to make sure your characters feel rounded and real. Become a keen observer of people: the twitchy young man sitting next to you at the bus stop, muttering to himself, earphones plugged in; the shop-keeper you see every day who never speaks but always smiles, showing yellow, crooked teeth; the cousin who you barely know but always overshares the lurid details of her personal life.

Just like ideas, characters require a little input from real life and from imagination. Ask yourself what lies beneath the surface, and don't settle for the most obvious answer. Look at the three scenarios above – as well as what you can see outwardly, are there any additional details you can guess at or imagine? What might they be carrying in their pockets? Perhaps the young man is listening to heavy metal or rap music, like you first thought; or perhaps he's got a French language programme on his phone, and that's why he's whispering. Maybe the sexually adventurous cousin has a tattoo on her bum that she's always bragging about but has never shown you. Does it really exist? Maybe she's not as wild as she wants you to think?

Apply this same process of working outwards (and inwards) to the things you can see. *Why* does the shop assistant have terrible teeth? Because he's addicted to the lemon sherberts he sells (fun detail but not especially illuminating)? Maybe he's afraid of going to the dentist for some reason (potentially intriguing psychological detail)? Perhaps he's fled a despotic regime after being tortured, and smiles permanently because he's desperate to blend in. Practise sketching in people's back-stories and it will become a skill that filters down to your writing, helping you portray your characters in a deep, nuanced way rather than just relying on surface detail.

There are lots of other tricks and tips you can use to help create characters. The following exercises are widely taught, with a few of our own twists; we won't go into them in too much detail, but encourage you to play around with a couple and find out which one/s work best for you.

- Note one or two **key words** that sum up what your character is about – the first characteristics that spring to mind. Is he/she *organized* and *considerate*? Now choose some related words: perhaps she's also *tidy, thoughtful, self-possessed, secretive, a good listener, introverted*. Add some opposing traits. If you've written 'She is organized and considerate,' add the word 'but…' and see what comes. You might get something like, *She is organized and considerate, but doesn't like it when her routine is upset.* Continue the exercise using pairs of your related words: *She is self-possessed and a good listener, but finds it hard to make her own voice heard.* Finally, delve deeper: look for explanations. She is organized and considerate – why? *Because she grew up in a chaotic household and ended up looking after her siblings a lot.* Or, *She is self-possessed and a good listener, but finds it hard to make her own voice heard because she's so used to putting other people's needs first.* This exercise can help to lead you away from two-dimensional thinking where characters are either good or bad.
- Write a **character questionnaire** including basics (age, sex, appearance, name, etc) and more advanced characteristics (their earliest memory; things that make them cry; a secret they've never told anyone). At this stage, ask yourself if the character is going to be appropriate for the genre you're writing in. For romance or chick-lit, for instance, your hero needs to

be sexy. For a children's story, your character should be the same age or slightly older than your target readership.

- **Switch POV** – if you normally write in the third person, try a few paragraphs in the 'I' voice, stepping deeply inside your character's head. Perhaps you're an author who struggles with inner voice, and first person might help you 'hear' your character's thoughts. On the other hand, if you normally prefer first person, and have trouble keeping your character's inner monologue in check, pull back into distant third; try viewing the character purely externally. How does their behaviour come across to others? Do they wear their heart on their sleeve or seem aloof and disconnected? When you delve within the character again, feed back some of these external dynamics into their own self-perception: are they self-conscious, aware of how other characters think about them, or too wrapped up in their own thoughts and feelings to notice?

- **Interview your character** as though you were writing an article about them for a magazine. What would you ask them to get them to reveal themselves? Would they respond best to humour or a more direct approach? Would you present them sensationally, like a tabloid, or seriously, like the weekend section of a broadsheet? Would they lie to you and if so, why?

- Consider referring to the **enneagram** or similar psychological models of personalities (there are a number of these out there, usually based on psychoanalysis techniques). These can offer surprising insights into how people conform to specific **types**, or sets of characteristics, as well as flagging up particular fears, weaknesses, strengths and preoccupations that are associated with each type.

Knowing which approaches to *avoid* can also be useful, particularly when you get to the self-editing stage: the point at which you're likely to be looking at your characters more analytically. Look out for the following warning signs:

- Do your characters seem very **black and white**, either wholly good or bad? If so, go back to some of the exercises above and imbue them with more nuance and depth. Look again at their inner lives and motivations.

- Do they act in **uncharacteristic or inconsistent** ways, lurching from one extreme personality trait to another? We worked with an author whose main character was a lot of things: sometimes righteous and honourable; sometimes back-stabbing and cowardly; sometimes determined to stick up for herself; elsewhere, allowing herself to be bullied and manipulated. We decided that there was a disconnect between the way the character liked to think about herself and the way she *acted*. We tried to make the character more self-aware, imbuing her inner voice with more understanding of the fact that whilst she aimed high, she didn't always make it. What was originally coming across as inconsistency became the basis of an intriguing, conflicted character.

- Are they **clichéd** (are your good characters wise and beautiful; are your baddies ugly and sneering; are your country characters ruddy-cheeked and wholesome)? Avoid the obvious choice: as with stylistic clichés, discussed elsewhere, anything that trips off the tongue too readily is probably something that's been done before. And, though there's arguably a case for using archetypes in certain genres, when you're trying to impress industry readers, originality and freshness is crucial.

- Have you 'told' us what your character/s are like, rather than bringing their personalities to life dramatically, through what they say and do? We'll talk about **Show not Tell** in Chapter 8, but a good technique is to apply this to characterization as though you were meeting someone at a party. If they say, *I'm not boasting, right, but people are always saying how funny I am! I'm generous, too…* then you probably won't believe them, or stick around to find out if it's true. But if they spend all evening making you laugh, then pay for your taxi home, you'll have seen their attributes for yourself and got to know them in the process. In real life, we can only truly begin to understand what someone's like by observing how they act. Likewise, in fiction the strongest, most enduring personalities are those which are gradually revealed through their actions, their dialogue, and the choices they make.

- Do your characters always **reveal their true intentions**, rather than dissembling, manipulating, and feigning emotions they don't feel – as we do in real life? Even 'nice' people (and characters) aren't always honest with themselves and others, and sometimes the most interesting and convincing characterization happens when characters are trying to hide their real natures. Look at the above analogy again. Suppose the person you meet at the party sees you into your taxi, but at the last moment tries to push their way in. Suppose you're waiting for the loo, about to leave the party, and you overhear them telling someone else, *I'm in there!* A sudden revelation that someone is not who they seemed to be can throw an episode into a new light, providing fresh sources of tension and conflict and challenging our perceptions both of them, and of ourselves; of our own ability to judge.

- In the same vein, do your characters always **speak their minds**? Dialogue that's too 'on the nose' – where characters say exactly what they think and feel – tends to be unrealistic, but it also robs you of the opportunity to exploit the tension between text and subtext; between what's said and what's not. A conversation where the character's inner voice is in direct opposition to what they're saying outwardly will go a long way to setting up inner, emotional tension: that special conflict that comes from within a character, rather than being driven by external forces, and that provides the main engine for challenge and change.

- Have you based your characters too closely on **real people**? This is generally a bad idea – not least because you can potentially get into trouble if people recognize themselves. And by basing your fiction on real life you tie yourself in to one way of presenting a character; you wed yourself to 'the true person' and aren't able to fictionalize them, play with them, and get beneath their skin in the way that you need to. You may also find that you're too kind to them… and as we'll discuss later, you do need to be prepared to put your characters through the wringer.

Paint me a picture

Description is your tool for bringing a character to life visually, so that we can 'see' them in our mind's eye. As discussed above, what's going on beneath the surface is more important, but good, sensory description nevertheless fulfils a vital role. We'll cover description in more depth in Chapter 6, but a few of the basics are set out here.

Again, it's important to **avoid the obvious choice**. Commonplace adjectives like *tall, blond, fat* and *beautiful* might be factually accurate, but they don't create an image that will zing off the page and stay in the mind. Zero in on more unusual, memorable features: the peculiar shape of a character's nose; the way their hair gets in their eyes; the mole on their top lip that they're obviously embarrassed about.

We need to know the basics like how tall they are too, but if you can avoid stating this outright – instead, showing us how they stoop under a doorway or hunch their shoulders, or walk with their chest out as though trying to seem bigger – the picture you're creating will remain **active and ongoing**, rather than being an isolated vignette that we're less likely to recall.

Remember that description doesn't just refer to what a character looks like: consider all the **other qualities** that go to make up our outward impression of someone. Their tone of voice might be husky, so that other characters have to lean in to hear them; they might have a physical tic like clicking their fingers whilst they speak, or twiddling their hair; they might move through crowds with head bowed as though trying not to be noticed, or shoulder people out of the way. The more thought you give to these details, the more vividly your character will spring to life.

What's the problem?

One of the main things that marks out a main character as memorable, whilst also being a key component of your **narrative drive**, is the problem they face, or the goal they're attempting to achieve. Almost every main character in the history of the novel will have started out as someone tackling a problem, who is forced into unfamiliar and testing circumstances because of their attempts to resolve it. This is, quite simply, the basis of fiction. Without a problem, goal, or conflict, there can be no story.

This question is tied in with plotting, so it's something we'll discuss in more detail in Chapter 4. However, when you're at the planning (and editing) stages, you should be asking yourself what your main character's problem is. It might be something as dramatic and sensational as having been framed for a murder they didn't commit, or, for much younger fiction, something as apparently innocuous as not wanting to go to bed: the problem's power, and the impetus it provides, will come from how **personal and meaningful it is to the protagonist**.

For example, consider fantasies in the Narnia model, where characters are summoned to an alternative world because it is their destiny to save it from a source of evil. On the surface, the destruction of an entire world does seem like a big problem, but because the protagonist has had their fate imposed upon them without any reason for becoming involved, and doesn't have a personal stake in the action, plots like these often lack tension.

On the other hand, when a problem *matters* to the protagonist – Thomas Cromwell in Hilary Mantel's *Wolf Hall*, for example, attempting to do his best by a king whose actions seem unforgivable; the future of his family and even his own life at stake – a story gains emotional pull, and a wide, potentially impersonal scope becomes something intimate and deeply powerful. Make things as difficult as possible for your main character – going easy on them won't result in page-turning fiction. The more serious the repercussions of failure, the greater the tension.

Sometimes it's possible to have too many problems or goals, or for these to stand in opposition, and that's something to keep an eye out for during editing, particularly if a story lacks tension in spite of being packed with obstacles. One novel we edited featured a main character whose younger sister had disappeared, and though initially the protagonist was devastated, he quickly got distracted by other, less pressing issues. For 50 pages or so the character barely thought about his sister, instead pursuing other, less emotionally significant tangents. The effects of this were twofold: the initial problem no longer provided narrative drive, because it wasn't present in the character's consciousness; in addition, the character seemed shallow and purposeless – as though he'd forgotten what was important.

The key point here is that you can come up with the most original goal or problem ever, but it must be connected to the character by an unbreakable thread; it must form part of the very fabric of their personality, otherwise it may work against plotting and characterization rather than helping them along.

The protagonist's attempts to solve their problem or achieve their goal are what drives the action – see more in Chapter 4 – but they also underpin the **emotional arc**: the character's journey of development. The problem or goal is fundamentally linked to who the character is – all those details of personality and backstory that you've worked so hard to uncover – often arising as a result of the character's flaws or mistakes. This can be boiled down to: *Because of who they are, the character faces an*

apparently insoluble problem. To solve it, they must change the situa-
tion and in doing so change themselves.

Someone deeply opposed to violence may put themselves in a position where they have to hurt or kill: what actions might they take as a result; where might these actions lead them; how would this experience re-shape them? Or, someone whose fear of commitment has prevented them getting close to previous partners might rush into a monogamous, claustrophobic relationship because they're so desperate to find love: what might this drive them to; how would they need to adapt; would they need to make a choice between losing themselves, or losing the relationship?

The emotional arc will not generally be spelled out on the page. We frequently see this: a character having an epiphany at the end of a novel, where they acknowledge how much they've changed. We all know the cliché, *I've really learned something from this*. Ideally the change should happen gradually and organi-cally, so that we witness the evolution of your character mani-fest in their behaviour and the choices they make. If they do have an epiphany (and we'll discuss this in Chapter 5) then it should be implicit; coming to life through their actions and decisions, rather than explicitly stated.

Finally, try not to substitute plausible character develop-ment for its nemesis: acting inconsistently. Often authors write with the fact that characters need to grow and change weigh-ing heavily on their minds, and of course a certain amount of wavering – within consistent parameters – is a human char-acteristic. However, if a character suddenly does something that doesn't seem like them; changes their mind about an issue they'd previously felt strongly about; or acts in a way that goes against their core personality, this can seem as though you're trying to force change on them. Genuine transitions in emo-tion and attitude take time.

The cast list

Your most important character is, of course, your **protagonist**. The word comes from the Greek and literally translates as 'leader of the action', and this is a great way to look at your main character: whether we like them or not, they need to be proactive, making choices, driving the plot forwards; changing themselves, and their situation, in a dynamic way.

The protagonist is our route into the story so even if we don't like them, we need to empathize with them and find them interesting. Look at the two lead characters in Gillian Flynn's *Gone Girl:* Nick, who's not inherently likeable, manages to capture our interest because of the impossible, emotive situation he finds himself in and because of the secrets he seems to be hiding. On the other hand, Amy, absent from the story but appearing on the page through her diary, is instantly engaging: warm, candid, vulnerable yet sassy … the fact that this characterization turns out to be an act is a deft trick by the author and one of the things that makes the book so successful.

Your **antagonist** is the story's bad guy. Not all stories have one, but it's useful for your main character to have a constant source of pressure and conflict driving them forwards. In some genres the bad guy may be obvious and, occasionally, over-the-top. Though the concept of pure evil is dated nowadays, in crime fiction you'll still find murderers, kidnappers, rapists, torturers … and in children's fiction, larger than life villains like Voldemort, or Lemony Snicket's Count Olaf still regularly make an appearance.

However, if you can, it's best to steer clear of cliché here just as elsewhere, as stereotyped, over-the-top baddies are often too familiar (and even comical) to be truly scary. Watch out for villainesque cackling, over-explaining their crimes, and rubbing their hands! As you do with your main character, think through your antagonist's backstory and motivation to try and piece together why they are who they are. It stops them feeling two-dimensional, and though we don't need to empathize with them in the same way as we do your protagonist (in some circumstances this can be counterproductive) a certain level of sympathy can create an interesting, nuanced dynamic – especially if you're feeling like your characterization is veering towards the black-and-white.

In addition, if an antagonist has a solid emotional motivation for acting malignantly, they're likely to be more menacing: harder to dissuade from their chosen path; harder to reason with. A character who is arbitrarily cruel may be unpredictable – but, a certain amount of predictability is a key way in which you build expectations and raise tension. If we know that a character is likely to act in a certain way because of who they are, the reader will be biting their nails, waiting for the incident that sets off this chain reaction. If the character may do anything at all, at any time, there can be no real suspense.

In other genres, the antagonist might be less obvious, more of a **secondary** or **supporting character** rather than someone who is obviously trying to undermine our main character from the outset. Look at Daniel Cleaver in *Bridget Jones's Diary* (Helen Fielding), or Tyler Durden in *Fight Club* (Chuck Palahniuk). These aren't villains – a romantic lead and the main character's best friend/alter ego, respectively – but they turn out to be acting against our protagonists' best interests in subtle ways, doing things which challenge and pressure them.

Other supporting characters include anyone who has an important role in the plot, and they're worth spending time over because they'll often act as foils for the protagonist – bringing out unexpected qualities, changing and shaping them, and influencing their choices. The bossy, busty best friend, the needy, diet-obsessed mum, the tattooed but sensitive boyfriend, the boss, the psychiatrist … these characters might be painted in almost as much detail as your protagonist and, like your protagonist, they should have their own **arc** – their journey of growth and development that takes place over the course of the story.

Minor characters will make a brief appearance but may not reappear. Sketch these in just enough detail that we can see them vividly, but don't give them undue weight and allow them to take up space in the reader's imagination that's better reserved for your major players. Spending too long describing a minor character can mislead us into thinking they're going to be more important than they are: we try to remember them, and guess at the role they're going to play, and when they don't reappear it can feel like a loose end. The trick with minor characters is to achieve a memorable and plausible, but not overwhelming, picture in a short space of time. Deft brushstrokes of description, without going into too much detail about personality, tend to work best here. You may not even need to give them a name.

You will want to give some thought to the **number** of characters in your cast. Too few, and the world of your novel may feel underpopulated; too many, and you may be asking too much of your reader. We sometimes do an exercise in Cornerstones workshops where we imagine all the characters in a novel in a lifeboat, each having to justify the space they're taking up and getting thrown overboard if they can't. Every character you include should have a clearly defined role – if you can cut characters, or merge them, those who remain will have more room to breathe and develop into real people.

Finally, try not to let your supporting cast take over. Often there's so much baggage attached to the protagonist that they can become overworked, staid and stodgy, whereas the antagonist, for example, free of the constraints of carrying the story, has a more vibrant presence. As you edit, ask yourself if you're spending longer on some of your secondary characters because you're secretly more interested in them or find them more fun to write (this is scarily true with villains). If that's the case, find a way either of bringing some of that energy to your protagonist, or of reworking the plot to allow you to change some roles around.

We mentored an author whose main character seemed weak and ineffectual, whilst her romantic lead was introverted but sensitive and practical, and in spite of not being especially outgoing was stealing the show. She wanted her protagonist to be vulnerable, but no matter how we underpinned this vulnerability with solid psychological motivation, the character was coming across as needy and self-justifying. The comparison to the hero and the dynamic between them wasn't doing the protagonist any favours.

In the end, we decided to try switching personality types, swapping some backstory and rejigging the plot so that the heroine was now the stronger character. Transferred to the heroine, the hero's quiet, thoughtful nature was just enough to create the vulnerability the author was looking for, but without slipping into weakness; in the hero, what had been neediness and self-justification in the heroine evolved and resulted in a man who was unusually in touch with his emotions; less introverted, but sensitive and intriguing in a different way. This had positive repercussions, taking the plot in some unexpected and fruitful directions.

Much as it is appealing to think of our characters as 'real', this needs to be tempered with a healthy dose of pragmatism. If you can't put the thumbscrews on your protagonist because you're too emotionally attached to them, then the story will suffer as a result. If a character isn't pulling their weight or justifying their role, then something needs to be done; whether that's cutting, merging or changing them – no matter how much you like them in their current form. And, if your character's personality simply isn't working, be prepared to take them back to the drawing board – try something you haven't thought of before: change their gender; throw something completely new into their backstory; force them to confront a huge tragedy out of the blue, and see what that does to them.

Perhaps the best way to think of your characters is as a group of actors on a stage. Each has their own role, dictated by the story, and each must inhabit that role fully and deeply, behaving in a way that's consistent with who they are. But you are the director and have the final say, and if you can see that the dynamic on stage isn't working, don't be afraid to give them the boot.

3
Viewpoint – the eyes of your story

The point of view you choose can have a big impact on everything in your story – from its mood and atmosphere through to the way the reader perceives and interprets your characters. Different viewpoints carry different expectations and conventions, and once you've made your choice there are a number of techniques that must work together to ensure a smooth, consistent read. In this chapter we'll look at head-hopping, and how to avoid it, along with some advanced approaches for bringing us as close to your POV characters as possible – aiming to get the reader right under their skin and inside their heads.

Getting some perspective

One of the first choices you'll make is what viewpoint (otherwise known as POV, perspective, or point of view) to tell your story from. Will the main character tell their story themselves, in their own voice? Will you use a third-person narrator, allowing a more objective, externalized perspective on the protagonist? Could you use multiple third-person perspectives, giving us a wide angle on the action and a broad emotional range? Might you employ a secondary character as your narrator – a less common choice that can work well, as in John Irving's *A Prayer for Owen Meany* or, famously, in Emily Brontë's *Wuthering Heights* – giving an alternative first-person view of your main character?

All of these options come with different benefits, drawbacks, conventions and challenges. Each carries expectations, too – for example, there tends to be an innate and often erroneous belief that a first-person narrator will be 'honest' with us, which can be used to your advantage. By making strategic choices about POV, not just in the story as a whole but for individual chapters, you can evoke an entirely different mood around the same material. Imagine a scene where someone is being kidnapped: how would it read differently told from the POV of the person being captured; the kidnapper/s, stalking and springing on their victim; an observer, hiding, too afraid to intervene; an omniscient author? Which perspective would provide the most gripping, tension-packed take on the action?

Viewpoint is a complex area; it uses several techniques which must all work smoothly together. In addition, it can be tempting to randomly break from your chosen POV to give us another character's perspective, drip feed plot and backstory that the POV character wouldn't have access to, or just provide variation. These shifts may seem harmless and you might feel they're working in the best interests of the plot, but they can create a background white noise; as though you're not quite in control of the material. Many readers won't be aware of this consciously, but it can subtly undermine our trust in the story and characters.

So, choose wisely: know the rules, and understand the effects of breaking them. Not all of these effects are bad, and it's not always a question of right and wrong – we'll look at some examples of where changing the game can work. But for now let's focus on the two most common viewpoint choices – first and third – and look at some of their associated techniques and pitfalls.

First person

The 'I' voice is a common choice for authors writing their first book, perhaps because it feels closest to the mode we adopt if we're 'telling stories' in real life. It can also have a powerful immediacy – by getting inside your character's skin it can feel easier to predict how they'd react in any given situation. And there are genres (women's or teen fiction, for instance) where the confidential style, that sense of being best friends with the character that first person can create, works very well.

However, this POV poses specific challenges; indeed, the very aspects that make it a strong choice can also be weaknesses. As we discussed in the previous chapter, it's not always desirable for characters to 'take over', and there tends to be more chance of that happening in first person, where your character's voice can run away with you. A strong voice – that very thing which makes the writing immediate and vibrant – can dominate to the point where plot, structure and the supporting cast get pushed into the background.

Of course, a big voice can be a big asset, too. There are many first-person novels – Mark Twain's *Adventures of Huckleberry Finn*, much of Irvine Welsh's fiction, Russell Hoban's *Riddley Walker*, Emma Donoghue's *Room* – where we remember the narrative voice as much as what happens in the story. But even with these hugely successful novels there can be a subjective element to the reader's response – powerful voices can be very marmitey – and if we don't love it, then the first-person form offers no respite. In addition, letting a character talk to us too much, commentating rather than *doing* things, will often result in flat writing, irrespective of how lively their voice is. So, if your first-person narrator is a big personality, it's crucial to balance this out with nuanced and vivid supporting characters, plenty of action and tension, and an awareness of the need to get the character out of their head and interacting with the world.

Let's look at an example:

> I'd had it up to here with Simon's antics. I was pretty sure he was cheating but I just couldn't prove it. I'd checked his emails enough times, and there were those middle-of-the-night texts that he'd always say were just a wrong number. But then they'd be deleted in the morning – and, honestly, why would you bother? I know I don't delete all those stupid texts offering PPI or whatever. That's why my sodding phone memory's always running out.
>
> Anyway, it got to the point where I knew I was going to have to confront him. I wanted evidence, something I could wave in his face, that he couldn't deny. All I had was a bank statement. Hotel bills; Hermes handbags that I'd never seen; dinners in restaurants I'd never been to. But when I asked him what the hell he thought he was playing at he had the nerve to laugh and say it was all related to work. Work! Can you imagine a scenario in which a software engineer needs to wine and dine someone at Nobu? No, me neither.

This could be considered an effective narrative voice – there's humour; the character's personality comes through; and she confides in a candid, intimate way that ought to draw us in. However, there's a lot of exposition and backstory – much of it peripheral and chatty – and as a result the voice feels breathless and unfocused. The conflict is skimmed over, offering no opportunities for building tension, and what could be a dramatic exchange instead feels like a directionless rant.

Consider instead a scene conveying the same information and emotion in a more immediate way:

I was dithering in the kitchen when Simon's key scraped in the door. The bank statement lay on the pine work-top, wrinkled where I'd screwed it up then unfolded it to read it over and over. I rubbed my hands on my jeans, heart skittering. Why couldn't I have slapped some makeup on, tried to look more together? Right now I was just a sweaty frumpy wife pathetically wait-ing for my ratbag husband to get back from whatever, or whoever, he'd been doing.

He clattered in, shrugging off his jacket and frown-ing as he chucked it onto one of the antique chairs that I'd spent half last summer re-upholstering. He planted a cool dry kiss on my cheek. 'What's for tea? I'm starved.'

'I haven't cooked. I …'

He pulled a face. 'Chinese again then, I guess.'

'Simon.' Couldn't he have at least tried to play nice? I picked up the bank statement, hand trembling. I couldn't let myself be derailed by stupid things like din-ner. As if it mattered! I felt my neck burning, a sense of righteousness making me grind my teeth. 'What the f- what the bloody hell is this?'

He snorted a little laugh out of his nose. 'Is that a trick question?' He spoke in the voice he usually reserved for foreigners or people he'd decided were too dense to bother with. 'It's … a … bank … statement.'

'Don't you dare try to make me look … I mean this!' I shoved the page under his nose. 'This … Look, this handbag. For example. And what about dinner at Nobu?' I'd always wanted to eat there, and he knew that, which somehow made it worse.

The briefest frown crossed his face, like he'd been caught with his hand in the cookie jar, then it was gone. 'Oh come on, you can't think…'

'I knew it! I knew something was going on. All those texts, and you changing your password. Who is she?'

He put a hand on my arm and I tried to wrench myself out of his grip. His nails dug into me.

Then his face softened – that face, I couldn't bear it. Like he felt sorry for me. 'Babe, look at me. I took the handbag back – it just wasn't you. And dinner – I do eat out after work sometimes, you know. I do have friends; colleagues.'

Here, the scene is dramatized – the moment of confrontation brought to life on the page, with the backstory and the narrator's feelings filtering in through the dialogue and brief snatches of inner voice. Rather than the narrator explaining what's happened, we're right there, and her viewpoint acts purely as the lens through which we see the action. A dry summary of events becomes an opportunity for tension and conflict.

The effect of a first-person voice can be dramatically altered by the tense and/or medium you write in. This is true of other perspectives too but the first person is a particularly good tool for manipulating perceptions. As we saw above, it's easy to assume that if a character is telling us the story directly, it must be 'true.' And if their story is in the present tense, then surely it must be even 'truer' – we're literally witnessing the action as it happens: there's no room for the character to dissemble, digest, or allow hindsight to distort their impressions.

The Hunger Games (Suzanne Collins) is a good example of a first-person voice that feels particularly 'honest'. This candour works in the story's favour – Katniss's first-person present tense narrative keeps us guessing as to whether or not she survives the ordeal of the arena, which is one of the key tension drivers. How can she make it out alive, with the odds stacked against her?

In addition, the viewpoint here allows us to empathize with some of Katniss's seemingly impossible choices. She fights, kills, and manipulates other characters in a way that could be called cold blooded, but because we live the story alongside her, almost in real time, we are acutely aware of both the external pressures that make these actions necessary in the moment, and the emotional repercussions of the violence that linger with Katniss long after it's over.

Earlier we looked at *Gone Girl* and this is another interesting example: Amy's first-person narrative initially takes the form of diary extracts in the present tense. Here, the seeming transparency of the diary form convinces us that the Amy writing these extracts is trustworthy — if it's hard to believe that a first-person narrator might be lying to us, it's even harder to imagine that they might be lying to their own diary. But this is an elaborate act, made more believable by the fact that it's in the first person and in the present tense. In a novel of twists and tricks, with our other narrator apparently unreliable and tacitly implying that he's withholding information, this first-hand account is the one thing we feel we can trust. The way the author plays with our expectations about what the first person should and shouldn't do makes this a deft use of the form.

First person offers a wealth of exciting possibilities for tension, and the opportunity to immerse yourself fully in a character's voice and world with stylistic flair. It's not surprising it's a popular choice. However, it can also be restrictive and emotionally overwhelming. Because of this, you may decide that third person offers a greater scope for expanding the world of the story outwards from your main character, and a less claustrophobic writing and reading experience.

Third person

A third-person perspective (he, she) can be useful when you're aiming for a deliberately authorial tone, a particular dramatic effect, or a broad canvas, as might be the case with crime, thriller, historical and fantasy fiction. It allows more distance from the main character, but ideally without sacrificing the reader's emotional involvement.

It's important to make a distinction between the two main types of third-person narrator: a third-person **intimate** or **limited** voice, which deals with just one POV character at once, and tends to stick quite closely to the experiences and impressions of the protagonist/s; and a third-person **omniscient** voice, which can dip in and out of any character's thoughts and feelings at will. This latter is a fairly uncommon choice for recent fiction, though it has been used widely in the past. Contemporary thought on narrative technique tends to be that the omniscient approach can weaken our bond with any one character; can be emotionally muddy (because we're expected to understand/empathize with multiple viewpoints at once); and can diminish tension in a story (since much tension is derived from both reader and protagonist *not* knowing what other characters are thinking and planning). If you do choose to write in this form, or a variant of it, then it's still worth following some of the guidelines discussed below under *Close to you* to help you make the most of each POV.

Here we will primarily discuss third-person **intimate** POV – a more popular choice for contemporary fiction and one which mimics the human condition more closely than an omniscient viewpoint. In real life, we can only know what other people are thinking and feeling by interacting with them, observing them, and guessing at the real motives below the surface. Similarly, with a third-person intimate POV, the narrative voice stays close to just one character at a time, getting beneath the skin of each POV character almost as deeply as in a first-person narrative – without simultaneously giving us access to other characters' emotions.

Let's look at the beginning of the scene above, translated into third-person intimate:

> Laura was dithering in the kitchen when Simon's key scraped in the door. The bank statement lay on the pine worktop, wrinkled where she'd screwed it up then unfolded it to read it over and over. She rubbed her hands on her jeans, heart skittering. Why couldn't she have slapped some makeup on, tried to look more together? Right now she was just a sweaty frumpy wife pathetically waiting for her ratbag husband to get back from whatever, or whoever, he'd been doing.

As you see, this can be as simple as changing the pronouns from 'I' to 'she' throughout. There's very little difference in emotional involvement or dramatic impact – we're still right inside Laura's thoughts and feelings. However, switching into third person here means you can subsequently step back and utilize other POVs if you want to. Note, too, that in third person a verb choice like 'dithering' implies external judgement on the character, as though we should see her as weak; whereas in the first person, when Laura refers to herself as 'dithering' it seems self-aware – honest and appealing. So, the perspective you're using can change the way your choice of language is interpreted.

To hop or not to hop

Using more than one POV character allows you to choose which POV makes best use of the tension and drama in any given scene; and lets you build up the inner lives of some of your supporting characters, perhaps opting for a dual narrative or more than one protagonist. However, if that's the approach you go for, it's important to handle shifts in viewpoint carefully, with a keen eye on their dramatic effect. Switches between POV in this kind of narrative are best delineated with a scene or chapter break, rather than taking place within a scene, known as **head-hopping**. (Some authors do this, but it can seem uncontrolled, whilst diminishing tension for reasons already discussed.)

Let's look at the above scene again, switching rapidly between both characters' POVs:

Laura was dithering in the kitchen when Simon's key scraped in the door. The bank statement lay on the pine worktop, wrinkled where she'd screwed it up then unfolded it to read it over and over. She rubbed her hands on her jeans, heart skittering. Why couldn't she have slapped some makeup on, tried to look more together? Right now she was just a sweaty frumpy wife pathetically waiting for her ratbag husband to get back from whatever, or whoever, he'd been doing.

Simon breezed in, shrugging off his jacket and chucking it onto a chair. God, Laura was looking tired, he realized. Old, just like those grotty chairs. It was no wonder he'd ... he plastered a smile on his face, trying to disguise these treacherous thoughts, and kissed her on the cheek. 'What's for tea? I'm starved.'

'I haven't cooked. I ...'

He couldn't help it – his mouth twisted. For goodness sakes, what now, he thought. 'Chinese again then I guess.'

'Simon.' She wished he could have at least tried to play nice. She picked up the bank statement, hand trembling. She mustn't be derailed by stupid things like dinner, she told herself. She felt her neck burning, a sense of righteousness making her grind her teeth. 'What the f– what the bloody hell is this?'

He laughed. 'Is this a trick question?' But he was nervous now, wondering where she was going with this. 'It's a bank statement.'

'Don't you dare try to make me look … I mean this!' She shoved the page under his nose. 'This … Look, this handbag. For example. And what about dinner at Nobu?' It was somewhere she'd always wanted to eat, which he knew, and which somehow made it worse.

He wondered where she'd found it. Was she opening his post now? He had to start being more careful. 'Oh come on, you can't think…'

'I knew it! I knew something was going on. All those texts, and you changing your password. Who is she?' He put a hand on her arm and she tried to wrench herself out of his grip. His nails dug into her. Now he was pulling that face, the one she hated – like he felt sorry for her.

He tried to keep his voice level; he could see she'd wound herself up and from past experience he knew not to push it. 'Babe, look at me. I took the handbag back – it just wasn't you. And dinner – I do eat out after work sometimes, you know. I do have friends; colleagues.'

In trying to encompass each character's thoughts and feelings we're whisked from one emotional standpoint to another, not sure how we should feel or who we ought to empathize with. In places, the thoughts we're accessing could now belong to either character (e.g. 'It was somewhere she'd always wanted to eat, which he knew…') which makes things doubly ambiguous, and pretty confusing. Even in real life it's hard to occupy two emotional spaces at once; when we try, we end up with our minds a jumble of feelings. Here, we can't grasp either character fully, and the dynamic of the scene feels diluted and uncertain.

In addition, we lose some of the previous tension of not knowing whether Laura's right about Simon cheating, and we're less connected to her. Of course, you could play out the scene differently, with Simon's thoughts revealing a more sympathetic side, perhaps suggesting that Laura's suspicions are unjustified and telling us something new about her as a character – but either way, you've missed the chance to let us share in her paranoia, which is the key emotional driver of the scene. Instead of presenting an ambiguous relationship, raising questions about both characters, you've given us answers upfront and left nowhere for the scene to go.

(Notice when you're head-hopping you can't be so direct with the characters' thoughts and feelings – to differentiate them from the surrounding text you have to signpost them with tags like 'he wondered', 'she thought,' 'she told herself' and 'he could see that'.)

One author we mentored had lots of great, nuanced characters in place, but perhaps because of this she often found it hard to stick to one POV per scene, flitting around to give us multiple perspectives which resulted in some slightly disjointed moments. In one scene, a character called Jenny discovered a crashed alien spacecraft whilst accompanied by another character, Cameron, who'd already seen the craft and met some of the aliens. Because of Cameron's familiarity with the scenario, which came through clearly in his inner voice, it was impossible to share in Jenny's wonder.

The obvious solution here might have been to cut Cameron's POV and let us experience the tension of Jenny's discovery; however, because we'd already lived the same journey alongside Cameron there wasn't much to be gained from living through another character's amazement. The best way to play the scene was sticking close to Cameron instead, participating in the glee he took in introducing Jenny to these sights as though it was the most natural thing in the world; watching Jenny's stunned reactions purely from the outside. The scene ended up light and funny, providing a nice counterpart to the tension elsewhere.

Avoiding head-hopping is probably the most important thing to bear in mind if you're writing in the third person. Certainly it's the one aspect of POV that tends to have the biggest impact on reader identification with your characters and tension within a scene. However, there are various other techniques and guidelines associated with third person; mastering these will help your POVs feel real, rounded and just as vivid as any first-person character.

Close to you

Intimacy with a POV character is a vital part of the reading experience — it contributes to that sense of total immersion that a really good book delivers. It's particularly crucial to stay close when what's going on is visceral, emotional or dramatic. Moments like these pack a bigger punch when we're experiencing them right alongside your character.

We discussed above how in first person it's best not to spend too much time inside the character's head, and that applies to third person too. So how do you keep close to a POV character without subjecting us to too much inner voice? Fortunately, there are lots of ways to build an intimate bond with a character that don't involve overwhelming chunks of direct thought. Most of these apply just as much to first person as they do to third.

Imagine a scene where someone gets into a fight:

> The big man glared at him. Nat wasn't sure how he'd managed to get into this situation, but now he was here and he was terrified. He took the offensive and threw an undisciplined blow, which swung past the big man's face and toppled Nat off balance, spinning him around. Before he could catch his breath, the big man had punched Nat's jaw. He saw stars and tried to collect himself. A crowd was congregating around them now, some laughing, some looking worried.

The action's engaging, and we're not switching POV, but we're lacking a deep, inner sense of how Nat is experiencing the moment. We don't feel the uniqueness or immediacy of his impressions; what makes them specific to him. Here's the same moment, rewritten to bring us closer to Nat:

> Christ the dude was huge. Nat's throat closed up, his skin puckering with cold, even in the close air of the bar. How had he gotten himself into this? What'd he been thinking?
>
> The guy was squaring up to him already, great beefy shoulders slugging into position like a tanker. Nat swallowed. He had to make the first move. He was smaller, quicker – he hoped, anyway.
>
> Without thinking he swung, but felt only air against his knuckles. The swoop of his arm spun him around and his vision wheeled, his legs twisting under him. Then there was a crunch in his jaw and a blinding flash of pain across his eyes. The hubbub of voices disappeared, then roared back in.

Nat shook his head and breathed deeply, tasting metal in his mouth, gagging on the smell of stale beer and sweat; the blood trickling down his throat. Through half closed lids he could see red, weaving faces. A girl with a skinhead frowning … a blonde smirking into her wine glass. Behind the bar, a sweating barman was mouthing something into the phone. Calling the police?

There's now a visceral intimacy: we can feel, see, taste and hear exactly what Nat does; we listen in on his thoughts and share in his emotions at this critical moment.

There are a few techniques employed here which you can use to bring us this close to all your POV characters, both during key scenes but also at more minor, insignificant moments. Firstly, we **establish the POV** character quickly. Rather than starting with *the big man glared at him* which leaves us vague about whose perspective we're sharing, we can see straight away that Nat is our main point of empathy. The POV character is our route into the scene, so knowing upfront who it is will guide our emotional response.

Secondly, the **writing voice** aims to stay close to Nat's own phrasing and vocabulary. Though we're not using a character voice here, the author's own style takes on a flavour of how Nat might express himself and view the world. So, instead of *he took the offensive* we have *he had to make the first move;* instead of *toppled off balance* we have *spun him around;* instead of a cliché like *he saw stars* we have *a blinding flash of pain across his eyes.* This seems more intimate, whilst reflecting the immediacy of the moment, where one would be unlikely to think in tactical, analytical terms like *took the offensive.*

Thirdly, there's a more naturalistic use of Nat's **inner voice** — his direct thoughts and reactions. So, instead of, *Nat wasn't sure* *how he'd managed to get himself into this situation,* we have, *Christ the dude was huge … how had he gotten himself into this?* There are a few accepted ways to include your character's thoughts in the narrative – using speech marks ('That dude is huge,' thought Nat); italicized direct thoughts (*That dude's huge!*); indirect thought (Nat thought how huge the guy was); or free indirect thoughts, as above (Christ the dude was huge). This latter tends to be the smoothest way of incorporating thoughts into a third-person past-tense narrative, as it avoids any jarring shift into the present and/or first person. It creates an almost seamless blend of the character's thoughts and the narrative voice, and contributes to the illusion of closeness between character and reader.

However – as we'd expect from a situation where Nat's running mainly on instinct, and doesn't have much time to think – his thoughts rarely take over; instead he's governed by **physical, sensory responses**. This is a key point because – as discussed in the section on first person – it's not enough to give us loads of thoughts: those thoughts also need to be pertinent, plausible and suitable for the context (i.e. always linked to what's going on in the action scene). If a character wanders off into reflection bang in the middle of an exciting incident, it will distract us from the drama and it simply won't feel believable.

This brings us to the fourth technique – making more use of the **character's physicality**. Rather than staying on the surface of what he's experiencing, we convey what it's like to be inside his skin – the *crunch of his jaw,* the *air against his knuckles,* the tastes and smells. The more you can rely on the different senses here, the rounder and fuller this impression will be; the more the reader will begin that dreamlike process of losing themselves inside the character.

Fifthly, we're **showing not telling**. We'll deal with this concept separately in Chapter 8, but at this stage it's worth noting that instead of saying *he was terrified* — a summary of an emotion that everyone may experience differently in any given situation — we're dramatizing how Nat's *throat closed up, his skin puckering*. This specific detail shows us how Nat's own, personal terror manifests, in this particular situation. It allows us to experience a little of the emotion for ourselves.

Finally, we're conveying the character's **external impressions**; flashes of what's going on around him that take us slightly outside the immediate POV. This can be hard to get right, as our awareness of our surroundings can vary hugely depending on circumstances. But generally we won't notice what a scene is 'broadly' like (*a crowd was gathering ... looking worried*), instead honing in on a couple of specifics — things that jump out as unusual or memorable. Little morsels of description tend to work better: they act as placeholders for the bigger picture and allow our imaginations to fill in the detail.

Can't get you out of my head

Creating a strong POV involves bringing us as close to the character as possible, as we've seen above, and part of this process is avoiding stepping away from them unless there's a good reason for it. As well as head-hopping, there are a few other tell-tale signs that your grip on POV may be loose. Initially these will be problems to watch for at the self-editing stage. However, as the techniques become ingrained into your creative process you should find yourself writing this way automatically.

We've discussed switching POVs to other characters and you might think that's easy enough to spot. However, be just as aware of **subtle shifts** outward, which can chip away at the integrity of your POV:

Lulu stared at her tea, a prickly feeling creeping over her neck. Why did Mum have to be so …? She speared a baked bean with her fork but couldn't bring herself to put it in her mouth. Instead, she glanced at Mum from under her eyelashes. Sue was frowning at her daughter, lips pursed.

This moment starts securely in the intimate third person. However, with the line *Sue was frowning at her daughter*, we shift minutely away from Lulu's experience of the scene: she'd be unlikely to think of her mum as 'Sue'; nor would she think of herself as 'Sue's daughter'. To maintain POV, this could be rephrased as something like, *Mum was frowning at her, lips pursed.*

Now, consider a passage that involves some description:

Lulu scratched at the back of her hand where the stamp from the club last night still hadn't quite washed off. Idiot— why hadn't she taken care of it? She shoved both her hands into her jacket pockets and jogged downstairs, biting her lip.

Mum was shouldering open the front door, loaded down with shopping. 'Great, love, you can give me a hand.'

Lulu took a breath, her eyes shifty.

Again, the moment starts off close to Lulu, rooted in her thoughts and voice. But how would she know what her own eyes look like? And even if she could see them, would she think of herself as *shifty*, or would she gloss over the negative aspects of her behaviour? This externalized view breaks our link with her; suddenly we're seeing her as Mum does, rather than sharing in Lulu's feelings.

Shifts away from your POV character that may seem minor can still have an impact on the way we identify with them:

Lulu plonked her bag down on the table, sticky with rings of spilled coke. Carrie and Lise were giggling about something but they shifted over on the bench to make room for her.

'Alright?' Lise said, twisting a strand of dark hair around her finger.

Carrie had gone quiet, her back slightly turned, looking at something on her phone. God, Lulu hoped she wasn't going to be weird about what'd happened last night.

A waitress in a leather mini-skirt stopped at the table, jaw working on a piece of gum. 'What can I get ya?'

They glanced at each other, biting down giggles. How try-hard was she?

It's better to avoid vocalizing your POV character's thoughts as part of a group (*How try-hard was she?*); since they can't know whether the others think and feel the same way they do, this can come across as mind reading. But here, the switch into third person plural – *they* – feels particularly out of kilter with the rest of the scene, which seems to be setting up a distance/conflict between Lulu and her friends.

An exception to this rule might be if you were trying to establish a sense of togetherness, where some manipulation of the pronouns can subtly contribute to this impression. If the thrust of the above scene was that the three girls were very close, you might use *they* more frequently, and the 'mind-reading' wouldn't feel so out of place.

(As an addendum to this point, a common error in younger fiction is to refer to a group of characters as 'the children'. It's not the way your character/s would think about themselves; it's an adult, external or authorial point of view. It's best, within a POV, to simply use the character's name or, even better, just 'he' or 'she'. If you're close enough to their perspective it will be obvious who you're referring to.)

Unless a specifically authorial stance is part of your narrative voice, and you've chosen to talk directly to the reader – a slightly old-fashioned choice but one that's sometimes used in children's fiction, literary fiction or comedy – then it's best to avoid breaking perspective to tell us things the POV character wouldn't be aware of. If they haven't been introduced to another character by name, then don't use that name in the narrative; if they're in a forest but know nothing about natural history, don't give us lots of factual information about the various plants they see – instead, focus on things that they *would* be aware of – shapes, sounds, colours, textures.

We worked with an author whose wider control of POV was great, and who'd written predominantly in limited third person. However, like many authors who aren't confident in their abilities, she'd developed a habit of concluding scenes and chapters with portentous statements about what was to come:

> Little did he know it, but he was being watched...
> He was happy ... but that was about to change...
> There was no way he could have known the horror that would await him...

The author didn't think the plot was gripping enough, so she couldn't resist these authorial asides. But whilst they seemed to build tension, it felt contrived because it relied on the authorial privilege of knowing everything about the story. It wasn't playing fair, because if she could reveal *this*, then what was stopping her from telling us *anything* – such as, how the story would end?! It also broke our bond with the POV character, and since our empathy with them and the fact that we care whether they succeed is a more organic, natural way to create background suspense, her **manufactured tension** was working *against* the real sources of tension.

Keep an eye out for observations, vocabulary, and figures of speech that the character wouldn't be likely to adopt. We talked about using lexicon to bring the reader closer to your POV character; at the editing stages you should be alert for things that don't ring true:

> Dan arrived home from school and entered the living room. On the carpet in front of the TV a cherubic toddler was engrossed in building teetering structures out of duplo.

Would Dan view his brother as 'a cherubic toddler', a distanced phrase that implies they don't know each other? Can we use language that reflects both the intimacy of their relationship and the way he feels about his brother?

> Dan slouched in from school and shoved open the living room door. The little monster was on the floor in front of the TV as usual, a sticky-looking yellow brick clutched in his fat fingers.

Or, imagine a scene where two adult friends are meeting for a drink:

> Andy was leaning on the bar, his chestnut hair swept back from his haunted eyes, when Dave arrived. Dave embraced him, feeling his friend's shoulders taut under the cashmere sweater.

The romanticized focus on the physical details doesn't ring true for the way two mates might think about each other (unless you're trying to set up some subtext). Ensure that the description remains in keeping with the genre, Dave's world-view, phrasing, and relationship with his friend:

> Andy was leaning on the bar, a pint in his hand, when Dave arrived. His dark hair was slicked back, like he'd been raking his fingers through it; there were shadows under his eyes. Dave pulled him in for a clumsy hug. God, had his mate always been this thin?

The actual description you're imparting is identical, but the flavour and tone are completely different.

There are numerous elements that work hand in hand here, but the two key points to remember are: **don't head-hop**, and **stay close**, which are two facets of the same principle. Once you've got to grips with these aspects, you'll be in a position to experiment more, knowing that you have a strong foundation in place: POV characters who draw us in, who we care about, and who we're getting to know on a deep level.

What next?

It's rarely as simple as choosing which POV you're going to use and running with it. As a writer in control of your material you'll be making ongoing decisions about which POV to use when; how to zoom in and out of POVs when the story demands a tighter or looser focus; and how to use POV to manipulate our perceptions of the action.

You may decide to do something groundbreaking or just more ambitious with viewpoint. Perhaps you want to use **multiple third (or first) person narrators?** That's fine, as long as you're aware of the above rules and how to apply these in a multiple viewpoint novel. On the whole, unless you have a specific purpose to head-hopping, and you know you can work it, it's best to **restrict POV** to one character per scene or chapter, separating any shifts in POV with a scene break (but keeping these fairly minimal to avoid the prose feeling too fragmented).

You'd probably also want to **limit the number of POV characters** you use overall, making strict choices about whose POVs we'll have access to and why. Each POV character places a demand on the reader — we need to remember who they are, how they fit in, how they feel, and how *we're* supposed to feel about *them*. You don't want to waste our energy on the POV of, for example, the postie who delivers a letter and is never seen again. It's usually better to have fewer POV characters developed in greater detail, so that we build a relationship with each significant character, and have an important, **meaningful** point of focus for each scene or story thread. So, the final point is that you'll still want to **bring us as close to each POV** as possible.

With multiple POV characters, you'll need to avoid any **loss of tension** arising from knowing each character's story simultaneously. One of our authors had written an ambitious historical novel, spanning centuries, with five or six intertwining threads, each with a main POV character. In the 'present day' thread, one of the key tension drivers was a mystery about who'd written a piece of music. In a parallel thread, the main POV character was the composer — so, whilst the mystery still existed for our main character in the present day, for the reader it had already been solved. Both threads contributed something to the tone and texture of the novel, so instead of cutting one we looked for other solutions: manipulating the POV to keep the identity of the composer secret; considering alternative ways to bring tension into the present-day storyline.

Similarly, authors of crime/thrillers sometimes include brief episodes from the antagonist's point of view. These tend to work best when they provide tantalizing snippets of detail (for example, revealing more about the nature of the adversary), rather than giving away too much in advance. In a police procedural, for instance, a key source of tension might be, *when will the killer strike again?* A positive way of using the killer's POV might be to show them preparing meticulously for the next crime; we can see that it's definitely going to happen soon, and the scene might reinforce just how dangerous the killer is, but we still don't answer the central question. The additional POV therefore builds on the main tension, rather than resolving it.

Whatever decisions you make about POV and whatever rules you follow, you will find published authors who do something different. That's no bad thing – it's through experimenting and playing around with conventions that new approaches are born and boundaries broken. You might find yourself in a position – like one author we worked with – of having used many different POVs already (first, intimate third, alternative POV characters, characters writing in diary/note form, emails, texts and even snapchat) only to find that to make one of your subplots work you need to incorporate *another* POV in the form of omniscient authorial segments inserted at intervals throughout the entire text. This is all part of the journey a novel can take you on.

However, by mastering the fundamentals of POV, you will have an understanding of the pros and cons of each choice, and ensure that you're writing cognitively, knowing exactly what you're doing and why. You'll be in complete control of the effect POV has on plot, character and tension – and ultimately, on the reader.

4
Plot and structure – finding your story's shape

Good plotting serves many purposes: a strong structure containing escalating tension keeps the reader turning the pages, but it also feels satisfying in a more intangible way, honouring the magical role of storytelling in our lives; fulfilling the reader's expectations about how story *works*. We'll show you how to employ the three-act structure to map your plot; use cause and effect to keep it moving forwards; and build your plot around your character arc to make the most of its underlying emotion and grab your reader by the gut.

Losing the plot?

Almost all authors will come up against plotting problems at some stage. It is often one of the most involved issues to address, especially once a draft is finished, because it can be both emotionally and intellectually difficult to deconstruct the skeleton that holds the novel together. This is why planning is useful: by having your story's basic shape in place before you start, you can save yourself hard work and heartache further down the line.

Authors often ask us why we are so firm about plotting. There are lots of answers to this question: firstly, and (if you're aiming to get published) most importantly, it's what tends to keep us reading – the burning questions of *what will happen next* and *how will it all end* work most effectively if a story has a clear direction. Secondly, your plot is what ties the novel together conceptually, turning random events into a story with meaning and purpose. Thirdly, plotting gives a story its emotional underpinning, linking what happens to the characters on the surface with their inner lives – giving a reader that satisfying sense of experiencing both a literal *and* an emotional journey.

Finally, the whole idea of plotting is very bound up with life. We're born, we grow, we strive against adversity and in doing so learn, we achieve what we set out to do (or not), we pass on what we've learned, and we die. We like to believe that our lives are a journey with a destination and a purpose, and that need feeds into our cultural reference points in many ways. A good plot is therefore a reflection of something greater than itself, tapping into something primal and universal.

In practical terms, a strong structure underpinning your story keeps it on the straight and narrow. You'll often notice, in stories without a clear plot, that the action digresses, stalls, backtracks and repeats itself; lots of scenes don't have a point; and characters don't seem to know what they're doing or where they're going. We may not be consciously aware of why something isn't working, but we all know that feeling of boredom and frustration we get from reading a story that doesn't seem to be heading anywhere.

Try to see this need for underlying structure as less of a stricture and more of a helping hand: far from hampering creativity, if the story is following a clear path it's easier to wander off and explore the hidden glades and shadows in the forest, knowing that we have a map to guide us back.

The three-act structure

This is the tool we use at Cornerstones to help with plotting, though it's only one of a number of models that are taught in contemporary theory. Most methods have a lot in common: the same rising and falling shape, with tension peaks, an inciting incident and a clear goal for the protagonist. Some are more prescriptive in terms of what happens when, and some are looser. This basic model is simple to use, and will probably already be familiar to you — most stories, from fairy tales through to gritty thrillers, follow some variation of it. It's based on a few proven tenets: that stories draw us in when a protagonist has a problem; keep us hooked when the protagonist takes active steps to solve that problem; and leave us satisfied when an ending rounds things off in a meaningful way.

Let's look at these individual components.

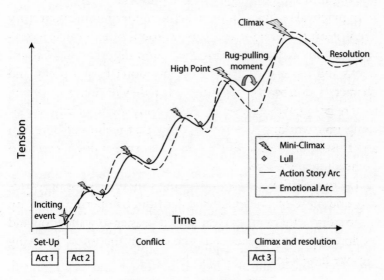

THREE-ACT STRUCTURE

Act 1

This is the story's **set-up**. We meet the main **character/s**; are introduced to the **universe** of the story (the setting, era, genre and tone) so that we feel grounded and have a rough idea about what to expect; and we find out the **status quo**: what is currently going on for your protagonist, what sort of person they are, and why we should care about them.

Once you've set the scene, we get to the **inciting event (or inciting incident)** when things change for the main character; something happens that upsets their normal life, presenting them with a problem that must be solved, or a goal to be achieved. It might not be massive or earth-shattering (we talked in Chapter 2 about how problems are significant because they *mean* something to the protagonist) but it tends to be irreversible. There's no going back from whatever's happened.

Act 1 is often the shortest of the three acts. Some genres may necessitate a longer set-up (like fantasy or sci-fi, which may require more world-building), while some stories might miss out the set-up altogether, starting with the inciting incident and filling in the set up once the next act is underway.

An author might even choose to withhold the inciting incident altogether and treat it as part of the backstory, making it a mystery for protagonist and reader to uncover. *Before I Go To Sleep* (S.J. Watson) is a good example of this approach: the protagonist has amnesia, caused by a traumatic event in her past, and her goal is to find out what triggered her illness. In these instances, there may be another, lesser inciting incident – something which sets the protagonist off on their journey towards the truth. In *Before I Go To Sleep*, this is the protagonist's decision to write a journal, keeping a record of things she'd previously allowed herself to forget and beginning to piece her memories together.

If you decide to play around with the three-act structure in this way, it can be helpful to write two synopses: one that is chronological, to help you check that the underpinning structure is definitely in place before you start tinkering; and one that lays out the plot in the order it will be read, which will allow you to check that the sequence works, presenting enough tension peaks and plot incidents to keep us engaged.

Act 2

The inciting event propels us into Act 2, which is where the bulk of the **conflict and tension** takes place. Here the protagonist takes steps to achieve their goal or overcome their problem, and these steps either solve the problem but create new problems, or get them into further difficulties that exacerbate the original problem. Either way, the protagonist must be **active** at this stage, making choices and doing things, rather than being pushed around by other characters, by fate, or by the needs of the plot.

Act 2 is where plotting problems frequently tend to arise. It's proportionally the longest section of a story, and it can be hard to keep tension rising over such an extended period. Mid-sections of stories often meander, without a clear direction; with lots of scenes where not much is happening or changing and a lack of suspense. Here plot and structure comes into its own: if your protagonist stays focused on their central goal, this creates urgency. At this stage the idea of **escalation** is important, too — the protagonist's situation should worsen, either in spite of or because of their actions. Each obstacle they encounter should be more challenging, and the plot should provide a mix of climaxes and lulls, of success and failure, so that the action and tension rises and falls, but on an ever-climbing curve.

Crucially, the action throughout Act 2 (and indeed, during the plot as a whole) must be linked by **cause and effect**. Events must have consequences, and these consequences should lead to the next plot incident/s. This can be a hard concept to identify and explain, so let's look at an example. We've chosen something simple and well known to make the exercise as clear as possible.

PLOT ONE

The three little pigs decide to build houses: the first out of straw, the second from sticks and the third from bricks. When the hungry wolf comes knocking one day, he's able to destroy the first house easily. The pig runs to the house of sticks, which the wolf is still able to break down. The two pigs flee to the house of bricks, where the wolf cannot get in. He climbs down the chimney, falls into the fire and dies.

This plot has a certain amount of rising tension, with the stakes increasing for the pigs as each house is destroyed, and a satisfying resolution. However, it could be much stronger in terms of cause and effect. *Why* do the pigs build houses? Why don't they all run straight to the brick house when the straw house has been destroyed? How does each stage lead inexorably to the next, and how does it make things *worse* for the pigs? It wouldn't, in fact, make much difference if some of the plot points were switched around; they could be changed or cut without much impact on the outcome. Consider instead a plot which pulls cause and effect into the foreground:

PLOT TWO

Act 1: After being ambushed one day by the Big Bad Wolf, the three little pigs decide they're sick of living in fear, and that they'll build a house for protection (*status quo, basic problem, inciting incident*).

Act 2: They find some straw and get to work. The wolf comes sniffing around and is easily able to blow their house down. They flee, realizing they must choose better building materials (*cause and effect – the fact that the straw house has been destroyed leads them to do things differently next time*). The pigs build a house out of sticks, which is much stronger. However, the wolf is still able to destroy the house, and when he does so one of the pigs is hurt by the falling sticks (*escalating problems; the steps taken to solve the previous problem have actually made things worse*). The pigs now choose to build a house of bricks, certain this will prevent the wolf from harming them again. (*Cause and effect – the consequences of previous mistakes have made them take further action – but will it be successful?*) The wolf arrives at the brick house and sees that he cannot break it down – perhaps he can trick his way in? (*Protagonists' actions have also made the antagonist up his game – escalating tension*). He claims to be the doctor, come to help the pig who's been hurt (*cause and effect – previous incidents feed into the current action*). The pigs are about to let him in when they realize that only the wolf knew about the injury. (*High point, rug pulling moment*).

Act 3: They know it's not enough to hide away – they must defeat the wolf for good. They tell him their door is broken and he must climb down the chimney if he wants to help. The wolf falls into the fire and dies. (*The climax and resolution again feature cause and effect: the pigs have learned their lesson from everything that's gone before, and even the wolf's actions follow on consequentially from the preceding scenes*).

The internal logic that the second plot delivers makes it stronger and more interesting to read, even though the basic incidents are virtually identical. In real life, events often happen for no reason at all; in fiction, and particularly in your second act, you should always be working to the idea that **one thing leads to the next**.

We touched above on the **rug-pulling moment**, which often forms the end of Act 2. At this point, the protagonist/s seem to have achieved their goal, or solved their problem. Then something else happens and we realize that their success was illusory; they're worse off than they were before and we can see no way out for them now. This is the **hero's darkest hour**. Something dramatic and extraordinary needs to happen, and that's the job of …

… ACT 3

Act 3 is firstly comprised of the **climax** – also known as the **denouement** – which is the culmination of everything the protagonist has been through. It's usually the apex of the tension curve: the point at which the stakes are highest and the protagonist has most to lose. The hero must use what they've learned to succeed, hopefully in a surprising or unexpected way and, vitally, by themselves or at least on the strength of their own qualities.

This is particularly important because it gives a story's resolution its emotional payoff. In essence, this is the finale of the protagonist's journey and/or transformation: implicitly, they are able to succeed now because of who they have become, whereas they couldn't have done so at the beginning because of who they *were*. They are now able to do things – make difficult choices; sacrifice something or someone they care about; do the right thing, as opposed to the easy thing – that they couldn't have previously contemplated. The completion of their emotional arc/character development is why it's so important that your protagonist faces the climax alone.

(NB, some emotional conclusions will involve a character realizing that to succeed they must *come to terms with who they are*, where the rest of the novel has shown them *trying to be someone else*. The narrative arc in this instance isn't as simple as 'a character changes', but still involves progress – acceptance of one's flaws and limitations is in itself a kind of growth.)

We worked with an author whose plotting was solid, but whose climax felt flat. When the protagonist was faced with a sink-or-swim moment, she chose to run away rather than tackle the final confrontation. Ultimately, she succeeded, but only because another character gave her a lot of help. We briefly tried out a new version of the climax, where the protagonist took charge, but it didn't feel believable. So, we retraced the character's arc of development, asking some questions about who she really was; and by setting up a clearer trajectory for her we created a climax that allowed her to be proactive but also felt right for the story. In this instance, it wasn't enough for the heroine to simply save the day; first, she had to acknowledge and overcome her own cowardice.

You may work a **plot twist** into your climax: a surprising event or decision that is key to the protagonist's success, but that the reader didn't see coming. This might take the form of unexpected and satisfying character development, as discussed above; it might involve the revelation of a secret; or it might be that some action that took place earlier in the plot, which we have almost forgotten about, reappears, proving to be the decisive factor in the denouement. We'll discuss plot twists in the next chapter.

The final element of Act 3 is the **resolution**, where we take stock, consider what's changed, and sow the seeds of what the future might hold. The resolution tends to set the tone the reader will be left with when they close the book – where the climax may have been whizzy-bangy, preferencing excitement, conflict and drama over *mood*, the resolution attempts to leave us with the feeling of questions answered, and destinies shaped.

Act 3 may also be short – once the action and emotional climaxes have been reached, you're tying off loose ends, and you don't want to spend too long over this. You may choose to leave some threads open – something we'll discuss in more detail below. Whatever you decide, the key to making an ending feel satisfying is the extent to which the **emotional plot** is resolved. Readers will forgive a lot, as long as the main character's journey is rounded off nicely.

Inside out

The action storyline (or external conflict) is what happens to your protagonist outwardly – the literal, physical events that take place, related to the initial problem they're tackling. It focuses on tangibles: real world conflicts and dramas that contribute to the character achieving their goal (or not). We've seen from our study of Act 2 how external conflict means keeping your main character proactive, taking steps and making choices, with action linked in a cause and effect way.

By contrast, the emotional storyline (also referred to as the **emotional arc**, the **internal conflict** or the **main character's journey**) focuses on the protagonist's thoughts, feelings and growth. It explores how the action plot affects them internally, and vice versa: how what's going on in the character's mind/psyche affects their choices and actions. As you'll see from the three-act graph, the internal and external plots should weave in and out of one another, so that each plot point changes the character in some way and these changes feed back into whatever happens next. The action plotline and the emotional plotline usually come together at the end, so that the resolution of one provides the key to the resolution of the other.

Whatever the physical goings-on of a plot, the emotional core tends to be its most compelling ingredient, providing the tension and keeping the reader turning the pages. This is part of the reason we place so much emphasis on getting your characters spot on, since it's their inner lives and journeys that form the spine of the story.

A crucial ingredient to the emotional plot is **inner conflict**. Where outer conflicts may be either literal (obstacles, incidents and other characters who stand in the main character's way) or ideological (the main character comes into conflict with others because of their core personality), inner conflict is more about how the character's own mind and emotions create problems **within themselves**. The character's personality traits, fears, doubts, prejudices and beliefs – all the quirks and flaws that make them human – prevent them achieving their goal. To succeed, they must grow, and this should take place gradually, over the story, intrinsically linked to the action plot.

Let's look at an example. Below is a summary of the plot of Helen Fielding's *Bridget Jones's Diary*. Here, we've highlighted Action Plot (AP) and Emotional Arc, which has been split into Inner Progress (IP) and Inner Setback (IS) so that we can analyse how the action and emotional arcs proceed simultaneously.

At the beginning of a new year, Bridget Jones longs to find a boyfriend – to fulfil her need to be loved, but also so that her family will stop getting at her (overarching plot goal/problem). She's a relentless self-improver, whose failure to achieve her own impossible goals makes her unhappy and insecure (overarching emotional problem).

Bridget's family want to set her up with Mark Darcy, an old family friend and international lawyer (AP) but Mark's perfect life and attractive girlfriend are Bridget's antithesis, and every time she meets Mark she ends up feeling silly (IS). Bridget starts a fling with her flirty boss, Daniel Cleaver (AP), which bolsters her self-esteem (IP). However, Daniel messes her around, and the relationship often leaves her feeling confused and worthless (IS).

Bridget bumps into Mark at a party, when she happens to be feeling particularly insecure, and he proves to be warmer and less snobby than he first seemed, giving Bridget a boost (AP/IP). Feeling brave, Bridget is ready to move on from Daniel (IP). However, when her miraculous weight loss doesn't result in the happiness she'd anticipated (AP), her confidence takes another dive (IS) and Daniel is there to pick up the pieces (AP).

She and Daniel have a honeymoon period (AP) and he continually tells her how much he likes 'real women' (IP). But when she discovers him cheating with her exact opposite – someone tall, thin, confident and successful (AP) this confirms her belief that she'll never be good enough (IS). Her life starts to spiral, and she realizes she can't stay in her job; working for Daniel is too humiliating (IS).

She manages to land an exciting new job (AP) and walks out of her old one on a high (IP). It comes as a complete surprise when Mark tells her he's no longer with Natasha and asks her out (AP/IP) telling her how much he likes the fact that she's unvarnished and real – exactly the sort of thing Daniel used to tell her and which she desperately wants to believe (IP). When he doesn't show up she's crushed (IS).

It turns out to have been a misunderstanding, and filled with the buzz of success (IP), Bridget throws a dinner party for her friends and Mark (AP). The cooking goes disastrously wrong and Bridget yet again feels that she's made a fool of herself (IS). But Mark saves the situation – and seems to understand Bridget almost better than she understands herself, recognizing her flaws, and liking her nonetheless (IP).

Just as everything is going well, Bridget gets a phone call telling her that her mum has got into trouble – has left her dad, and shacked up with dodgy Julio, timeshare seller, who's now on the run from the police (AP). Mark steps in to help out (AP), and Bridget is convinced she's seen the last of him – how can he love her when she has a mum who's a criminal? (IS)

Mark disappears and Bridget spends a depressing Christmas (AP) trying to find solace in socializing but in reality lonely, beating herself up because she's failed to keep any of last year's resolutions (IS). But when Mark and Julio make a dramatic reappearance over Christmas dinner (AP) and Bridget steps in to save the day (action climax) she realizes she's achieved more than she thought: she's grown up in many ways, she no longer needs her family's validation, and (it turns out) she's managed to bag a great boyfriend after all (emotional resolution).

Bridget's emotional arc constantly shifts as the action plot lifts her up and down. Progress and setbacks proceed in a series of peaks and troughs, linked to what's going on around her. Likewise, her inner life – comprised of all these ups and downs – impacts on her future choices, and shapes the action plot as it progresses. Bridget's insecurities often stand in her way and it's her lack of self-awareness that's her biggest flaw rather than any fault in her character. Because she always feels that she needs to be doing better she cannot see her existing strengths.

If you're struggling with creating plausible and naturalistic inner conflict, consider dealing in extremes: make your characters face their fears. In this example, Bridget's deepest fear is that she's not attractive or together enough to keep a boyfriend. Daniel's actions seem to confirm this, and it's devastating for her because it suggests that everything she secretly believes about herself is true. However, the emotional arc of the novel resolves this conflict by showing her that it's possible to find love with someone for whom her flaws and eccentricities are, in themselves, attractive. Everything she's done to try to improve herself has blinded her to this possibility, and only once she stops trying to be someone she's not can she recognize Mark's genuine affection.

In essence, the thing that makes Bridget an appealing and empathetic character – her earnest desire to be the best she can be, combined with her continual failure to meet her own impossible standards – is both a strength and a weakness. The humanity of this inner conflict gives the plot depth and resonance and makes her more than just a comic heroine – she's an everywoman we can all relate to.

Scene structure

Once your overarching plot is in place you'll get down to the nitty gritty of writing, chapter by chapter and scene by scene. Here, too, it's important to keep the idea of structure and direction in mind; anything you include should be there for a reason. So, rather than writing absolutely everything that happens, think in terms of key scenes – moments where something significant takes place – and use these as your building blocks.

A scene is an **action and dialogue sequence** (as opposed to **narrative sections** which may be reflective prose, backstory, exposition, scene-setting etc) – but that's its most basic definition. A scene is also, more importantly, a point at which things **turn** for the protagonist; an episode of conflict; a moment where the direction changes. It's not enough to simply show two characters going for a nice walk, for example; the scene must also advance our understanding of the characters in some way, change the dynamic between them, or take the plot down a new path. Each scene should contain a definite **point of tension**, and exist for a **specific purpose**.

Scenes should also follow their own internal structure and logic. You'll often hear the adage 'get in late, and get out early' and whilst that's helpful, it's not the be all and end all. If you start *in medias res* (literally, 'in the thick of the action') but then need to backtrack to fill in where the scene is taking place and/or who's present, the scene may feel static and retrospective (where the ideal should be dynamic and immediate). A good scene will usually roughly follow the sequence:

- brief scene-setting
- establishing character's goal
- action, dialogue or interaction leading to conflict
- success or failure/resolution of scene
- cementing or reflecting on the change that has taken place.

As you can see, this is like the overarching structure of a story in miniature. And as with the overarching plot, some of these aspects will be implicit rather than stated outright; they form the emotional subtext or the inner conflict that underpins the action. The one aspect that you can't afford to miss out is a **tension driver** which may come either from the main character's goal (whatever it is they need to achieve at this point, as opposed to the overarching plot goal); or from the conflict (which may be inner or outer); or from the fact that they've failed; or from a plot question you've set up. Perhaps it will be a combination of all these things; either way, a scene must have tension underpinning it, otherwise it will feel flat and purposeless.

The best scenes usually accomplish several things at once, so look for ways to make every scene work harder and don't be afraid to lose some altogether. If you have a few in a row that are making broadly the same point, stuck in the same location, or going over similar ground in terms of conflict, consider merging or cutting. If you have one scene containing a key, dramatic plot twist, followed by one where your characters aren't doing much, then think about how you could combine the two.

Let's examine how all the elements fall into place:

Tilly looked at the invitation which sat, innocently enough, on top of the loose manuscript papers that covered the worn green baize of her desk, and drummed her fingers. What was she going to do about it? It'd been over a week now, and Lucia would be expecting an answer. Tilly really, really didn't want to go to the vile wedding, which would doubtless be full of immaculate beauties like Lucia herself; perfect couples basking in the glow of their ideal lives.

It was gold-edged, on thick, creamy paper. Classy, Tilly would have said, if she hadn't known better. With Lucia (whose name at school had been plain old Lucy) it was definitely pretentious. She'd always thought she was that bit better than everybody else.

'RSVP by post' the invitation said. Tilly sniffed. Trust Lucia to make it difficult. But there was an email address too, and a phone number. Maybe she could just whizz off a quick note, keep it casual.

Her fingers hovered over the keyboard for a moment then, as always happened once she started typing, the words seemed to flow without her even thinking about it.

'Lucia! Gosh, long time no speak. What a surprise. I would love to come but unfortunately I have so many deadlines hanging over me at the moment; my editor is breathing down my neck! I hope it all goes well for you. Best wishes, Matilda.'

The email carried her usual signature — her professional title (though at least Matilda was her real name and not some ghastly made-up handle) and an Amazon link to her latest novel. She scanned the email quickly, planning to hit send before she could reconsider, then glanced back at the invitation, flipping it over to double check she hadn't missed anything. And there it was: a handwritten note in Lucy's still-childish script, right underneath the date:

'Dearest Tilly. Please come. We have stuff to talk about.'

Her throat constricted, and her hand fluttered to her mouth. The words on the page wavered. What did Lucy mean? It couldn't be … surely … but what else could she be talking about? The two of them had never been truly close; that one holiday really the only thing binding them, stopping them from losing touch altogether. But they'd promised never to talk about it, so why bring it up now?

Tilly felt the world tilt. This couldn't — could NOT — happen. She looked almost unconsciously at the neat rows of books on her grandmother's old oak bookshelf, each with her name, Matilda Deere, in different fonts and sizes. Her pride, her security. Herself. And there was no way she was going to let Lucia start interfering now, whatever her reasons.

Quickly she fired off a response –

'Lucy, I'll be there.

Tilly.'

Then she slammed the lid of her laptop down with a shaking hand, and went into the kitchen to make a cup of tea.

The opening briefly pencils in the location and gives some hints about the character: a novelist, successful, self-possessed, at her desk. The main point of tension/Tilly's goal, is to decide what to do about this obviously unwelcome invitation. All is not well between Tilly and Lucia, though we're not sure why, and Tilly's first response is classic deflection: I'm too busy and successful to attend, look how I've moved on. This establishes both inner and outer conflict.

Then, with the revelation of Lucia's personal note to her, Tilly changes her mind, and the scene is resolved, though not necessarily in the way we expected. Something has shifted – we know now that there's some darker mystery, something that strikes at Tilly's sense of security and self' – and that she's willing to do anything to protect this secret. The conclusion of the scene cements Tilly's decision, but leaves us with plenty to figure out. The point of tension of this specific scene has been resolved, and the overall story moved forward, but the scene has established follow-up questions; tensions which may or may not be addressed and resolved in subsequent scenes. The scene is both a mini-episode in its own right, and a key cog in the wider plot.

You will also want to think about how to move between scenes. There are a couple of options here: a **scene break** or

hiatus will make a clean cut, perhaps to change character, POV, time frame or setting. Employing scene breaks in early drafts can be particularly useful because it encourages you to rely on the scenes themselves, helping you avoid digressing into filler material or becoming bogged down in narrative segments.

This method can feel fragmented, however, particularly if you're using lots of short scenes, so in later drafts you may want to think about substituting some of these for **segues** – longer pieces of connecting prose that link one scene to the next. Ideally, keep these fairly brief; look towards the next scene and the next point of tension, and prevent yourself wandering off down narrative side trails that aren't adding anything.

A juggling act

Above, we've looked at some of the fundamentals of plotting, with reference to straightforward structural models. However, as with character and POV, once you've mastered the fundamentals you may well want to play around with them. It's rare to see a novel with just **one main plot thread**, for example: the chances are that there will be a number of interconnecting storylines going on at once, and it can be tricky keeping all these balls in the air.

We suggested above that if you start tinkering with structure you might want to write more than one synopsis and certainly that's the case if you have multiple plot threads. It can be useful to write several separate summaries to check that each one works, with tension peaks, a cause and effect structure, and an emotional arc underpinning it. And your various threads must come together by the end – one recurring problem we see in novels with multiple subplots is a feeling of disconnectedness. Be sure that all your subplots feel as though they knit, even if much of the novel is spent concealing or circumnavigating their connections. (This is another good example of how to work a twist into your ending – subplots that prove to mesh in a surprising and satisfying way.)

As well as checking that each subplot functions in isolation, and that they all feel like integrated parts of a wider whole, you need to decide *how* you weave them together. Will you make use of alternating chapters, each presenting a parallel, chronological narrative? Might you choose a non-chronological approach, perhaps incorporating a series of non-sequential flashbacks to reveal pieces of a puzzle that will only become clear once the final element is in place? Might you even work backwards in one of your narratives, starting with the thread's conclusion and deriving tension from the individual steps your protagonist has taken to get there? David Mitchell's *Cloud Atlas* is a wonderful example of a novel that defies structural expectations, presenting a narrative in which several seemingly distinct stories are connected in unexpected ways.

Some subplots aren't separated out from the main plot at all; they take place alongside the central action and provide a different focus for the protagonist's energies at various points in the plot. Though it seems simple, this latter can be the hardest technique to pull off. The definition imposed by establishing a distinct structure and narrative for each of your subplots can help each to function successfully; squeezing them all in together requires an enormous amount of concentration, detachment and discipline if you're not to lose your grip on each thread.

We mentored one author whose multiple plotlines each contained fascinating, tense material, drip-fed into the main plot piecemeal, here and there. However, he'd been so subtle – wanting to pace his revelations gradually and use them to build layers of mystery – that a great deal of each subplot was missing altogether. Rather than feeling like a series of cleverly intertwined subplots, the overall impression was incomplete and confusing.

First, we went through a printed copy of the narrative highlighting any material relating to each subplot in a different colour — this is a great trick that we sometimes use with authors when plotting isn't working — to get a visual impression of where the various threads appeared, how frequently, and the relative amount of material they contained. We then summarized the existing material in several separate synopses, one for each subplot, and set about filling in the gaps. Once we were satisfied that each subplot functioned individually, we reintroduced it into the main storyline in a way that still paced it carefully, but didn't leave the reader feeling lost. In this instance — as is often the case when it comes to plotting — it was a question of meticulous planning and preparation, approaching the task in a rigorous, almost mathematical way.

It can be uncomfortable applying such a methodical process to something that's basically an act of creativity, but it often makes all the difference, turning a tortuous task into a rewarding and liberating exercise. We mentioned earlier that plotting in advance can save heartache, and certainly it's easier to know where you're going before you start than it is to unpick a finished draft and begin the process of plotting from scratch. Some authors do have an instinctive sense for story structure, and the universal resonance of story arc undoubtedly helps us to *feel* when something isn't working. However, the art and technique of plotting isn't something we get taught at school; it's not surprising that it doesn't come naturally to everyone.

Many professional writers don't start until they've completed a full synopsis (often much longer than the one-page summary you'll eventually submit to agents and publishers). Others might prefer to use notecards, which can be spread out to create a visual picture of how the story flows and how different threads are weighted, and physically moved around to see what fits best where. It doesn't matter how you do your planning; the important thing is to find a technique that makes the process manageable, then remind yourself as you go that nothing is set in stone. Let the security of having a plan give you the confidence to branch out and experiment.

Our preference – and this is good advice whatever stage you're at – is to come up with a basic synopsis prior to starting, which outlines the key points on the three-act graph (or whichever structural model you're using) but leaves the detail vague. That way, you can still 'discover' the story as you write (which is where much of the creative energy comes from) but with a clear direction in mind.

Building a certain amount of freedom into your plan/synopsis helps a story feel spontaneous and lively, with a magical sense of your characters living and breathing; existing independently of you, and of the plot. In the redrafting process, if an author has become bogged down in restructuring, we may advise them to stop planning and just write – perhaps a brand new scene, one that they're excited about, where they know broadly what happens but there's loads of fun incidental detail to explore and the conflict might go in various directions. This can help to refresh their energy and let them find out something new about the story and characters, avoiding the staleness and stasis that can creep in with over-planning.

Help!

Even if you plan your story to within an inch of its life there's probably going to come a point where somebody says, *something about the plot isn't working*. Feedback like this can be difficult to deal with, unless the commentator really knows what they're talking about. Plot problems aren't always easy to pinpoint, and sometimes fixing one leads to others. There are, however, a few issues that crop up repeatedly; keep an eye out for these if you have a creeping sense that everything isn't hanging together as it should, or if your mid-section particularly is feeling flat:

- If you're writing a story with **multiple threads**, check that there aren't too many, and that they're not competing for space or taking the story in conflicting directions. Check that the material is balanced, (i.e. that each thread progresses regularly and the material for each isn't too squashed together or spaced apart) and that the threads feel connected.

- Ensure that your main character's **core goal** is in place – and that they **stay focused** on it. If they get distracted by other less pressing incidents, the goal will diminish in urgency and cease to provide narrative drive.

- Do you have **too many goals or problems**? Just as a missing central goal will result in a lack of purpose, so too many problems mounting up may lead to a protagonist who's not sure what they're supposed to be doing, and a plot that flits around without a strong central driving force.

- Have you used too many **flashbacks**, or does the narrative tend to backtrack in other ways (starting mid-scene then regressing to fill in how the characters got there; or having characters think back over events rather than dramatizing them directly)? Too much retrospection can stall forward momentum, and make the reader feel that they've missed out on something important.

- Check that there aren't too many **coincidences** sprung on the main character. Though these happen in real life, in fiction they create a sense of unreality and unpredictability. You might think it's good to be unpredictable, but actually predictability helps build tension. If absolutely anything can happen at any time, then there's no way to engage our expectations.

- Is the action **repetitive or static**; does each scene progress things in a new way?
- Is your plot material **too thin** for the length of the mid-section? Do you need more incidents; particularly more tension peaks and mini-crises?
- A common problem we see is **over-complicated backstory**; whilst it's great for a character to have a secret to uncover, if the truth they're trying to find out is excessively dense and complex, it will drag the whole story backwards. Make sure your backstory doesn't require too much explanation, or it's likely to take over the plot altogether.
- Finally, are there **too many ideas** jostling for position? This can dilute your focus, leaving us uncertain what the story is really about. If you have two or more big themes in play, be sure that these complement each other and you can give each the space it deserves. If you can't, then consider separating them out into different novels. Don't feel you have to pour all your creative output into this first book.

This brings us back to perhaps the most important thing to bear in mind when you're editing your plot: your **Big Idea**. If you find that you've wandered off course, then take some time out to mull over what you originally wanted to write about: what was your inspiration; what was the story you wanted to tell? You might find that somewhere along the line that initial idea has been swallowed up by other material, and you need to do some pruning to foreground it again.

Conversely, in exploring your Big Idea, you may have discovered that there's a different story to be told, but you're still wedded to your first vision for the plot and that's now holding you back. Either way, ask yourself, what is important to you about this story; what is the one premise that you cannot stop thinking about as you lie awake at night? By refocusing in this way, staying true to that vision, you should be able to see which bits of your plot are pulling in the right direction, and which are leading you astray.

5
Brilliant beginnings and cracking conclusions

Your opening is your first chance to wow the reader. What do you need to aim for in these crucial first pages, and how do you know what to prioritize? In this chapter we'll look at choosing the best way to kick off, depending on your genre, whilst avoiding exposition and making your style work for you. By the time you get to the final twist you'll know exactly how to achieve closure – both for your characters, and for your readers.

Start as you mean to go on

When Philip Pullman was asked how he wrote such wonderful books, he replied that it was easy: all you have to do is write a brilliant first page … and then a brilliant second page … and then a brilliant third page … He's right: it's not enough to have a fabulous first chapter – the whole book must deliver the same energy and sparkle. Editors often see this: an opening that's obviously been polished until it gleams, only for the story to drift apart further in. Hopefully, the work you've done on plotting and character will ensure that doesn't happen.

However, your first chapter does need to be extra-special. It's the first thing we'll see, and if it doesn't captivate us, we may not read on. It needs to work hard, achieving several things: it should be a breathtaking introduction to the **world of your story**, immersing us vividly in your setting and establishing tone and genre. It will normally introduce your **main character**, or at least some of the supporting cast – and these characters need to be intriguing. It's your first opportunity to showcase your **style and voice** – so no room here for imperfection; we're looking for strong, confident prose. And perhaps most importantly, it should begin to **build tension** – posing a compelling question, establishing your main character's key goal or problem, or launching into edge-of-the-seat action.

The best openings will usually present a combination of these elements. Certain genres, like fantasy or sci-fi, may spend longer on world-building but might have this underpinning a dramatic, extraordinary scenario to provide momentum. Others – crime fiction, for example – may foreground tension and suspense; literary fiction might preference theme and style. Below, we'll look at some successful opening gambits from published authors; at the same time, we'll flag up a few problem areas associated with each beginning, and look at what you can do to avoid them.

Take us on a journey

Plunging head first into an unfamiliar environment can certainly be a great way to hook a reader. Sometimes the **world of a story** can be wonderful enough on its own – we're happy to sit back and enjoy the ride because the scenery is so fantastic.

Jeff Noon's sci-fi classic *Vurt* throws us into a setting that's both familiar and strange, and it's a compelling, psychedelic blend. His main characters are waiting in a van outside the *all-night Vurt-U-Want* – a dime store selling mind-altering 'Vurt' feathers. Outside the shop is a *genuine dog, flesh and blood ... the kind you don't see much any more.* And in the van, hunched between the protagonist and his partners in crime, lies *the Thing-from-Outer-Space.* Deft touches of otherness amidst semi-recognizable flashes of realism provide sharp, unsettling little glimpses of this world.

This alone would make for a page-turning opening, but Noon also incorporates multiple questions and lots of tension: these guys are breaking the law, and on the very next page a *shadow-cop* arrives on the scene and the friends are forced to flee, with the story briefly turning into a high-speed car chase; we then see the characters indulging in the drugs they've acquired (which do strange and scary things); next, the second chapter blindsides us with a different narrative voice – the *Game Cat*, a reviewer of Vurts, who speaks in a kind of cyber patois and describes some of the terrifying things that can happen to you during the Vurt experience (and these, he says, are the 'safe' ones. What must the 'unsafe' ones be like?). This opening features a lot of world-building alongside action, tension and stylish prose.

If your opening is likely to revolve around your setting, then the main pitfall to beware of is an excess of **expositional material** explicitly explaining elements of the story, setting and background. When you've created a whole fictional universe, it can be tempting to lay it all out upfront, telling us everything you know about it, digressing to describe things that aren't immediately relevant. In these circumstances, even the most fascinating setting can become dry and dull to read about.

We worked with an author whose world-building was exceptional: every detail of her futuristic fantasy universe had been thought through with precision and consistency; her creations were original, and they all felt as though they *belonged* – with a homogeneous background, a cultural and historical through-line tying them together. She also had a lot of exciting action; however, she frequently halted scenes to give us lengthy explanations about locations and artefacts, which stalled the action-tension. Because of this, what ought to have been fascinating details of setting were becoming frustrating interruptions – writing many readers would skim. The side-by-side combination of these two individually strong elements was doing justice to neither.

We encouraged her to think of the world-building she'd done as background research, informing the present-day action but not essential to spell out. We worked through the first few chapters doing some ruthless red-penning of any detail that was interesting but peripheral, and finding ways to **hint at** the underlying background rather than explaining it all. This sped up the action scenes and maintained tension, but it also made the setting more involving, requiring the reader's own imagination. Subtle suggestions that pointed towards a huge, unspoken past; little titbits of juicy detail; characters who took the history of their world for granted. With a lighter touch, the author started to feel like the master of her universe – seeing everything but revealing only what she needed the reader to know – rather than a tour guide trying to cram too much into one day.

Make the character count

A **strong main character** can be a good draw in your opening pages. Your main character is a conduit into the story – often a confidante; someone who the reader may come to know almost as well as their own friends and family. In fact, sometimes better, because we can get inside the minds of fictional characters more closely than we can with real people. If that character is vivid, with an especially compelling problem or outlook, then it makes sense to introduce them upfront. And for certain genres, like teen fiction or women's commercial – where caring about the main character is perhaps one of the main reasons readers choose and stick with a story – this is particularly true.

An interesting example here is Sue Townsend's *The Secret Diary of Adrian Mole*. From the first pages this mordant, pretentious teenager, old before his years, manages to draw us in in spite of his pessimistic outlook, because of his wit and insight. He's not especially likeable, and perhaps that's why this is a useful study; we don't have to fall in love with the main character for them to be compelling. But we do have to see something in them – something of ourselves, perhaps – and Adrian Mole speaks both to teenagers, with his concerns about his spots, his non-existent sex life, and his excruciating family; and to older readers too, as a spokesperson for his time and his experience of life under Thatcherism. We have to care about the main character; to mind what happens to them; to want them to succeed, which it's hard not to when Adrian is so beset by troubles.

Though this sort of opening works particularly well with first-person narrators, we don't have to hear from a character in their own words for them to draw us in. Sophie Kinsella's Rebecca Bloomwood, the eponymous *Shopaholic*, is a hugely memorable and engaging creation. In the first book in the series we meet her not in her own voice, but in a series of letters from her bank in dry, corporate language, during which it becomes clear that she's in dire financial trouble and resorting to increasingly desperate and funny measures to avoid a meeting with the bank manager. By the time Rebecca speaks to us directly we're already on her side, intrigued by her predicament and wondering how she got into it (and how she'll get out).

Strong characters can have their downsides. We worked with one author whose protagonist was particularly striking: a hero whose ambition and fearlessness – in spite of the expectations imposed on him by his social class – should have made him sympathetic and appealing. However, he was deeply self-analytical; he spent a lot of time thinking about his place in the world, and as a result his inner life was more developed than his interactions with other characters. He came across as arrogant and detached, and because of the time we spent inside his head there was less space in the story for action-tension. His interactions with other characters, which ought to have been providing tension and drama, seemed almost absent from the story: he spent more time dwelling on them than we did on witnessing them. In this instance, we did some work on scene structure and Show not Tell so that, rather than cutting the inner voice and losing one of the things that made the character special, we allowed both character and reader to be more *present* in each scene. We'll talk about this more in Chapter 8.

As we discussed in Chapter 3, an overpowering narrative voice can make or break a novel depending on whether the reader likes it or not, so ask yourself if it's worth risking alienating some of your readership by handing over the reins to a character who may divide the crowd – especially in those all-important opening pages.

Rock your style

Some genres place a higher value on a **conspicuous narrative voice** – prose where you notice the writing almost more than the story. Some historical fiction, for instance, might employ a more varied or colloquial vocabulary; more complex sentence constructions; more focus on rhythm and the sounds of the words; and might have a tendency to linger over narrative segments for longer, rather than diving straight into scenes and interactions. In literary fiction, authors may use the lyricism and flair of their writing to impress us in the opening. Even in genres where you might not expect style to be so significant, like women's or children's, the trade often cites 'a strong voice' as the thing that convinced them to read on. Rich language, used with an expert touch, can work in all genres to elevate a book into bestselling territory.

Kevin Crossley-Holland's *Arthur* novels carry the rhythm and rhyme structures of Anglo-Saxon poetry – not necessarily an approach you'd expect with teen fiction. And Iain M Banks's *Culture* novels – science fiction – are often beautifully, poetically penned reminders of the fact that their author was also a successful writer of literary fiction. The opening of *Use of Weapons* begins as a reverie on a glass goblet, described in lush, sensual language, before the author reveals a backdrop of faded grandeur, violence and dissolution, and the scene descends into war-ravaged chaos.

Fundamentally, there's nothing to stop you using lyrical or impactful language whatever genre you're writing in … as long as you have a solid reason to do so, you know your writing is good enough (don't confuse stylish prose with overwriting) and as long as it doesn't detract from the story or push your inciting incident and sources of tension into the background. And that's the key point: relying too heavily on style as the driving force in the opening chapters is risky, because for many readers it's just not their number one concern. If you're a literary writer, or one who feels style is particularly important, give some thought to what *else* your opening pages are offering.

In contemporary publishing, even 'serious' literary fiction tends to have more going for it than just its style. Michel Faber's *The Crimson Petal and the White* hooks us in the opening pages with its unusual second-person voice that whispers directly to us – tales of secrets, shame and sordid assignations. However, it also presents a compelling story and a diverse cast of characters who pass the reins of the storytelling on from one to the next, as though they're leading the reader by the hand. What could feel like a self-conscious literary device is used for a distinct purpose: giving us an opportunity to experience Victorian London with great intimacy, as though we are literally exploring its back streets alongside the characters.

Or, look at Kevin Powers' *The Yellow Birds*, a prize-winning novel set during the Iraq War which features memorable prose – lyrical but not romanticized – and whose first line, *The war tried to kill us in the spring*, contains the promise of violence, pathos, self-reflection and richness of setting: all the things that make the novel special. As well as a thoughtful literary piece this is, however, a coming-of-age story and a harrowing, tense exploration of the emotional and physical consequences of conflict. Its opening sets up this blend in measured style, with descriptions of war-ravaged settings and communities and insight into the main character's ambivalent attitude to death, all running alongside the tension and drama of an ongoing military offensive.

So it's important that, even when you know your prose is a selling point, you don't allow your opening to drift off into self-indulgent waffle. If you're a strong writer, this will be just as evident if your prose is restrained, and the action is allowed to speak for itself; understated writing is often the mark of a stronger, more confident writer, who has enough faith in their talent to know that they don't need to show off.

One author we mentored had a beautiful writing voice; his descriptions were lush without being overwritten, and his characters were deft and nuanced. However, he was uncertain when it came to plotting and tension and had therefore relied on his style to carry the opening, which was basically an extended stream of consciousness. Because he wasn't as confident in other areas the novel never developed beyond this leisurely, reflective pace. There was no clear inciting incident and several chapters in, we were still meandering; the story lacked direction. We went back to some plotting basics, ensuring each scene or chapter had a definite point of tension (though, as this was literary fiction much of this tension was subtle and character-based) and checking that the story contained enough drama and incident to keep it moving.

Finger on the pulse

A great way to grab us by the gut during your opening is to present a situation that's full of tension and questions. These don't have to be explicitly phrased in the narrative, which might feel contrived. It's more about establishing scenarios that seem mysterious; creating a conflict with no obvious resolution; introducing the main character's apparently insoluble problem. You should be encouraging us to wonder, explore, and question: *What's going on here? How can this possibly be resolved? How are they going to get out of this one?*

Stephen King's *The Stand* opens like this: Charlie, who may or may not be our protagonist, wakes up his wife/girlfriend (we don't know) in the middle of the night and orders her to get dressed. They have to get away, *now*. Her words to him are a question that voices the reader's own sudden uncertainty: *'What is it? What's wrong?'* He's desperate, terrified, but the author resists the temptation to tell us what's going on. Instead, the opening keeps us guessing, and by the end of the short chapter all we've found out for certain is that Charlie's mysterious colleagues – where he works, and what he does, remains unanswered – are all dead. Charlie should have died too, but he's managed to escape. But he's sick: the last line of the chapter makes that clear in an understated way: *By dawn they were running east across Nevada and Charlie was coughing steadily.* We might think we've figured out some of what's going on, but much of the situation is unvoiced because of the assumed knowledge between the characters, so we can't be sure. We can't resist turning the page to find out more.

If you want your opening to be mysterious, there are a couple of things to be aware of. Do be sure that the questions you set up, which may seem beautifully tantalizing at the time, don't **hold back your plot**; that they are **pertinent**; and that they can be answered in a way that **progresses the action**. We've worked with a few authors who've chosen to deal with the afterlife in their work; in one novel, the opening scene was of a character being shot after a bank robbery went wrong – and awaking in hell. It was an intriguing scenario posing plenty of questions: why was the character involved in a life of crime; what went wrong; what will happen to him next; is there any way back; can he undo his past mistakes (and does he want to)?

However, the next few chapters spent a long time dwelling on these questions, skirting around the answers in a way that began to feel as though the author was deliberately withholding the truth to manufacture tension. The 'real' plot, which was about the devil's grand plan for the character, didn't get going until almost Act 3. To address this, we came up with an opening that established slightly different questions; the story needed to start in a different place, one that was more reflective of the story's *real* central concerns, and that didn't lead us down false trails.

If your opening sets up some compelling questions, then as a rule you should answer these in the next few chapters, using the answers to take the story off in new directions and pose *new* questions. It's like the principles of scene structure, discussed above: in addition to your overarching central plot tension, individual scenes can and should have their own point of tension, but this should generally be something that will either be answered in the same chapter, or at least within the next couple. If your plot is full of scene after scene of unresolved tension points, we will begin to feel cheated; similarly, if your opening gambit is a thrilling, mysterious question which you then refuse to answer, you're not playing fair.

However, authors do break these rules. Michael Grant's *Gone* series is a good case in point. Here, the very first line introduces the story's main question, which is also the teenage protagonist's problem: during class, the teacher disappears ... and we later find that *all* the adults in the town have disappeared. The immediate question is: *what happened to them?* And the author doesn't answer this definitively until almost the last volume in a seven book series.

How does he get away with it? It's a balancing act: he drip-feeds answers that give us some of the picture but not all of it; substitutes further questions that may or may not hold the answer to the original question; and above all, includes so much action-tension that we can't help but keep reading. The story becomes a battle for survival in a world with no adults, where kids do whatever it takes to live. Each book in the series reveals more about what's taken place, gradually piecing together a fascinating puzzle; but the individual plots are much more about the power struggles between the characters, and the limits of human cruelty and endurance.

So, if you opt for an opening that layers questions on top of one another, know that you can only tease us up to a point: you must either answer these before too long; or, offer alternative sources of tension that are sufficiently gripping and intriguing that we don't mind the fact that you've sidestepped solving your original mystery.

Be extraordinary

If you want your opening to make an impact, then presenting a situation that's strange and out of the ordinary is a less subtle device, but it's certainly effective. There are various ways of approaching this, many of which we've already discussed – an unusual setting, a compelling and original main character, a vivid, unique writing voice – however, to be truly extraordinary you're looking at coming up with a scenario that, ideally, the reader has never encountered before; something that makes them sit up and go *wow!* Or maybe, *what the…?!*

Patrick Ness' *The Knife of Never Letting Go* is a great example of an author gripping us with a premise that feels genuinely original. In the opening pages we meet Todd and his dog, Manchee, and we learn that Todd and Manchee can effectively 'speak' to one another – at least, Todd can hear Manchee's thoughts. So far, pretty intriguing – we may have read novels where characters talk to animals before, but we might not have seen one where the author deals with the subject in so literal and humorous a manner (Manchee's first words to Todd are, *'need a poo'*).

We quickly find out that not only can Todd hear Manchee's thoughts, he can hear *everyone's* thoughts, and everyone else can hear his, too. The novel's location remains mysterious, but its inhabitants are blessed – or cursed – with the ability to read everyone's minds, all the time. Again, we might have seen novels exploring the idea of mind-reading, but the concept of it being wholly involuntary, and all-encompassing, feels fresh, and sets up some nicely creepy tension: if anyone can know what you're thinking, how can you have secrets? How can you ever tell a lie, and what happens if you try?

If you're using an extraordinary scenario as a hook, then do exercise caution. It's easy enough to come up with a weird idea – let's say, an opening chapter in which a woman gives birth to an octopus – but ask yourself if there's a reason why no one's done it before. Maybe it's just so shocking and strange that it would put most readers off altogether (though doubtless it will intrigue some). Maybe it leaves nowhere for the story to go. Maybe it's obviously a schlock tactic that doesn't offer any subtleties of tension or nuance, leaving us not with questions, so much as a question mark: what's the point? Be certain that your opening isn't just there *because* it's unusual, but because it's **intrinsic to the story**.

We worked with an author whose opening scene featured characters taking part in a race on wonderfully steampunk mechanical horses – a race which ended with a devastating accident. It was wholly original, thrilling, fun and unusual enough to make me take notice. However, as the story got going it became clear that this opening had very little to do with the ongoing plot. If anything, it appeared to introduce an extremely anachronistic element into a setting that was broadly Roman Empire-era.

It turned out that the opening was indicative of a key issue: a lack of focus; a sense of overcrowdedness that extended into all areas including plot, setting, character, genre and tone. The author had so many ideas that she'd been reluctant to let go of, and as a result the novel was a mishmash of disparate elements. We looked for ways to strip back the story so that it wasn't trying to achieve so much (a crucial point for the author was accepting that this didn't mean losing her ideas, just deferring them for future projects) and finding an opening that show-cased the novel's originality but also foregrounded its *most important* themes and characters. The scene we settled on was different, but no less extraordinary.

Start with a bang

The final sort of opening we will look at is one rooted in **action-tension**: a story which starts with a whopping punch, either by joining the action *in medias res*, as something exciting is hap-pening, or by flashing forward or back to a dramatic moment from elsewhere in the story. This technique is commonly used in thrillers, for obvious reasons: what better way to get the heart racing than by jumping in at a point of crisis or chaos?

Dan Brown's phenomenally successful *The Da Vinci Code* is a great example: the opening scene is a curator staggering through a museum, yanking a painting off the wall to set off the alarm and call someone to his rescue – but too late; his attacker finishes him off. In the seconds before he dies, Saunière must find a way to pass on the secret he's been killed for in such a way that it will only fall into safe hands... It's a violent, dramatic scene that establishes the book's central mystery up-front. On top of this, it gives us a character we can relate to in a desperate, life or death situation.

Killing Floor, Lee Child's first Jack Reacher novel, opens with the line, *I was arrested in Eno's Diner* and goes on to describe an initially placid scene of the protagonist having breakfast, before armed cops screech up and drag him in for murder. What can possibly justify such an over-the-top arrest, we wonder – but as the protagonist muses on the various mistakes the police are making and cold-bloodedly evaluates the ways in which he'd be able to overpower them, if he chose to, we start to realize what a dangerous adversary he is. Though the rest of the scene plays out relatively quietly, it's underpinned by the constant possibility of violence. If anything, the protagonist's deadpan exterior ramps up the tension, as we wait to see what he might do.

Some novels might merely hint at huge action about to take place. The opening paragraph of *The Girl on the Train* by Paula Hawkins is a sort of epitaph, beginning: *She's buried beneath a silver birch tree.* Who is buried; when and how did they die; at what point are we going to find out? Again, this works well because it foreshadows some cracking action, but also because it lays out the story's tone and themes so uncompromisingly: death, loss, secrets, lies. For a thriller, this is meat and potatoes: *yes*, we think, *this is going to deliver.*

If you want to kick things off with action, or the promise of action, then there are a few considerations. First and foremost: is your action scene **relevant**? The sequence you open with should be essential to your plot, rather than something you've selected purely because it feels so exciting. We worked with one author in the developmental stages of his manuscript whose sample opening chapter was a kick-ass scene featuring martial-arts wielding monks from ancient Tibet. However, looking at his synopsis and subsequent chapters we couldn't see any sign of these characters reappearing. When we discussed it, it transpired that this was backstory, laying the groundwork for a plot that featured wholly contemporary characters. Much like the mechanical horses discussed above, the Tibetan monks were scene-stealers, mainly there to catch the eye. Though the author was sorry to lose his attention-grabbing opening, the replacement we came up with was a truer reflection of the main thrust. And it was ultimately more gripping, because it featured characters who were far more invested in the remainder of the story.

Another of our authors opted for a flash-forward as a prologue, using an action scene from later in the novel in which the main character was close to death. However, the scene gave too much away, so that when we arrived at the point in the novel at which the scene appeared in 'real time', it wasn't as surprising or shocking as it could have been, and it felt predictable. So, if you do choose to lift a scene from somewhere else to use as your punchy opening, be sure that the new sequence doesn't **undermine tension**.

Finally, be sure that you don't ramp up the action at the expense of **character**. Most successful action-tension openings also offer us something in the way of emotion to hook us in on a level that's about more than just crash-bang-wallop. If the action is happening to someone we don't care about, it will carry less impact irrespective of how dramatic it is. We worked with an author who had grasped this necessity beautifully: the character he chose as his POV died in the first scene, so didn't reappear in the novel (much like the Dan Brown example above) but nevertheless, the author wanted us to empathize with her; she felt like a living breathing human. However, he'd taken it a bit far, incorporating so much of the character's emotional life and backstory that the chapter was stodgy and overlong. The reader's attention was less on the thrill of the scene than it was on filing away all this data, which eventually turned out to be peripheral. So, you need to give us enough of an emotional inroad that the action feels meaningful, without skewing our focus onto misleading elements.

If you're still unsure about how to open, play around with a few alternatives. The right first page might not be the first one to occur to you, and often the solution may be to start somewhere completely different. This can be both daunting and liberating: since the first page is often the very first thing you'll have written, it's natural to be wedded to it. However, this attachment can blind you to other possibilities, so do try something else – even if it's just an experiment, and you end up going back to your original, you may come up with some refreshing new ideas.

The best opening will probably present a blend of these ideas. It might include your inciting incident, though, as we've seen, this can be obliquely referred to, happen off-stage, or take place long before the action of the story; it doesn't have to be dramatized before our eyes to be an effective starting point. Your opening should, above all, excite, intrigue, and captivate – so that we cannot help but read on.

Finishing with fireworks

Ending a novel is very different from beginning one: in the opening pages, with everything to play for but nothing on the table yet, you can afford to take risks; be bold and adventurous. A novel's ending, however, is all about satisfaction (note that this is not necessarily the same thing as making us feel happy) and you can get away with less than you can in the beginning: the reader is looking for a just reward for sticking with the story and without that, the whole experience of the book may be soured for them. Even if you've told a cracking tale, the feeling they're left with at the conclusion is what they'll remember.

A great deal of a denouement's success depends on how well it resolves what's gone before. So, in this section we will look primarily at some key targets to hit in your conclusion, so you can be sure your reader will go away feeling good about the story. We'll also discuss a few little tricks you can implement – once you know all the essentials are in place – to give your denouement more sparkle, and to help you break the rules if you want to.

Finish what you've started

This is probably the most important point, and the main purpose of Act 3. As well as providing an exciting or emotive climax, an ending should resolve your central narrative arc; the problem or goal that you've set up should have been addressed, and even if the main character hasn't achieved what they set out to, something fundamental should have changed.

In most novels the conclusion either directly or indirectly answers the novel's central question. To pick a couple of the above examples, in *The Da Vinci Code*, Langdon, the protagonist, solves the last part of the puzzle literally in the final scenes, and is led to the resting place (we suppose) of the holy grail, the secret that the museum curator was so desperate to protect. In *Before I Go To Sleep*, Christine remembers the incident that caused her amnesia, and uncovers the identity of the person who threatens her. We may not know whether she'll have her memory back for good, but that was never the point: we have found out what happened to her, and are confident that she's now safe.

But what if you don't?

There are, of course, novels that don't offer a completely neat and tidy resolution, as with *Gone*, discussed above. In these cases, authors will generally present us with a denouement that satisfies a narrative need for progression; that delivers a sense that something has been learned and the characters have moved forward. If you do decide you don't want to tie off absolutely everything, at the very least you should still answer many or most of the story's central questions, and provide a climax that resolves the main action plot.

In *Gone*, the denouement resists answering the key question about what has happened to the adults. However, the children left behind after the adults vanished have discovered that in this new world many of them have supernatural powers, and that some of them are prepared to use these in violent and manipulative ways. By the conclusion the main antagonist, Caine, who has provided the bulk of the novel's conflict, has been vanquished, and the dynamic is stable – for now. In this way, the main plot – existing alongside the overarching problem – has been resolved.

Simultaneously, at the moment of the denouement, the characters learn something new about their prison – something that fills in at least part of the puzzle. When you turn 15, *something* comes to summon you away and take you to wherever it is your parents have gone. This *something* seems sinister, and cannot be trusted, and our hero has to make the impossible choice between leaving and finding his mother, or staying in this place of danger and chaos. The choice he makes may not address *all* our questions, but the answers we get are **just enough to give us closure**.

Complete your character

Just as important as rounding off the action plot – indeed, often more so – is delivering **satisfying character development**. In David Nicholls' *Us*, the character's main goal is winning back his wife, and at the end she's with somebody else – not, on the face of it, the happiest or most complete outcome. However, the protagonist has realized that getting to know his son and making up for his mistakes was more significant; and it's enough that he's done the right thing, even if it didn't get him what he wanted. This bittersweet mood, where a character has on the surface failed but in reality has progressed in a deeper, more intangible way, is often the type of conclusion that will linger longest and resonate most.

By contrast, a lack of character development can feel purposeless – if nothing has changed, what has the *point* been? We worked with one author whose contemporary novel featured a protagonist whose drug addiction was ruining his life. By Act 3, he'd successfully resolved the various problems and obstacles the plot had thrown at him, but he hadn't grown as a character and it was obvious he was going to continue down the same path. Though in action terms the plot was essentially complete, the novel still felt *emotionally* unresolved.

The author was keen to retain this nihilistic sense that some people just can't change, no matter what they go through. Since he was writing literary fiction (where a 'happy ending' isn't such a prerequisite as it might be in certain other genres, and where it's almost expected that your denouement challenges expectations) we agreed on a compromise, making the ending more ambiguous. We left the protagonist at a turning point, about to make a decision that would demonstrate his character development (or lack thereof). We wouldn't find out for certain whether and how he'd changed, but we'd have the option of interpreting his actions in a couple of different ways, thereby allowing the author to keep hints of the darker tone he was after, without forcing a negative/non-progressive outcome on the reader.

Using ambiguity

Ambiguity in the resolution can be useful, as above: either to counteract too much negativity, or temper an unequivocally happy ending if that's not what the author's looking for. In *Us*, a more commercial novel that needed to deliver a more positive ending, but where a neat return to marital bliss wouldn't have been true to the characters, the story's coda offers the prospect of a new relationship for the protagonist, but doesn't answer the question of whether it will definitely happen. In spite of (or perhaps because of) its ambiguity, the story's ending suggests a new beginning; a hopeful, uplifting direction for the protagonist.

Or, consider a crime story where the killer is unmasked but not apprehended – as in Agatha Christie's *Murder on the Orient Express*. Outwardly this might defy all convention and expectation; an ending that fails to deliver on its genre's most basic requirements. However, here, the story takes care to reveal the secret lives of the characters and the devastation wreaked by the 'victim' – someone who can truly be said to have got their just deserts. The resolution, which allows the killers the chance but not the certainty of freedom, is far more satisfying than a straightforward procedural ending would have been.

Don't be depressing!

As with the author above, who wanted his ending to be reflective of the darker side of human nature, we often have to convince authors to avoid too much negativity in their denouements. If the tone set by the final chapters is the one the reader will take away with them, you don't want to leave them feeling too bleak.

This approach might be more common in literary fiction, where the demands of theme and style may outweigh any need for emotional satisfaction: perhaps an author wants us to think, more than they care about our feelings.

In F. Scott Fitzgerald's *The Great Gatsby* the eponymous hero is murdered in the final act, and no one attends his funeral in spite of the fact that he is, on the surface, a popular socialite. Pursuing its theme of the illusory nature of the American Dream (Gatsby has accrued wealth and influence by shady dealings to seduce his childhood sweetheart, but has still failed to win her or learn from his life), the novel's denouement encapsulates the idea that it's impossible to create a new, real self by means that are so wholly shallow. To make such a convincing case – and to create a story that has resonance both as an echo of the era and, arguably, now more than ever – this ending is a stark necessity.

However, there are few authors, particularly those writing more commercial fiction, who could get away with such a hopeless picture of humanity in general or their own characters in particular. Indeed, there are not many novels that – like *Gatsby* – seem to actively *require* this approach. That said, there are many novels that don't end 'happily'. So how do these avoid leaving the reader with a bitter taste in the mouth? To look at another example by David Nicholls, in *One Day* the heroine dies just a few chapters from the end. Having followed the central love story throughout – and in a tone that is generally light and warm, suited to romantic fiction – this feels like a tragedy. How can the author spring this on us? Here, the sadness is tempered firstly with a redemptive scene featuring the protagonists' daughter, offering the possibility of a hopeful future; and secondly, with a flashback to the lovers' parting after their first ever meeting – a goodbye kiss, a blossoming friendship, a promise to stay in touch. It's a farewell that feels far less permanent than the one we've just endured. In this way the novel's conclusion allows us to revisit some of our earlier, happier emotions, and that sweetly poignant mood is what we take away.

Keep the focus

Particularly when an author has planned follow-up stories there can be a tendency to layer in multiple new threads in the last few chapters. You'll often see this in long-running TV dramas – the penultimate episode in the series or season is spent bringing the narrative arc of this season to a close, and the final episode begins to set up new arcs that will be followed through in the next. It's an approach that may work with the visual, immediate medium of television (though even here it can be frustrating to have new characters and ideas introduced when we're more interested in those we know and love). But in a novel – inherently a more self-contained form – it can feel very digressive.

Whichever structure you've used, the main purpose of the final Act or closing chapters is to resolve the threads of *this plot*, ensuring that the reader's investment is paid off; that the central storyline is given space to be concluded satisfyingly. The final Act tends to be fairly short for a reason: we have expended a lot of energy and emotion getting here and once the climax of this story is over we're generally about ready to sign off, say good-bye to the characters, and reflect upon what we've read. If too many new threads are introduced, our attention and focus may wander, and we may leave the novel feeling as though we've missed something. And in the fickle world of publishing, where the fate of follow-up books can depend on the success of the first, you can't afford to give us any reason to feel downbeat. You want the reader to rave about your book to their friends;

review it favourably online; buy it for their mum's next birthday present ... the irony is that, in using the closing chapters to prepare for your follow-up, you may scupper your chances of that sequel ever making it into print.

In addition to this, filling a conclusion with 'teasers' is risky. We worked on one novel whose ending featured several brand new characters and ideas, including an enticing reference to a supernatural theme – something which had been absent from the plot so far. It felt as though we were now hearing about characters and situations which were potentially more dramatic and interesting than those we'd spent a whole novel following. We did some cutting to streamline the conclusion, but also replotted so that tantalizing titbits of this new material were woven into the current story, informing the action and ensuring the conclusion felt less out on a limb.

Leave us hanging ... At your peril

This is a related but subtly different point: do you want to leave us on a cliffhanger? It's a risky strategy that can work under certain circumstances. The first book in Philip Pullman's *His Dark Materials* trilogy ends on a wonderful cliffhanger, with the heroine Lyra, a long way from her humble origins in Oxford, having both failed and succeeded in harrowing ways, stepping over a bridge into a new world with no idea what awaits her. There are clear parallels between this and the story we discussed above: it's a new idea, introduced right at the end, that takes the story off in a very different direction and leaves us with no solid answers about what might happen next.

However, in Pullman's case this works, for a number of reasons. Firstly, Lyra's voyage into the new world is a continuation of her quest to find her father. It's the start of a new quest, too, but it's also the inevitable end point of everything that's gone before – if she didn't cross that bridge, she would always remain incomplete, with unanswered questions. Secondly, the main dramatic focus of this first story (Lyra is trying to find and rescue her best friend) has been resolved – albeit tragically – and the resolution to that thread is what has brought Lyra to this pass. Finally, hints towards this 'new world' have been subtly set up throughout the story, providing an underlying layer of mystery and strangeness so that, as well as posing new questions, this bridge into a new world is also an answer to questions the first story has established. So this finale might be a gateway into the next novel, but it's also an ending.

If you want to conclude your story with a cliffhanger or an unanswered question, this is an excellent model. Ask yourself: if the next book in my proposed series never gets published, will a reader feel cheated by the ending I've delivered? Does my cliffhanger feel like too much of a loose end, or is it integrated enough to work as a satisfying resolution to *this* story? If you think you might be guilty of leaving things too open, it's time for some honest self-questioning.

Perhaps your climax is lacking punch, and you used a cliffhanger to give it more impact. In this case, you might need to look again at the structure of Act 3, and maybe even at the plot overall, and find a more organic way to ramp up the final scenes. Perhaps – as with the author who introduced an unexpected supernatural element – you are secretly more interested in the subject of the second book than in that of the first, in which case you must ask yourself: is this the book I should have written instead? Or, is there a way to work this material more fully into the current novel? Perhaps you simply couldn't let go, and ended up leaving the novel open-ended because you weren't sure how to say goodbye. In that case, it's a question of working backwards, trying to figure out the story's natural end point. Accepting that a novel really is finished will allow you to conclude convincingly, rather than limply fading away or leaving the reader hanging.

Tighten the tension

This advice applies more to the end of Act 2 and the earlier part of Act 3 than to your final scenes. Sometimes, an author might reach their climax too soon, perhaps deal with it too quickly, and spend longer over the denouement in an attempt to restore weight to the final chapters. But a reader may start to lose interest once we feel the main action is over. Make sure you bring the action plot to a dramatic close, giving it due space, and incorporating your main character's progression. Then, tie up any remaining story threads fairly quickly and make the final scenes a swift winding down, focusing primarily on the mood you want to leave us with.

Alternatively, authors sometimes use a series of mini-climaxes instead of one major climax for their conclusion, and this can be more problematic to address. Have you ever watched one of those action films where the denouement goes on forever, with one explosive moment after another, and each time we think 'this must be it – surely!' something else happens? We can't help feeling that we ought to be excited, but with each climax our involvement and the background tension diminishes.

We worked with one author whose major climax featured a huge confrontation between the heroine and her mother, along with some explosive revelations about the true identity of the heroine's father and the secret he had died trying to hide. It was clear that this was a defining moment: the answer to the riddle the protagonist had been trying to puzzle out – both emotionally and literally – and the point at which she was finally able to move on. However, following this there were two or three more, smaller climaxes, each revealing a few more of the story's secrets. In contrast to what we'd already discovered, these details felt like small fry, and with every revelation (and the amount of narrative prose and action required to link these moments together) the tension slackened.

We needed to do some juggling – it wouldn't work to incorporate the smaller 'reveals' earlier, since they would have been too obvious hints towards the major revelation. Instead, we ended up merging some scenes and speeding up the progression of the final chapters so that these mini-climaxes didn't drag things out too much. At the same time, by keeping one part of the major revelation back, we withheld the protagonist's emotional resolution for a little longer so that the desire to see her happy and fulfilled kept us reading.

The final twist

In Chapter 4, we touched on the use of twists. These are most frequently associated with certain types of novel: psychological thrillers, crime and murder mysteries. However, the twist can be useful in almost any type of fiction, and you may well have tried, whether consciously or not, to work one into your novel. Having a point at which things take a dramatic turn in a different direction can help you in a number of ways – by allowing you to draw previously disparate threads together; by ramping up the tension just when you need it most; by delivering a gut blow which makes us think all is lost before you resolve things satisfyingly. Indeed, the rug-pulling moment is itself a form of twist.

There are a number of different approaches you can take – the art of the twist is almost a book in itself – but it can be helpful to think of them as falling roughly into a few (main) categories, including the **reversal**, the **revelation**, the **reappearance**, and the **epiphany**.

Rebecca (Daphne du Maurier) contains a great example of a **reversal**: our heroine challenges the aloof and impenetrable Max to admit he still loves his ex-wife, fully expecting him to confirm her worst fears. However, instead he floors his young wife with the truth – he hated Rebecca, and indeed, he *killed* her. This is also a superb example of a **double twist**, where one dramatic revelation is superseded by another that's even more stunning. From that point the novel is a series of twists, as Rebecca's body is found and the truth about her death starts to come out in a way which keeps the reader hanging for as long as possible.

In *Finding Nemo* (2003), Marlin has been terrified of the dangers of the ocean after the death of his wife, and this has made him mollycoddle his son, Nemo, causing Nemo to deliberately take a risk that leads to him being lost at sea. Marlin, embarking on a dangerous journey to find him, meets Dory, whose recklessness and lack of forward planning is anathema to Marlin. Only by letting go of his fears and throwing himself into things as Dory does can Marlin succeed in finding his son, and coming to this **epiphany** is the point at which the plot shifts irrevocably into a new gear; we suddenly feel that success might be possible after all.

The **reappearance** tends to be action-based; a simple example would be the end of *Jurassic Park* (1993), where the T-Rex who we've almost forgotten about in all the excitement returns at the end to save the day – despite the fact that for the majority of the film it has been trying to kill our heroes. This surprising reappearance turns our expectations upside down, and provides, in retrospect, the only possible escape from seemingly certain death. Another quite different example is Nabokov's *Lolita*, where a titbit of information presented in an 'editor's note' at the beginning comes full circle to reveal, in the last moments of the story, that the heroine dies in childbirth.

Some authors use a **Deus ex Machina** as part of their plot twist – an out-of-the-blue event or an intervention from other character/s that we have no chance of predicting, as in *Us*, where the protagonist is stung by jellyfish and saved by his son, repairing their fractured relationship. However, be wary of this device as it can leave the denouement seeming disconnected from what's gone before, and make the protagonist feel passive.

In *Us*, the healing process had begun before this incident, and the emotional climax that has already taken place satisfies the reader that the protagonist has, largely, saved himself. The jellyfish incident serves as a bathetic reminder that even though the protagonist has changed and grown, he is always going to be the kind of person *to whom things happen*, even when he's trying his hardest to *make things happen himself*. In that way it forms a thematic bridge towards the story's coda, where the hero does something completely out of character and pro-active, and which marks the watershed between his old life and his new one.

Twists featuring **revelations** are probably the most common: consider how many novels and films you've encountered where the denouement hinges on a secret being revealed, a true identity being unmasked, or a truth that we thought was certain being turned upside down: *The Sixth Sense* (1999), *The Hound of the Baskervilles*, many of the *Harry Potter* novels, *The Crying Game* (1992), *The Matrix* (1999) … this sort of twist is commonly, but not exclusively, used in crime fiction and thrillers. Though it's used a lot it's one of the hardest twists to pull off successfully because it requires such a subtle handling of the preceding material – you don't want to give the truth away, but nor should you obscure it so completely that we feel you've tricked us.

Whatever you choose as your plot twist, the ideal scenario is one where you take us by surprise, but which still feels *right* – where we can look back at the action and think, yes, that makes sense. The twist feels like a logical, natural outcome.

The above is a fairly comprehensive checklist of things your climactic scenes should be achieving, and though it might seem a little prescriptive, we've also tried to demonstrate some ways in which you can break the rules without compromising your vision and intent, and **without disappointing the reader**. The most important thing to consider is the tone and feeling we're left with – if the main goal of a novel's conclusion is satisfaction, then ask yourself what demands the rest of the novel has set up that now need to be fulfilled.

Because of this, the mood you leave us with may partly depend on genre, your plot, and what tone you've aimed for elsewhere. Broadly, romantic fiction tends to carry the expectation of a happy ending; crime fiction would feel incomplete if we didn't find out who the perpetrator was. As we've seen, it is possible to play with these conventions and expectations up to a point. But having invested often considerable time in reading a whole novel, the reader will want **an emotional payoff** at the end. This doesn't have to be obvious or saccharine; as long as *something* has changed for the better … even if it wasn't in the way we were expecting.

6
Dialogue and description – bringing your story to life

Great dialogue is about striking a balance between naturalism and purpose – knowing how you want your dialogue to sound, but also what you want it to achieve. By approaching your text with an awareness of context and subtext, you will help your characters communicate with the reader not just through what they say, but what they *don't*. And when strong, nuanced dialogue is supported by description that is specific, sensory, and unique to your characters, you're on your way to creating a story-world that sings from every page.

Getting your scenes to speak

These two elements involve slightly different creative skill sets, but they also have a lot in common: if dialogue allows us to 'hear' the voices of the characters, then description lets us 'see' the world of the story. Used in combination, the two techniques are perhaps your key tools when it comes to engaging the reader's senses and letting the words come to life before our eyes (and ears, and noses). Because these are such fundamental building blocks of the writing process, they're referred to elsewhere, too; here, we'll pull the key points together and look at taking your dialogue and description to the next level.

What is dialogue?

And no, this isn't a trick question! It may seem obvious, but it is worth asking yourself: what, exactly, is dialogue supposed to do? This applies both in macrocosm and microcosm: be aware of what dialogue needs to achieve (and what it doesn't) in the grand scheme of things; and question each individual exchange: why it's there, and whether it earns its place.

Dialogue does not need to **mimic actual live speech**, or at least, not too closely. When we talk to people in real life, thinking as we go, we pause a lot, backtrack, repeat ourselves, and use fillers (like *um* and *ah*) to cover silences. Whilst a certain amount of naturalism is desirable – a character may speak haltingly *for a good reason*, something significant in terms of their characterization or the plot – a little goes a long way. If you've ever listened to a talk given by someone who was nervous, and inadvertently honed in on their pauses, or a verbal tic, you'll know how distracting it can be. We don't hear what they're saying – all we hear is the tic.

On the other hand, dialogue **shouldn't sound too perfectly-formed**. People rarely speak in full sentences; they use idioms and contractions; they might employ pet names and in-jokes; they speak differently depending on context and who they're addressing. So, your dialogue needs to be **readable**, but it also has to be **realistic**.

Let's look at an example where the author has striven too hard for lifelike dialogue:

> 'Well,' said Pete, 'It's like this. I mean, I only went over to see if she was OK but when I got there she was … well … there were all these candles and … um … she'd already poured the wine. I didn't – I wouldn't have – nothing was going to happen, but I just, I thought …'

'Nothing was going to happen?' Nick snapped. 'But you thought you'd sit down and have a candlelit dinner with my wife, right? You thought I'd be OK with that, yeah?'

'I knew it wasn't OK, but what was I supposed to say? I couldn't – I couldn't just walk out, could I? It was completely innocent! It was you who asked me to keep an eye on her, wasn't it? I didn't want to be rude. She's so ... she's, well, you know what she's like!'

'What the hell are you saying about her? That's my wife you're talking about! God, I can't believe you'd...'

This is easy to 'hear' in your head; it sounds authentic. But it's also tedious – repetitive, verbose, with a feeling that the characters could ramble on indefinitely. Try some pruning, and see how it reads:

'I only went over to see if she was OK,' said Pete. 'There were all these candles and she'd poured the wine. Nothing was going to happen, but I just thought ...'

'That you'd sit down and have a candlelit dinner with my wife?' Nick snapped. 'And I'd be OK with that?'

'I couldn't just walk out. You did ask me to keep an eye on her. And... well... you know what she's like!'

'What the hell are you saying?'

The tone of the exchange is the same – we haven't lost any of the uncertainty (on the one part) or belligerence (on the other), but it's a much smoother read. We've cut any repetition (including any instances of the characters repeating each other's words back to them); we've cut 'filler' – the *ums* and the *wells* and the *I means* – along with interjections like *yeah* and *right*. We've also cut rhetorical questions like 'could I?' and 'wasn't it?' since Pete's defensiveness is already clear from the substance of his dialogue.

The one bit of filler that remains carries more weight because it stands alone. When Pete says, *'And... well... you know what she's like!'* we have a real sense that he's aware he's crossing a line. Nick's final, accusatory, *'What the hell are you saying?'* no longer feels like a mere continuation of the argument, but is a genuine challenge. Instead of allowing the conversation to roll ever onwards, it's been brought to a crisis.

Here's an example that's gone too far in the opposite direction:

> Cathy stared at Steph. 'I know it was you who stole it. I left it on my dresser, and no one else has been in my room since. It must have been when you offered to come and fetch my sunglasses. I knew there was something off about that. When do you ever do anything helpful? You are the only one who could have done it.'
>
> 'That is not true,' Steph said. 'What about the cleaners? What about room service? Any one of the hotel staff might have slipped in whilst you were sunbathing. Why are you so certain it was me? You always think the worst of me. It is like you are looking for reasons to pick a fight.'

Grammatically this is correct, and there's no 'filler', but it's lacking in naturalism; the characters sound identical. As a result, it's impossible to really 'hear' them; they're like robots who've had the English language programmed into them with no guidelines on how to fit it to purpose. Try cutting to allow for smoother speech patterns and some assumed knowledge between the characters:

> Cathy stared at Steph. 'I left it on my dresser, and no one else has been in my room. When you were all, "Oh don't worry, I'll get your glasses." I knew it.'

'Hey,' Steph said. 'What about the cleaners? Room service? Anyone could've come in while you were baking yourself. Why's it always me?'

Here, the characters' suppressed animosity is implicit, less overt − the conversation skirts around their feelings; they use contractions (like *why'd* and *you're*) and the odd, pertinent interjection. It feels like a real exchange, albeit one that's trimmed back to fulfil a distinct purpose.

This brings us to the next general point about what dialogue should do − and that is *something; anything*, but it **must have a purpose**. If your characters have come fully to life then you may well find them having meandering, directionless conversations just as real people do. So be vigilant; check that every exchange you include has a *raison d'être*.

Imagine a scene where your characters are having dinner, discussing the meal. It might provide scene-setting and colour, but those are not reasons enough to include it. Ideally, whatever the characters are discussing over dinner should also be *revealing*. Just like each scene, dialogue should be moving the action forwards, creating conflict or tension, building up a relationship or dynamic, increasing our understanding of the character/s, or posing/answering questions.

However, that doesn't mean the characters *can't* mention the food. Successful dialogue may be about something banal on the surface, with other things going on underneath:

'How's your pork?' John looked at her over his glasses.
'Mpff.' Alice poked at it, then set her knife and fork down with a clatter and waved at a waiter. 'This is far too pink,' she said. 'Take it back, please.'
'Oui, Madame, but …'

'Oh for the love of – it's supposed to be served pink, Liss. It's called "blush".'

She downed her glass of wine in one. 'Well, I'm sorry I don't know as much about fancy food as you do. Just because I don't want to eat raw pig doesn't make me some sort of philistine.'

'Keep your voice down. People are looking.'

The waiter whisked up her plate; probably desperate to get out of there. Alice's eyes had that dangerous sparkle to them.

In this example, what starts out as an innocuous comment about the food escalates into conversation full of unspoken resentments. The dialogue makes use of the balance between **text and subtext**.

However, forcing conflict into dialogue won't automatically make it worthwhile. A pointless argument, or one that goes on too long will be just as tedious as a placid, amicable conversation. If it doesn't serve a purpose in terms of the overall plot, even the most explosive argument might end up feeling like **manufactured tension:** conflict that you've wedged in purely to hold our attention.

We worked with one author whose two main characters tended to bicker, and whilst this was useful in early scenes, establishing a certain dynamic, it eventually began to feel repetitive. In addition, allowing the interactions between the characters to remain one-note left the emotional arc static – neither of them was developing. We realized that a lot of the characters' arguments were disguising sexual tension between them, which was a perfectly valid emotional subtext but one that needed to progress more and move things forward in new ways. Once the characters stopped merely sniping, their deeper feelings started to exert a more intriguing pull on the plot.

Because of its key role in conveying emotion and relationship, dialogue should always be **specific to each character**, as far as possible. In Chapter 3 we talked about how narrative voice may modulate depending on POV, and this is the same principle. Your characters should sound like individuals, with distinct speech patterns, vocabulary in keeping with their age and background, and their own lexicon dependent on deeper characterization — the books they read when they were growing up; the TV shows they watch; what they're trying to achieve from a particular conversation. **Context is just as important as character.**

Let's look at a scene featuring three characters with different agendas:

Lianna hovered in the doorway, holding Oliver's hand. 'I didn't think you were back until tonight,' she said.

Jeremy cleared his throat. 'No, I'd planned to stay late at the office but my meeting was cancelled. I'm sorry — did you have plans for Oliver?'

'Not really. Of course, if you want to take him out I'll leave early.'

'Can we go out somewhere? Maybe you could take me to the park?' Ollie let go of Lianna and took a step into the study.

'Maybe some other time.' Jeremy glanced at Oliver and lowered his voice. 'I have a date, you see. Is that alright? Could you stay a bit later with him tonight?'

'OK. We can go to the park anyway, Oliver.' Lianna crouched and drew Ollie back into the hall; into her arms, looking at Jeremy over the top of his blond curls.

'But I don't want to go with you. I want to go with Daddy.'

'Daddy's got some things to get on with. Come on, we'll go and buy ourselves some ice creams.'

There's nothing massively wrong with this dialogue, and the exchange is obviously serving a purpose. However, it feels dry and formal because all the characters' voices are so similar – it could be working harder to distinguish character, whilst bringing the tension to the surface and revealing more about the underlying emotions:

Lianna hovered in the doorway, holding Oliver's hand. 'Oh! I thought you were pulling a late one tonight,' she said. She glanced down at Ollie, sucking his finger. 'I mean, the meeting and all …'

Jeremy cleared his throat. 'No, I'd intended to, but it was cancelled. Did you have plans?'

'Nope. If you want to take him I'll head off. He'd love to hang out with you. Wouldn't you, Ols?'

'Can we, Daddy? Go to the park?' Ollie let go of Lianna and took a step into the study.

'Another time.' Jeremy glanced at Oliver. 'You misunderstand me. I'm sorry.' He lowered his voice. 'I've got a date, and I'll be late – even later, I mean. OK?'

'Oh.' Lianna crouched and drew Ollie back into the hall, into her arms, looking at Jeremy over the top of his blond curls. 'Don't worry, Ols, we can still go to the park, you and me.'

'But it's not fair! I want Daddy!'

'Shush, poppet, let's leave Daddy to it. We'll get ice creams. Promise.'

Here, we're foregrounding more interesting and nuanced subtext – Lianna, presumably a nanny or an au pair, is less formal than Jeremy but still professional, having to weigh her duty to her employer against her love for Ollie; Jeremy is cold and distant, taking Lianna for granted (his tone is less apologetic in this version);

and Ollie is breathless and childlike, quicker to express emotions that the other two don't voice. The dialogue differentiates the characters whilst making more of the scene's emotional underpinnings. A good exercise with a scene like this might be to remove one of the characters and see how it plays differently — if Ollie weren't present, would Lianna speak her mind more freely?

Another broad point to remember about dialogue is that it should not be used as **a tool for exposition**. It's tempting to make your dialogue do some of the work — it feels more elegant, somehow; a cheat, perhaps, but one that you might get away with. However, readers can be alert to conversations that don't sound realistic because the characters are saying things they wouldn't voice in real life. So, if you do want to sneak in a few details of backstory or set-up, keep them pertinent and plausible, taking account of the characters' relationship and any shared knowledge:

'But, Daphne, after everything we've been through — we were at school together, don't you remember? You can't, surely, abandon me now?' Lucas said, bottom lip stuck out like a child.

'Lucas, you really haven't made it easy for me. Embarrassing me in front of Greg like that — did you have to tell him absolutely everything about that time at camp?' Daphne was carefully tearing strips off her beer mat, not meeting his eyes.

'Maybe not, but you provoked me! You started it by bringing up my crush on Mr Evans!'

'That was years ago! Why does it even matter? But Greg — I mean, I want him to like me, I don't need him knowing all the slutty things I did when I was a teenager. I was young and stupid. So no, I just don't feel very inclined to help at the moment, I'm afraid.'

There's too much going on here – not just about the distant past, but about a more recent event when that past resurfaced. This has shifted the characters' relationship in the 'now' of the story – Lucas wants something from Daphne that she's reluctant to do because of the way he's embarrassed her. The exposition creates a couple of problems: firstly, the dialogue doesn't sound plausible – why would Daphne and Lucas rehash specific incidents at which they were both present – and secondly, the extent to which we linger on past incidents risks obscuring what's significant, which is the impact of the backstory on the present plot.

This example also illustrates another common (and related) problem, which is **dialogue that feels too 'on the nose'**. We touched on this in Chapter 2; here, note how both Daphne and Lucas open up without any reticence or self-censure. This contributes to a feeling of unreality, since people rarely speak their minds so candidly. Since these characters know each other well, you could possibly get away with it, but as a general rule it's best for characters to be more circumspect – it creates more tension, and allows you to make more use of subtext and nuance.

How would this dialogue read if we removed *all* the exposition, and all the telling of emotion?

> 'But, Daphne, after everything we've been through …?' Lucas said, bottom lip stuck out like a child.
>
> 'Lucas, you really haven't made it easy for me.' Daphne was carefully tearing strips off her beer mat, not meeting his eyes.
>
> 'Maybe not, but you started it!'
>
> 'Why does it even matter? But I want Greg to … I don't need him knowing … everything. So no, I'm not going to help.'

This is more intriguing, posing more questions and hinting at a shared past. However, it's perhaps a touch too opaque now, and might benefit from a little extending to help us unpick what's going on. How might you do this without sacrificing naturalism? A good start would be to firm up the POV and make more use of inner voice; you might also allow the characters to *start* to say what's on their minds, then cut themselves off mid-sentence. Shared knowledge can work to your advantage — a lot can be conveyed in a subtle reference to something they both know about but don't need to voice explicitly. And on a minor note, since these two are so familiar, would they keep using each other's names?

Let's implement this:

> 'But after everything we've been through — school, all that stuff back in the day. Please — I … I need you.' Lucas stuck his bottom lip out like he always did when he wasn't getting his own way.
>
> 'You haven't made it easy.' Daphne was carefully tearing strips off her beer mat, not meeting his eyes. How could he have brought up what'd happened at camp? It was — God, she couldn't even think about it without feeling sick.
>
> 'Don't tell me you're still stewing over what I said to Greg? You started it!'
>
> 'Maybe, but … Greg — I mean, I want him …' She couldn't bring herself to admit what she wanted, so instead she finished lamely, 'I just don't want him knowing everything I did back then. I was a different person. So maybe I don't feel like helping you right now.'

Here we have access to the facts necessary to understand the current situation, and the lens of Daphne's POV to help us interpret past events, but without too much extraneous expositional detail (e.g. the crush on Mr Evans) to distract us from the present moment. The conversation sounds natural – it gives a true sense of their intimacy and the conflicts between them without laying everything bare.

Your dialogue tool box

As well as these general, overarching points about dialogue, there are some line-by-line considerations: useful tools to fine-tune your dialogue; and problems to watch out for at the self-editing stage. Some of these – like **repetition, use of characters' names**, and **interjections/padding** – we've already touched on; here are a few other things to bear in mind.

Swearing and slang

Swearing is still fairly taboo in some genres, particularly children's fiction. Anything younger than YA tends not to feature swearing at all and even YA requires a light touch; save swearing for when it will carry most impact.

There are ways around this if you have a character or situation that demands fruitier language. Consider inventing words that are unique to your universe, but that are obviously offensive in context (imagine a world where everyone is a vampire, or undead, and something like *breather* becomes an insult). You can also make use of words that *sound* worse than they are: things like *flipping, fricking* or *for crying out loud* (read the first two syllables aloud and you can hear the swear word hanging in the air).

Slang is more acceptable, but it can date contemporary fiction as it changes so quickly. Consider the evolution of words like *gay, long, bare* and *sick* – it's hard to know which of these will hold their meaning, and which will continue to mutate. If you're writing historical fiction, you can certainly refer to primary and secondary source material to find slang which gives a flavour of the period. However, it still needs to feel naturalistic and organic. If you just use a little here and there, it may feel too tentative, as though you're not sure of yourself. And if you go overboard, it may seem as though you're striving for authenticity (like a Shakespearian character continually saying *'forsooth!'*).

Like much of the writing process, it's a question of consistency: ensure that any slang you use fits in with the tone and writing voice elsewhere. If you use mainly contemporary vocabulary, then throwing in the odd archaism, even into the dialogue, may jar; similarly, if you've written an historical novel and broadly avoided anachronism, then modern words will stand out. We worked with one author whose Wars of the Roses novel favoured archaic phrasing; however, because he wanted a noirish detective feel, he'd also used twentieth-century figures of speech. It created a clash, so instead we looked for ways to bring the *mood* of noir voiceover into the language of Tudor England.

Dialect and accents

Even if your novel is set solidly in contemporary England, it's likely to feature at least one character with different speech patterns; and if you've set it in Scotland, say, or Hackney, you may be wrestling with the notion of how to get across an entire cast of accents. It can be tempting to render your characters' voices phonetically, spelling out every distinct sound:

'Wheesht, ah cannae breng masel to tail ye whit ah've jist seen!'

Whilst there are writers who do use a lot of phonetic dialogue, like Irvine Welsh, Alice Walker and Roddy Doyle, trying to replicate this kind of accuracy if you're not a native speaker is unwise: it can feel hokey and condescending, whilst making dialogue unnecessarily impenetrable. Look for ways to bring an *essence* of the region into the dialogue – perhaps using the odd dropped letter (but be sparing – lots of apostrophes are just as hard on the eye), a few carefully chosen expletives, and just one or two phonetics. Again, be consistent: allow each character to be distinct and stick to their verbal signifiers, so that we can tell who's speaking without becoming overwhelmed by accents:

'I can't bring myself to tell you whit I've just seen!'

Or here, where you can tell the speaker's nationality without spelling anything out phonetically:

'Get your clothes on, bach. You'll be late for school now, is it.'

The same applies to a character who lisps or stammers, or to any vocal habit, as discussed earlier: if you attempt to convey this in every line, the tic is all we'll hear. Consider *describing* the character's voice when we first meet them (for instance, *she spoke as if she had a mouthful of cotton wool*) then include subtle reminders each time they speak, and trust the reader to hear their voice. It may not be the exact version of them that *you* hear, but it will be more resonant for having been born partly from the reader's own imagination.

Dialogue attribution vs accompanying action

Also known as 'dialogue tags', **dialogue attribution** is the name for the combination of pronoun and verb that tells us which character is speaking, like *he said, she said, he asked*, and *she replied*. In first drafts and manuscripts where the author is still learning self-edit skills, we often see a wide variety of dialogue tags:

> 'Where are you off to?' he demanded.
> 'I'm just going to the shops,' she croaked.
> 'So why are you sneaking out?' he growled.
> 'I'm not sneaking!' she wheedled. 'I didn't want to disturb you.'
> 'Fine,' he grunted. 'Pick me up some fags then, OK?'

With a language as rich and versatile as English, it's tempting to make the most of the variety at your fingertips. Why wouldn't you choose the word that exactly conveys the tone of the dialogue, if it exists? However, just like dialect, and vocal tics, too many variants on 'said' can become noticeable; the reader ends up focusing on the author's language, rather than on what's being said. 'Said', on the other hand, is so commonly used in both speech and writing that it's virtually invisible. If in doubt, use a more mundane verb, and let the dialogue itself do the talking.

If you can, and if your characters sound sufficiently different, then it's preferable to cut dialogue tags altogether. You will want to use the characters' names early on in the scene, to establish who's present. But thereafter, you might use accompanying action to demonstrate who's saying what. This has the double benefit of allowing you to remove clunky dialogue tags, whilst also making use of dramatic, visual 'showing' to bring the tone and subtext to life.

Below, the accompanying action works harder to convey the dynamic between the two characters:

> 'Where are you off to?' Dean leant back against the front door, blocking her way.

'I'm just going to the shops.' Louise held the bags up to show him.

'So why are you sneaking out?'

She swallowed, her tongue sticking to the roof of her mouth. 'I'm not. I … I didn't want to disturb you.'

'Fine.' He opened the door for her and gave a gallant bow as she shuffled out. 'Pick me up some fags then, OK?'

You don't need action in absolutely every line – this can lead to stodgy prose and an overwhelming amount of visual information to assimilate. Just include enough cushioning around the dialogue to keep things brisk, clear and implied.

Two of the most common problems associated with attribution are things that are easy to deal with but can make a big difference to how professional your dialogue looks and how smoothly it reads:

1 **Check your punctuation**. If you're using attribution, then the verb should be separated from the dialogue by a comma, exclamation mark, or question mark, but not a full stop; and the attribution should carry a lower case letter:

'Where are you off to?' he demanded.

But if you're opting instead for accompanying action, the action should be separated from the dialogue using a full stop, and should begin in upper case:

'Fine.' He shrugged.

This rule applies whether the attribution or action comes before or after the dialogue.

2 **Check your layout**. It can help us to visualize the scene if the action and dialogue belonging to any one character sits on the same line/paragraph. So:

'So why are you sneaking out?'
   She swallowed, her tongue sticking to the roof of her mouth. 'I'm not. I … I didn't want to disturb you.'
   'Fine.' He opened the door for her and gave a gallant bow as she shuffled out. "Pick me up some fags then, OK?"

But not:

'So why are you sneaking out?' She swallowed, her tongue sticking to the roof of her mouth.
   'I'm not. I … I didn't want to disturb you.'
   'Fine.'
   He opened the door for her and gave a gallant bow as she shuffled out.
   "Pick me up some fags then, OK?"

Italics

These can create emphasis and stresses within a character's speech, or give it an urgent or dramatic feel. However, too much can be jarring, and make the characters sound breathless and hysterical. If you have a character who speaks in an over the top way, you might use italics to convey this; or, if there's a risk that the dialogue could be misinterpreted without the addition of italics − then go for it. But be sparing; most devices work best if you save them for when they're really needed.

Clichés

In general, we advise authors against using clichés altogether. There are two notable exceptions: firstly, in a synopsis/blurb (and sometimes in non-fiction), where your purpose is primarily to convey information rather than be creative; you need to be brief and concise, and a figure of speech can encompass a lot of meaning that it would otherwise take you too long to convey. And secondly, in dialogue, where people do, in real life, often resort to idiom. However, again it's crucial to be both selective and sparing with the way you make use of these.

What can sound perfectly realistic for one character to say can sound like a foreign language in the mouth of another. We often read manuscripts featuring young or contemporary characters who use phrases like *'What've you got up your sleeve?'* or *'I made it by the skin of my teeth!'* Dated figures of speech like these are rarely used by teenagers (although much younger children do sometimes ape the way adults speak, resulting in some funny juxtapositions). On the other hand, older (or more formal, or pompous) characters might reasonably use these expressions, and it can form part of their characterization. As elsewhere, check that anything in the dialogue is appropriate for both **context** and **character** – as well as considering the **genre**, **writing voice**, and the **mood/atmosphere** of a scene.

Think about these techniques as bright, bold colours in a paint palette. Used deftly, they can add light and shade and emphasis, but splashed around all over the place they risk obscuring the picture. In dialogue, what's not said is often just as important, and too much colour and idiosyncrasy can leave no room for that secondary level of meaning to make itself felt. Your dialogue needs to be strong enough (by which we mean direct, purposeful, simple and *to an extent* distinctive) that you can trust the reader to understand both what's being said on the surface, and what's beneath it.

The big picture

Let's now move on to explore some ways to bring the same level of realism to your descriptions. Description roughly falls into three categories: firstly, there's what we think of as **infrastructure**: the wider setting and era; the novel's broader locations; its seasons, weather and atmosphere. Secondly, there's chapter-by-chapter **scene-setting**: the specific places where things happen — houses, transport, school, the doctor's surgery, a mountain side, a beach hut, a swimming pool. Finally, there's line-by-line **cushioning**: little reminders of what characters look like, what they're doing, and where they're interacting that accompany dialogue and allow us to picture scenes as visually shifting, evolving scenarios rather than static window displays.

Give some thought to the infrastructure of your story at the planning stages, because it will affect how much **research** you do. In some genres — historical fiction, fantasy and sci-fi — your wider setting can be as much a part of the texture of the novel as the characters, and planning in advance will help you give it weight and personality. A good setting is more than just a backdrop; it is intrinsic, as though the story could not have taken place anywhere but *here*.

It's important to avoid cliché and generalization, aiming for pertinent specific detail rather than too-broad brushstrokes. And again, be consistent — don't casually or accidentally drop in elements that feel anachronistic or out of the blue, unless you're going to work them in fully. If you're writing fantasy, be aware of the tropes and conventions associated with your sub-genre, and know when it's OK to follow them, and when it's better to be original.

If you're writing about a real place or scenario that is not already known to you, then research it carefully so that you can present a rounded impression of the location that makes use of all five senses. For novels based in historical fact, try not to rely solely on the sources of information that are widely available – you want to expand the story outwards (and inwards) from what's already in the public domain. There are many resources available: direct experience – if you want to write a novel set on a submarine, then see if you can find a way to spend some time on one yourself; archives/records libraries; the internet (within reason); speaking to people who've lived that experience personally. Bring the setting to life, without letting the facts you've uncovered take over the story.

If you're writing about somewhere or something you're already familiar with, don't assume that you know everything – visit it again, perhaps with someone who's never been before to see it with fresh eyes. This will help your setting feel authentic, but with that almost intangible essence of exploration and excitement – the discovery of something new – that draws a reader in.

It's reasonable to think that much of the description related to infrastructure should be front-loaded, as this is where you have most invested in setting out the story world. However, as we discussed in Chapter 5, excessive exposition and world-building can weigh down an opening and distract from tension, action and characterization. It's therefore advisable to treat your infrastructure as an ongoing process of drip-feeding; the odd line/paragraph here and there implying a wider backdrop. Then, in places, where the pace can withstand a lull (for instance after a big action scene or a tension peak) you might include some lengthier detail.

Notting Hill (1999) contains an example of more protracted infrastructure: around the mid-section, a montage shows the seasons changing as Hugh Grant's character walks along the Portobello Road market after having his heart broken. The section vividly reminds us of the setting, demonstrates the length of time that's passing, and re-establishes the character's relationship with his home, underlining how his perceptions of it have changed. This is pitch perfect – downbeat but watchable; slow-paced but reflective, providing a nice contrast to the emotional tension that preceded it. It serves several functions and feels pertinent rather than intrusive.

How might you replicate this effect in a literary way? Let's imagine that your protagonist has just taken part in a battle to save his homeland, and is returning victorious but shattered by the experience. The description should go beyond the immediate detail of his surroundings to take in the wider picture – his sense of how he and his country have changed, the time that's passed whilst the war raged on, his expectations about the future. But you don't want to spend too long on this:

> He stopped by a brook to water Thunder, rubbing down the horse's sweating flanks; feeling, as he did so, the bones jutting through his beloved companion's coarse grey hair. His own brow was damp too, and as he sank onto the dusty ground, scooping clear water into his cupped palms, he realized just how hot it was.
>
> Summer. When they'd ridden out to Greypeak the snow had lain thick on the ground. Now that same snow was meltwater, running from the scarred ridges of the Arrock Mountains and feeding the stream where he, Arlo, now drank. He was lucky to be here. How much of the blood of his kinsmen must this water have carried with it from the battlefields and mountainsides? The winter had been hard, even for those on the outskirts of the fighting. Like Thunder, Arlo too was thinner.
>
> He swallowed, allowing himself to wonder for the first time what he might find when he got back to the farmstead. If the soldiers had suffered, what must their families have endured? What had they given up to ensure the fight could continue?
>
> Not their lives, Arlo prayed. Not that.

This picture aims to be specific but also broad, encompassing small-scale scene-setting but allowing the detail of that to draw us outwards, taking Arlo's mind onto the wider world, and the impact of what he's been through on himself and his surroundings. It also attempts to introduce a point of tension so that the description doesn't feel too dry and 'out of time': the question mark over what horrors might await Arlo on his return.

Moving on now to **immediate scene-setting**, your watchwords here should be **brief but specific**. Scene setting is important: it grounds the action, which is particularly crucial if you've shifted settings, or if you're returning to a location after a while spent elsewhere. It also sparks off the reader's visualization, helping the imaginary world feel tangible. And it brings clarity and precision to your action: it's disorientating to begin a scene with several lines of dialogue, for example, without establishing where it's taking place, what the characters are doing, or who else is present. (Some of this will come under the aegis of ongoing **cushioning**, discussed below, but at this stage, bear in mind that some upfront scene-setting – even just a line or two – is vital if your reader isn't going to feel at sea.)

So, firstly, remind yourself where the action is taking place; picture it in your mind. (Let's use an old-fashioned tobacconist's shop here.) Close your eyes and see what's in front of you. You might make a list: *chipped walnut counter ... dusty jars of sweets ranged on shelves ... peeling posters in the windows ... a glass case with cigars ... the shopkeeper (maybe he's old with yellowing fingers, as we might expect, or maybe he/she is incongruous in some way – a motherly woman in a flowered apron) ... a back door with beads hanging over it, etc. etc.*

Now, ask yourself if you've relied too heavily on purely visual images: it's an easy first resort, because sight can feel like the 'primary' sense. But it's not always the most evocative one.

How often do you walk into an unfamiliar house and notice the smell (new paint, coffee, an overflowing cat litter tray); of what sounds is 'silence' actually comprised? These more sensory details get the reader's own creative juices flowing. There may be some obvious choices, and some less obvious: *the smell of tobacco... a blocked drain ... a ticking clock ... the creak of shoes on the wooden floor ... the gritty feeling of dust under her fingertips ... the sound of children playing outside...*

Next, think about which of your details are the most revealing — what atmosphere are you aiming for, and how do your chosen titbits of description support that mood? Your job as author is not to paint an exact picture, or include every detail about the character's surroundings; give us a flavour, allowing our imaginations to fill in the blanks.

Finally, think about your POV character: we're viewing this scene through their eyes. What is the character hoping to achieve in this new location? What plot-action are they currently involved in? What are their expectations and how does the reality of the setting reinforce or confound these? As we discuss elsewhere, the most memorable description — the stuff that we read, rather than skimming over — tends to be attached to action, tension and interaction so, ideally, give your character/s something to do as they move through the setting:

> Karen stood outside, peering through the greyish window. She could make out almost nothing, just wobbly shapes and shadows — it was that old-fashioned, moulded glass, with ridges that seemed designed to obscure the interior. Her heartbeat quickened. It was stupid to get excited, but she couldn't help it. What if the answer was behind this door?
>
> She pushed it open.

A bell jangled cheerfully somewhere further inside, and Karen heard footsteps clumping and a voice calling, 'Just a minute!' She took a couple of paces into the shop, feeling the crunch and scuffle of dust under her feet, breathing in the scent of old, old tobacco, and ... was that cumin?

She leaned over the formica counter, craning to see through the curtain of blue beads that separated the shop from what she assumed must be the living area, where whoever it was was still thumping around. She was about to call out when the footsteps clattered downstairs and an almost impossibly small woman swished through the beads.

'Yes, love?' The woman raised her eyebrows and grinned. Her brown face was deeply wrinkled, impish, and as Karen opened her mouth, suddenly unsure what it was that she wanted to say, the woman whisked the glass stopper off a sweet jar behind the counter and waved a chipped porcelain scoop towards Karen. 'Humbug?'

Here, we've made the mood surprising, the idea being that Karen expects a lot from the encounter, but ends up getting both more and less than she was hoping for, taking the story in a slightly different direction. The description is rooted in Karen's experience, viewing it through her lens; and we've engaged all the senses so that the scene draws us in on several levels. We've also introduced tension – the initially empty shop; Karen's uncertainty; the woman's unexpected response.

The passage isn't overloaded with adjectives, however: don't give us too much to take on board. Though it sounds counter-intuitive, this can be just as confusing and hard to picture as no description at all. We worked with an author whose fantasy land was populated by fascinating invented creatures which she was keen to keep. However, the sheer volume of description these required was overwhelming, so we struck a compromise. Her descriptions worked best when her invented creatures had an earthly parallel, so we tried to make use of similarities where we could, giving the reader a helping hand before expanding the picture (but only using a few descriptive markers). The story's cast sprang into focus, and the author's concerns about losing her originality were unfounded. With fewer, but more recognizable, descriptors in place, the strangeness and wonder of her world was much clearer.

The final element of description to focus on is what we've called **cushioning**: the ongoing, brief snippets of description that accompany dialogue and interaction, allowing the reader to picture the action. The main function of cushioning is to keep a scene alive and moving, so that dialogue doesn't read like a stage script, and so that the characters interact with their surroundings in a dynamic way. Without cushioning, a scene can become dry; a purely factual retelling without any colour or life.

Cushioning also helps circumnavigate longer, more intrusive scene-setting. Authors are often tempted to halt the action to paint a little vignette of a character or setting when they first appear. Some genres are better suited to this style of description than others (certain types of historical fiction and comedy, for example), but in general it can be a disengaging and static way of doing things. This kind of portrait may be less involving than the surrounding action, prose that readers are likely to skim over and therefore quickly forget. In addition, it can feel unrealistic, depending on the POV you're using, since we rarely do stop and observe people and surroundings in this level of detail.

This brings us to the final and perhaps most important purpose of cushioning, which is to bring the POV character into play. Using their inner voice, and the particular things they notice, allows you to spark the scene into life not just *generally*

– as anyone might view it – but *specifically*, as it appears to this character. The cushioning therefore works on several levels, telling us what we're seeing, but also helping us interpret it.

The most effective way to use cushioning requires a couple of steps. Firstly, sketch a **brief but memorable** picture of a character or location upfront, ideally weaving the description into the action of the scene, as discussed above, so that we're still drawn along by the tension of what's *happening*.

As we've already discussed location, let's look at some examples that apply to character:

> 'Thanks for fitting me in at such short notice,' he said. 'Do you run every day?'
>
> Alexa pushed her bleached blond fringe back from a forehead that was shiny with sweat. Her chest heaved against her pink lycra top, and she took a swig from her water bottle, the tendons in her neck taut.
>
> Damon realized he was staring, and cleared his throat.

Then, expand on this initial description as the scene progresses:

> As he shook her hand, he felt the bones in her wrist click. She had what his nonna would've called bird fingers: jutting, cold. When he looked up into her face, there was the slightest curl to her thin lips. Was she laughing at him? Flirting?

Include snapshots of the characters throughout the remainder of the scene so that we don't lose sight of them: bite-size chunks of action, description, gesture, inner voice and sensory information so that we can 'see' the scene as well as 'hearing' it. Consider how the scene might progress *without* cushioning:

> 'Do you run every day?' he said.

'Of course,' she replied. 'I'm a trainer. It's pretty much my job to stay in shape.'

'I wish I was that good,' Damon said. 'Since my wife died, I just can't seem to …'

The dialogue is fine, but there are no other clues about what's going on in the scene. Cushioning gives you an opportunity to build up a stronger picture both of what the scene looks like, and of what's going on beneath its surface:

'Thanks for fitting me in at such short notice,' he said. He fell into step beside her, feeling the creak and rub of his new trainers as he struggled to keep pace. 'Do you run every day?'

'Of course,' she replied, giving him a sideways look. 'I'm a trainer. It's pretty much my job to stay in shape.' Her pony tail bobbed, her arms swinging almost lazily.

'I wish I was that good,' Damon said. 'But since my wife … since Ellie died, I just can't seem to …' He was already panting, his belly aching.

Alexa slowed, a pinkish glow spreading over her pale shoulders. 'I'm sorry,' she said. 'I didn't realize.'

A key thing to remember about ongoing description is that it should always build on the picture you've established, rather than repeating, contradicting, or springing something new on us too late. If you haven't mentioned a hat, then a few pages into the scene you say something like *he tipped the peak of his cap down to cover his eyes*, this can create a jarring effect, taking us by surprise and undermining the image we've started to build.

We discussed above an author whose main character was introspective and self-analytical. This author also tended to delay many of his descriptions so that, having met *Eric* (for instance) several times, we would only learn a few scenes later that *Eric's hair was fair, and he kept the collar of his tweed jacket pulled up around his ears*. In this instance, the main character's obsessive inner life meant that he often failed to record external details, and the author had to pencil them in whenever he (or rather the character) noticed them. This had further repercussions on the protagonist's likeability, exacerbating the sense that he was aloof and disengaged from the other characters. But it also resulted in a confusing lack of description and scene-setting. Here, the work we did on getting the main character out of his head and into the world also had a positive impact on the author's descriptions.

Description perfection

In addition to what we've looked at above, there are a few things to keep an eye out for as you come to re-read and edit your descriptions. Some of these are also discussed elsewhere, but hopefully this will be a useful checklist.

The obvious choice

It's important to avoid cliché if you can, and if it's appropriate. Sometimes clichés exist because they're simply the best, or the only, way of looking at something. But as a writer, you should always go beyond your first impressions, beyond the way other people might see the world: it's part of your job to help us view things afresh. So, ask yourself: does a forest need to be *dark and gloomy*? Might it instead be *sun-speckled; dripping with rain*; the floor *carpeted with flowers*, rather than the more common choice of something like pine needles? Must a bus shelter be *covered in graffiti, smelling faintly of urine* or could it surprise us in some way – perhaps it has a fancy new computerized timetable with a screen that shows adverts for something incongruous or ironic – earplugs, or driving lessons ... this will help your descriptions feel real and unique.

Objective vs subjective

Consider the following:

- *The sunset was awe-inspiring* (subjective)
- *The sunset burnt the rooftops orange* (objective)

The first description tells us nothing concrete – only how this particular character (or author) feels about the sunset. But their idea of what's *awe-inspiring* (or *beautiful*, say, or *magnificent*) may not be the reader's. If we're to understand what the character is seeing in a way that's unique to them, you need to get **specific**. Here we substitute colour, detail about what part of the landscape the character is looking at, and a mood implied by the verb *burnt*.

Know your genre

Some genres require more upfront infrastructure and world-building; others more cushioning and ongoing description. Women's fiction, which tends to be concerned with the nuance of relationship and interaction, may benefit from more in-scene markers about what the characters are doing and the dynamics between them. A focus on outward appearances – clothes, hair, accessories – might also be more suitable (this isn't suggesting a lack of depth – it's partly about how these markers represent what's going on beneath the surface). In, say, courtroom dramas, character description might zero in on signifiers of status, career, or class. Crime fiction/thrillers might use lengthier scene-setting to build up tension, atmosphere and suspense before a scene gets going. Be aware of your genre's conventions, and pace/place your description appropriately.

Avoid stage directions

When we discussed cushioning, we talked about snippets of action and gesture that keep a scene alive. However, it's vital that these are genuinely revealing and useful, rather than just being dry, bald information about who's doing what and where they're standing. For example, we don't need to know that *Kate reached out her left hand, picked up her teacup, and lifted it to her lips.* None of these details tell us anything that couldn't be conveyed by a simple phrase like *Kate took a sip of tea;* all the description is doing is taking up space. If this is significant in some way, however, then let's see that. Perhaps she's in a job interview and trying not to appear nervous: *Kate took a sip, tried to set the mug down quietly and ended up slopping tea across the desk.*

Description is a balancing act between giving us too little and too much. You don't want to miss out anything genuinely significant, but nor should you overload us. A narrative that's weighed down with visual imagery – masses of adjectives; every single part of a character described; a reliance on stage directions – will be dull and confusing to read: the brain can only hold a finite amount of description before it starts to short circuit. On the other hand, a lack of description means we're unlikely to lose ourselves in the world of the story: if we can't 'see' something, we can't engage our own imaginations. Give your reader enough to go on, and ensure that it's high quality, vivid description, but hold back from telling us absolutely everything. Leave us with some work to do ourselves.

7
Pacing, tension, overwriting and cutting

Perfect pacing means knowing your material inside out. Not only do you need to make each scene carry the right weight, but you also need to exercise restraint and subtlety when it comes to pacing your plot – often a big ask when you have a lot of surprises you're keen to reveal. By listening to your writing's heartbeat you'll learn to feel when a scene should be speedy or slow; and by forcing yourself to keep your story's secrets for as long as possible you'll ensure that there's a constant thread of tension pulling your reader onwards.

Pacing is often one of the last things an author thinks about. It tends to be the area that we, as readers, are least aware of – whilst we may judge characters or writing style, we don't regularly think, *gosh that was well-paced*. But readers are conscious of the pacing, whether we realize it or not: we all know that feeling of being swept along by an exciting action sequence; or the frustrating sense of stasis when a story's going nowhere. Using pacing, the writer can control these responses, guiding us through the action at an appropriate rate.

There are two levels to pacing. Firstly, it provides a heartbeat for your scenes and chapters, dictating how fast the action moves, minute-by-minute. This is partly about **tension** – how much conflict, threat, and mystery is present in a scene, and how much it grips us. But it's also about **prioritizing your material**: what is each scene doing, and how much weight do you want to give it? Big, important moments need more time spent on them.

Secondly, pacing acts as an *overarching* pulse for the story and again, here, tension plays a big part. A story that's full of questions, leading us inexorably towards their answers, will grab a reader, whereas one that lays out everything upfront creates less motivation to read on. Prioritizing your material is important here too: deciding what a reader absolutely *needs* to know at any given time, and saving revelations until the last possible moment.

When thinking about this overarching pulse, there are a few factors to take into consideration. What **genre** are you writing in? A thriller will endeavour to evoke maximum tension and suspense, with lengthy description by-passed in favour of action sequences. By contrast, historical fiction might spend longer over scene-setting and character development; the story might feel as though it's building slowly and deliberately, rather than racing along. Fiction for children might feel very fast-paced to adults, but for young readers, still building their comprehension skills and attention spans, it presents bite-sized and digestible story chunks.

The mechanics of your **plot and structure** will also have an impact on pacing. If your story contains multiple interweaving narratives then you should ensure that each thread develops steadily, rather than bunching all the material for one thread together and then abandoning it for long periods. If your story is simple and linear, then you may need to use pacing to hold the reader's interest. And if you know your plot is action-heavy, with many dramatic scenes, then you will need to give some thought to breathing space. You can't keep a reader's heart racing indefinitely, or the returns will start to diminish.

Speedy scenes and slow sizzlers

We'll look first at pacing on a scene-by-scene level, as it's more in keeping with the term 'pace' as most people already understand it – the speed at which something moves. There are two parts to the process here: deciding what a scene is doing, and how important it is; and then pacing it accordingly.

There are some fairly simple rules of thumb about what material is worth lingering over, and what to whizz us through. If a scene is *emotionally significant*, presents a *key plot point*, contains *good conflict or tension*, or is a *dramatic event* or *sudden happening*, then it will need time spent on it. On the other hand, if a scene is *primarily inner voice, description, repetitious, non-dramatic* (i.e. filler or segue material) or *mainly there because you love it* then you should keep it briefer or cut it altogether.

Let's consider some scenes that might appear in a novel:

- A woman discovers that her father is dying *(emotionally significant/key plot point)*
- A couple are in a car accident *(dramatic/exciting/sudden happening)*
- A man thinks about a woman he may be falling in love with *(emotionally significant)*
- A foster child arrives at his new home for the first time *(emotionally significant, key plot point)*
- Two travellers argue about which path they should take *(conflict/tension)*
- A teenage girl confronts her bullies *(key plot point, dramatic moment, conflict/tension)*
- A man lovingly describes the sea shore where he collected driftwood as a child *(emotionally significant)*
- A woman tells her husband why she was fired from her job *(key plot point, conflict/tension)*.

Hang on a minute, you might be thinking – this sounds as though we need to linger over *all* of these scenes! That's why this is a good exercise to hone your ability to **prioritize and**

be selective about your material, because when you're passionate about your story it's natural to think that *everything is equally important*. But think about what kind of scene would actually appear on the page: some of these moments would be quite dry and reflective, or repetitious, and a few scenes that seem to feature conflict and tension may be less engaging than they first appear.

Characters discussing which path to take, for instance, may feel repetitive/pre-emptive, assuming we see them acting on their decision. In general, it's a good idea to avoid showing characters planning what action they're going to take unless something else significant is taking place during the conversation. The same applies to the material about the woman telling her husband she's been fired – chances are, we've already seen the scene where this took place, which was probably dramatic enough. Any subsequent retelling of the same events will feel like recapping.

By contrast, any scenes that feature live events – dialogue that is emotionally significant or pertinent to the plot, or action that's intrinsically exciting – are worth spending more time on. The one scene that's ambiguous here is that featuring the foster child arriving at his new home. It does sound emotionally significant, but you might want to avoid making it too reflective, bringing forward other elements – perhaps some tension with the new foster parents, conflict with other children etc. If it's a scene rather than just a descriptive sequence, it will earn its place.

Let's look at how to apply the idea of pacing to the decisions you've made. Firstly, we'll take the example of *characters arguing over which path to take* to demonstrate how to whizz through unexciting material.

In this instance, we'd suggest cutting the argument, and weaving any relevant conflict into a later action scene:

Elayne turned the map round, squinting in the gloom. 'This doesn't look right.'

'I said we should've taken the other path.' Athmos scowled at her. 'We're lost, aren't we?'

She shivered. A breeze stirred through the bracken; behind her the path disappeared into hollow grey darkness. 'I – I think so. I'm sorry.'

Athmos growled and snatched the map from her trembling fingers. When had it suddenly got so cold? She peered over her shoulder, gripped by a sense that they were not alone; that something was coming – and quickly. Athmos was paying no attention, muttering to himself.

'I think we should get off the path,' she said, tugging at the sleeve of his jerkin.

'I don't care what you think, girl. I'm in charge from now on.'

Here, the earlier conflict is implied, and it feeds into this action scene, creating a reason for Athmos to mistrust Elayne and thereby place both of them in danger. We miss out the potentially tedious argument, but take away its more useful elements and make something new out of them.

Or, *A man thinks about a woman he may be falling in love with.* Perhaps the reader needs to know that the man is dwelling, but you don't need a full scene showing this. There are a couple of options: firstly, you could use a brief line of segue to establish this fact before leading into another scene...

Lyall woke early with Marina's face still on his mind. Every time he closed his eyes, she was there. By the time Kristof arrived to collect the package, it was everything he could do to focus on what the other man was saying ...

(This is very 'told', but that's not necessarily a problem in these instances, as we'll discuss in the next chapter.)

Alternatively, you could cut straight to the next big scene and show that Lyall is still thinking about Marina within the ongoing action:

> Kristof slung his leather jacket onto the table. 'You have it ready?'
>
> Lyall rubbed his eyes. God, the package, he'd almost forgotten. He could hear Marina laughing at him. You're so scatty, I don't know how you've managed without me for so long. Her eyes, dancing.
>
> Kristof was staring at him. 'What's wrong with you today?'
>
> 'Nothing, yes, just let me get it.' He jogged into the bedroom and rummaged in his top drawer. He had to get his head straight.

The main thing is to ensure that the material you've opted to deal with summarily doesn't end up being the focus of the scene; you've made the decision to include it but not prioritize it, so establish it quickly, then move on.

Let's now look at one of the scenes that we might want to extend – the moment where a woman finds out her dad is dying. How might this read if it were paced quickly?

> Mum handed her a cup of tea. 'We've got something to tell you, sweetheart.'
>
> 'Oh?'
>
> Dad said, 'I went to the doctor yesterday. I'm afraid it's bad news.'
>
> Delia's chest constricted. 'What?'
>
> 'It's cancer, love. Inoperable. I'm sorry.'

This all happens so fast that it doesn't have the chance to evoke much emotional response; they may as well be discussing the football scores. Your aim with a scene like this should be to immerse us deeply in the moment – Delia's personal experience of it – so that we can feel what it's like to be her at this point, both physically and mentally. This means adding inner voice (though not too much!), description, Delia's physicality, and sensory impressions. Allow us to live the moment alongside her:

> Mum handed her a cup of tea, clattering the spoon against the saucer. It was the flowery china, the stuff she only got out on special occasions. Delia glanced at the half-drawn curtains; the cushions rumpled and squashed on the sofa that was normally so plush and neat. Everything seemed suddenly out of place, subtly mismatched. What was going on?
>
> 'Dad's – we've – got something to tell you, sweetheart.' Mum cleared her throat, opened her mouth, and then looked at Dad, her grey eyes soft. He sat very still, staring down at his hands clasped in his lap.
>
> Delia's tongue felt thick and sticky, but she managed to croak, 'Oh?'
>
> Maybe if she didn't ask, they wouldn't say, and whatever this weirdness was would just go away. But when Dad looked up at her, she knew what was coming. His voice shook – just the tiniest bit. If you didn't know him you wouldn't have noticed.
>
> 'I went to the doctor yesterday, love. I'm afraid it's bad news.'
>
> She swallowed; her chest constricted. 'What? Tell me?'
>
> 'It's cancer, love. Inoperable. I'm sorry.'

The scene carries more impact – the additional detail helps us to understand what Delia's going through, deepening her relationship with her parents, delaying the moment of revelation, and maximizing tension. However, the last few lines, where she learns the truth, are fairly similar. We've done most of the development in the build-up so that when the truth comes we can keep it clean and brief, avoiding overcooked language which might undermine the raw simplicity of the emotions. You can see how, even within one scene, it's possible to alter the pace as you go to make the most of the material and guide our responses.

Let's look at another scene that we want to extend – *a couple are in a car accident*. This falls under the description of *dramatic moments/sudden happenings*. As such, it might sound counter-intuitive to think about slowing the pace down here – surely, if something happens suddenly, then it should be dealt with quickly? Let's see how well that works:

> Suddenly there was a huge crash, and Lily felt herself spun upside down. Something must've hit them! The car tumbled over and over. She could hear Jonny screaming. Then they came to a standstill.

This conveys an impression of the events happening quickly, but there's not much drama because the picture is just too sketchy to draw us in. Here, again, we should experience the moment alongside the characters, and to do this effectively you need to crank up the action and description to an almost hyper-real level. People often talk about experiencing catastrophic events like this 'in slow motion' and that's the effect to aim for:

> Lily leaned across to the satnav, frowning as she tried to tune out Jonny's voice. She jabbed at the screen. Why was it these bloody things always decided to conk out just when you–
> 'Jesus! Lily, there's a–'

She looked up. The road had vanished, the windscreen full of metal. A truck, red and grey, grill decorated with flowers, its lights boring into her. She wrenched the wheel sideways and the car slewed across the road. The breath slammed out of her as the truck hit, side-on, and she felt glass spattering into her cheek like scalding rain.

Jonny yelled, 'Shit!' but his words turned into a scream that snapped off as the car vaulted over and the world wheeled around her. Metal screeched, and an icy pain tore through both her legs; something heavy as lead thumped into her chest, and she gasped, trying to haul air into her lungs. Then quiet, except for a low creaking hiss and the hot black smell of oil.

Her seatbelt was biting into her shoulder and she realized it was because she was upside down, hanging. She rolled her head, neck seized and stiff, and saw Jonny next to her, face twisted at an angle that looked all wrong.

She screwed her eyes shut.

Here, the slower pacing allows you to convey the speed and drama of events more successfully. Think sensory overload at moments like this – it doesn't matter if you lay it on too thickly; you can always pare it down, as we'll discuss under overwriting and cutting.

With scene-by-scene pacing it's probably more helpful to think in terms of *weight* rather than *speed*, because – as we've seen from the above example – the term 'speed' can be misleading. Something that happens quickly in real time might happen slowly in fiction. But if you ask yourself *how much weight do I want to give this?* that tends to be a clearer indicator of how much space the scene should take up.

Pacing your plot

If you flick back through Chapter 4, particularly the section dealing with scene structure, you'll remember that we talked about using scenes as building blocks to advance the reader's understanding. We studied how a scene can reveal or withhold information, and by doing so either move the plot forwards, keep us guessing, or take events off in a new direction. This balancing technique, knowing how to **handle your exposition**, is at the heart of wider structural pacing.

It can help to use the mystery genre as a model. Mystery writers tend to be experts at pacing because a successful mystery is all about drip feeding clues. Some of these might be red herrings; some might be significant; and part of the writer's job is to weight each revelation delicately enough that it's not too obvious which is which. The aim is to maintain intrigue by *keeping the story's secrets* for as long as possible.

When you've got a great banger of a secret in your story – something dreadful that happened in the protagonist's past, for example – it can be hard to keep this back, particularly if the secret affects the protagonist now, in the present. For instance, *Layla was fostered after her dad killed her mum. She doesn't know where her dad is now.* It might be very tempting to lay out at least some of this secret in the opening couple of chapters because obviously it will have had a huge impact on Layla; will have defined and shaped her. However, can you get more out of this if you withhold it? Think about all the questions you could raise: why is Layla so fastidious about locking all her doors at night? Why does she treasure pictures of her mum, but doesn't have any of her dad? Why does she pay particular attention to strangers with a certain hair colour or way of standing? Playing out these sources of tension will create an atmosphere of suspicion and uncertainty so that, by the time we find out the true reason for Layla's anxiety, we should be sharing in her paranoia.

It can be difficult to keep secrets to yourself, and you'll need to take care that your attempts to do so don't feel contrived – leaving readers dangling with a vague sense that something is wrong, but no real specifics, will ultimately frustrate rather than intrigue them. It can be good to divide a bigger secret into smaller mysteries, as above, because it allows you to answer some questions as you go, before posing new ones, giving a sense of progression. It's like dishing out small pieces of a jigsaw puzzle: each one reveals more – enough to tantalize us and satisfy us, up to a point, but not enough that we can guess the full picture.

You may need to do some juggling and character rationalizing to prevent the full secret coming out too quickly, particularly in a first-person or intimate third-person narrative. Why wouldn't the secret about Layla's dad be at the forefront of her mind, visible to the reader? Well, perhaps Layla might have suppressed this information, or find it hard to think about. Perhaps she's fallen back on rigid order and routine to try and feel secure, and now the routine and the vague sense of threat it protects her from is all she thinks about – the reasons behind these behaviours remain shut up in the darkest recesses of her mind. You can see, hopefully, how thinking about the way you pace the story may also have fascinating repercussions on characterization, and vice versa.

Let's look at a published example of overarching pacing, so that you can see the technique in action. Stephen King's *Misery* is both a great example of suspense, and an intriguing exploration of the process of pacing. In it, King introduces the idea of the 'gotta' factor – that quality that keeps a reader turning the pages, staying up late because they *gotta* finish just one more chapter. The overarching tension in *Misery* comes from the fact that the main character, an author who has been imprisoned by his psychotic fan, must grip her with his storytelling, making her so desperate to find out what happens next that she can't bring herself to kill him.

In addition to this overarching tension driver the story delivers suspense on a scene-by-scene level. There are many individually dramatic incidents which benefit from that slow-motion time-stretching we discussed earlier. But more importantly, King handles his exposition cleverly, delivering just enough answers to keep us satisfied, but continually posing new questions that mean we have to read on. Meanwhile he layers in hints about what's coming, creating an atmosphere of menace and fear before we're even aware of why we should be scared.

Let's unpick the first few scenes: we open with blurred sounds. We have no idea what these sounds are, who's hearing them, or what's going on. In the next couple of segments we learn that our protagonist is male, called Paul, and in some sort of coma. All he can remember at this stage is pain – we don't know why, or where the pain has come from – but we guess that some accident has brought him to this place – wherever that might be.

In his hallucinogenic musings one image recurs – pilings, jutting out of the sand on a seashore, sometimes covered by the tide. This image comes to represent his pain, and later we find out why: it signifies his legs, shattered in the accident. In between these dream-visions, something real intrudes – a mouth clamped over his, whose kiss of life feels like a violation. Who is this angel of death? When she introduces herself as Annie Wilkes, Paul is able to pre-empt her words, *I'm your number one fan* – these are the sounds he's been hearing at the edge of consciousness. So we now know: Paul is a writer.

As Paul begins to regain his mind, his glimpses of this woman become clearer and he begins to understand the danger he's in. His narrative leaves the immediate present where he's been locked in his fugue state, and starts to jump forward, offering brief, cryptic hints about incidents we haven't yet witnessed. By the end of chapter four, these hints are crystallized into three realizations: Annie Wilkes has a big stock of pain medication; Paul is hooked on it; and Annie Wilkes is *dangerously crazy*.

Having resolved these initial questions, Chapter 5 moves forward into new territory: how did Paul end up here, and what might be about to happen to him now? Paul is fully awake, and able to ask about his situation consciously, so the narrative becomes less dreamlike and more of a conventional dialogue between two people. However, with the increase in interaction between Paul and Annie we are able to see her more clearly, and this is unsettling: why does Annie sidestep Paul's questions about where they are and why he isn't in hospital? When he asks where his wallet is, she will only tell him that she's *kept it safe*, and she becomes angry. We realize, as Paul does, that he must be very careful what he says. However, the way Paul talks his way out of this – spinning a yarn which smooths over the conflict – tells us something else: Paul is not completely defenceless. His ability to tell a good story may save him yet.

Observe how the questions and answers work together here. The author poses a question, which he may not answer immediately, but in the interim he answers one or more of the other questions he's set up – before hitting us with another mystery or a hint towards something else lurking beneath the surface of the action. The questions keep us reading, whilst the answers move the plot forward and lead us into new areas of tension. None of these secrets are heavily signposted: they feel like an organic part of each scene and the way the two characters interact; indeed we may not even consciously notice the significance of some elements until later. All we are aware of as the story progresses is building unease and fear; a feeling that Paul is in deep trouble.

Pacing can be one of the hardest elements of fiction to get right, partly because it's not as commonly talked about as other aspects of writing, and partly because it involves such a delicate touch. It requires you to know your plot inside out, with a clear overarching sense of everything that has happened and is going to happen, so that you can gauge exactly when and how each vital piece of information should be delivered. And it also helps to have a kind of innate drumbeat in the back of your head that tells you how fast the story is progressing and what the reader's pulse is doing. That's not something that can be taught, but learning how to spot overwriting and cut effectively will help you to listen out for the rhythm of your scenes and sentences, so we'll go on to talk about that next.

Overwriting

Almost all authors will overwrite at some stage because it's a natural outcome of the imaginative process – and a side-effect of the extensive vocabulary most writers possess. Even authors who start with lean, spare prose may go through a phase of overwriting; perhaps an editor will tell them that they need more description, or that their writing lacks colour, and they'll take things too far in the opposite direction to compensate. This phase is no bad thing. It means you're visualizing your scenes well and you're employing a wide lexicon. It's only a problem when you can't spot it or figure out how to correct it; or when overwriting becomes your default mode.

Overwriting can sometimes happen after an author's been on a certain type of writing course; any process that focuses on unlocking creativity can lead to a sort of imaginative splurging – where thoughts pour onto the page – and a sense that every-thing you write is equally important. Overwriting can also become a problem when you're self-consciously trying to write literary fiction, or striving for a style that doesn't sit naturally with you. And it can creep in, as we touched on above, when you're writing dramatic or emotional scenes – places where elevated language seems appropriate.

Those are the danger areas to be aware of – but what constitutes overwriting? Overall, it can be summarized as *writing that leaves nothing to the imagination*, but like most areas of self-editing this broad stricture can be broken down into smaller chunks.

So, firstly, keep an eye out for **overlong description**. Perhaps you're depicting something prosaic, but you've got caught up in the moment and let it run away with you:

> As she left the house for work in the morning, she stopped to talk to Mavis over the garden fence. They'd put the fence up the year before, after the old one had been torn down in the summer storms, and it still felt new and pristine, the clean white paint masking the rough woodchip beneath. Small splinters pricked at her fingers when she laid a hand on the top…

Hopefully you can see why this feels overcooked – do we need to know about the fence in so much detail? Is it relevant or interesting? Is the conversation with Mavis what's important here – or is even that a distraction?

Excess information can appear in many contexts. It's often a kind of writerly geeing up, or padding out – perhaps you're not sure where a scene is going, or you're killing time until the next big moment, and your heart's not in the passage you're writing. To inject life and colour you start giving too much weight to peripheral happenings:

He stepped into the white-tiled shower, placing his right hand against the wall and leaned in. The hot water poured down over his back and shoulders. He lathered himself up with shower gel and let the water rinse off the suds, etc…

There's no need for most of these details (which are basically stage directions, as discussed in Chapter 6) and the whole scene can probably be cut, or reduced to a single line like *He took a shower.*

Or perhaps you're describing something that will be familiar to most people, but in striving to make it feel fresh and new you've used language that feels too **complex, florid or unusual**:

The elephant was mountainous, its voluminous leaden sides straining against the horizon.

We know an elephant is huge and grey (the main things this description aims to convey in a 'new' way). To make us see the animal differently, perhaps there's something else you could focus on, something readers might not be aware of:

She'd read somewhere that an elephant could stand on your hand without hurting you if it liked you. Up close, she could almost believe it – the skin that looked so rough was warm and velvety. Moisture matted its thick eyelashes.

Overwritten prose often suffers from **tautology, redundancy** and **repetition**, which are three fractionally different aspects of the same problem: saying something more than once.

Tautology can take a number of forms, including **unnecessary decoration** of an idea (*The prison's uniformed guards patrolled the perimeter* – we know prison guards wear uniforms so unless you're going to tell us specifically what they look like this isn't needed); using **two words** where one has already done the job (*she put on* *a pair of shoes* – the word 'shoes' is already plural so 'pair' serves no purpose); **superfluous description** (as with including both *mountainous* and *voluminous* in the above example); and **pointless additions** (like *she heard a loud banging noise* or *she was enjoying the sunny weather* – why not just *a loud bang* or *enjoying the sun?*)

Statements can also be tautologous if they reframe a point without adding anything useful: *That's it, she decided, she was leaving for good. She would never come back.* Or, *The road stretched into the distance, as far as he could see. He couldn't make out its end.* These kinds of repetitions can feel waffly.

Redundancy is similar to tautology but subtly different. Redundancies *seem* to contribute something, but can be removed without losing any sense. For example, *she shrugged (her shoulders)* or *he nodded (his head)* – in both these instances the body part is implicit within the action. Details of positioning and action often feature redundancies – like *they followed (behind), they were (completely) surrounded, they descended (down) into the pit* or *the warriors clashed (together).* And in general, many qualifying words aren't needed as the words they're attempting to modify are already sufficiently concrete and specific: *this is your (final) ultimatum; I will (completely) eliminate any opposition; this is (absolutely) essential.*

If you decide to get evangelical about redundancy, you can do a lot of minor but worthwhile decluttering – removing or making sparing use of modifiers like *very, really, quite, mainly, almost* and *nearly*, along with questioning every adjective and adverb. Even very basic syntactical changes can remove redundant words and make a sentence more efficient. Without getting too deep into this issue, the gist is, ask yourself if every single word is essential.

Repetition is similar but tends to be easier to spot. Most authors have **pet words**, and the more unusual these are the more they will pop out. We worked with an author once who adored the word *fulsome* and had used it around five times over the course of his novel. You might not think that's particularly frequent, but when a word is fresh and uncommon, we will notice it even if you only use it twice. Or, you might inadvertently have used the same ordinary word several times on the same page but because the instances are in close proximity they still sound repetitious. Even a simple word like 'back' or 'off' will stand out if it appears a few times in one paragraph.

Authors occasionally repeat **whole sentences or phrases** – either because they've moved something around but forgotten to cut the original instance, or because they've invented a phrase they particularly like and decided, perhaps unconsciously, to use it again. Clichés like *he tossed his head*, *he bared his teeth* or *she snorted with laughter* will be noticeable if used more than once. (Repetition happens frequently with clichés, perhaps because these are phrases that flow from the pen a little too easily.)

Ideas and concepts often get repeated. Perhaps it's something that's significant in plot or character terms, something like *She had hidden the letter in a book on the shelf*, and you want to make sure we've noticed it. Or perhaps it's to do with the setting or infrastructure – you might have told us several times, for example, that *the castle was full of twisting corridors and secret passages* – a detail you particularly like. Try to avoid this: trust the reader, and trust your own writing. Convey something vividly enough the first time around, and you won't need to tell us again.

Finally, watch out for **recapping and summing up**. Perhaps you've just written a scene in which something important happened, and can't resist the temptation to recap, either in the form of narrative or inner voice:

> So, Ryan thought, the gangsters had never intended to release Emmy. They'd taken the cash, and kept hold of her

anyway. She'd stared at him out of the back window of that Mercedes, as though she already knew they weren't about to be reunited. And then they'd just driven away.

Assuming we've already seen the scene in which this happened, the recapping serves no purpose.

Or, you might have one character needing to tell another what's just happened to them. Again, avoid recapping here – opt for a brief line or two that doesn't restate any of the fine detail. This summary will generally feel like telling, so keep it short and vivid in its own right, rooted in the now of the story rather than diving back into the scene you've left:

Ryan explained what had happened. He realized he was still gripping Emmy's scarf, and he scrunched it to his face and breathed in her lemony scent. God, how had he let her go?

Adjectives and adverbs are a useful part of the writer's lexicon, but you can have too much of a good thing. We've talked about these elsewhere so we won't go into too much detail here, but in the next section, on **cutting**, we'll look at the effect removing this decoration has on a passage.

Writing the author is in love with is usually one of the hardest forms of overwriting to accept and remove. There's a great quote attributed to Samuel Johnson: 'Read over your compositions, and wherever you meet with a passage which you think is particularly fine, strike it out.' It's sometimes possible to tell which parts an author is proud of because there's no obvious reason for the material to be there; it's only present because the author couldn't bear to part with it. Pay particular attention to lyrical, reflective passages featuring vivid imagery or poetic language; leisurely descriptions of people and locations; authorial grandstanding about issues that are important to you (but perhaps not to the characters).

If you can't tell if you're being self-indulgent, the best bet is to try cutting the passage anyway. Do you miss it? Would a reader? Lee Weatherly told us about one such passage that she'd reluctantly cut, but was convinced she ought to put back in. When she asked her editor, 'But what about that scene in the pub?' the editor had no recollection of the original incident.

One of the most common forms of overwriting is **overcooked figurative language** – metaphors and similes that draw too much attention to themselves; that cloud rather than clarify whatever they're attempting to convey; or that are simply not appropriate in context. Look at these examples: can you visualize the thing that's being described, or does the writing get in the way?

- *He catapulted out of his chair like a whippet after a rabbit.*
- *Her heart pounded like a cannon.*
- *It was as dark as if someone had poured black paint over the windows.*
- *Her eyes were two deep lakes on her face.*
- *His words tore into her like a samurai sword.*
- *She was wearing a t-shirt like the one that Britney wore in the video for* 'Hit Me Baby One More Time'.
- *His ears probed around the house for any strange sounds.*
- *Her hair was the same yellow as the inside part of a banana.*

There are a few different issues with these – mixed metaphors (like *catapulted* and *whippet*); similes that convey a slightly different impression from the one intended (*like a cannon* doesn't work because it's such a noisy image and a cannon fires only one shot whereas a heart is rhythmic and repetitive); images that are so strange or vivid that we can only see the metaphor, rather than the thing it's describing (*two deep lakes on her face* or *someone had poured black paint over the windows*); and ideas that come out of nowhere (*like a samurai sword* would only be apposite if the two characters, or the setting, or the conversation, was somehow linked to ancient Japan). There's a comparison that assumes knowledge (if we don't know what Britney's t-shirt looked like we have absolutely no way of visualizing this, and in any case the simile feels jarring – too culturally and temporally specific). And there's the image that doesn't work because it imparts agency to an inanimate object (*his ears probed around the house*). Finally, there's the simile that's so weird that we're not sure what it's trying to do – a banana is so far removed from hair that the image jars us out of the writing; and is this supposed to be a pleasing colour or is the comparison somehow detrimental?

With imagery like this we get so caught up in trying to comprehend the author's intention that we lose sight of what's important. One notable exception to this rule is comic fiction, where outlandish or quirky similes are often used to undercut the drama of a scene in an ironic way, and children's fiction, where authors might be deliberately more playful with their language to draw in reluctant readers or raise a smile.

(NB once you've settled on the right imagery, exercise some restraint. If you've come up with a couple of good metaphors it can be hard to choose between them, but several strong images close together will lose their impact and end up feeling just as overwritten as one bad piece of figurative language. If you're regularly using more than one metaphor or simile per page then the chances are you're getting trigger happy.)

Lastly, overwriting can sneak in within your **syntax and sentence structures**. Good writing tends to be varied in terms of sentence lengths; it will have an ebb and flow between sharp, pithy sentences and longer, more reflective phrases containing more clauses. However, don't strive to find convoluted ways of expressing something; clarity is paramount. And this is the main problem with overwriting of any kind. Simple prose works because it gives us a direct view of the characters. It allows the background emotion and atmosphere to take precedence over the language you're using, and draws us into the world of the story without our being aware of the writing. But if a reader is too busy trying to figure out what you're saying they won't lose themselves in this way. They'll always remain on the outside, looking in.

The first cut is the deepest

There's no two ways about it: cutting can be hard. It's galling to excise prose that you've worked hard on and that you love. However, once you realize the effect it can have on your writing it can be hugely liberating, and indeed we know many authors who love it; who even find it addictive.

The benefits are clear: first drafts of novels often tend to be too long, and agents and editors may baulk at a huge doorstep of a manuscript – either rejecting it outright or shoving it to the bottom of their pile – whereas shorter texts may get read more quickly, and with a more sympathetic eye. Longer texts can be more expensive to publish and harder to sell, and there's sometimes an assumption that a long text hasn't been carefully edited.

Aside from these pragmatic considerations, cutting does generally result in a tighter, more readable manuscript – one where every word counts – and when we read a tight manuscript we tend to turn the pages more quickly; slow down less; enjoy *all* the writing rather than skimming through to the next 'good bit'.

So what do you look for when you're wondering what to cut? Well, the areas discussed above form a pretty good checklist:

- inner voice
- overlong description/excess information
- unnecessarily florid language
- repetition, tautology and redundancy
- overcooked figurative language and clichés
- non-dramatic material or passages where nothing much happens
- recapping and summing up
- passages you love

Some of these things may warrant cutting altogether; some may just need trimming back, as discussed under pacing. Some cuts can be huge – whole paragraphs, scenes or even whole chapters. Some might be just the odd word here and there. And, in some areas, where you need to give a moment more weight or space, you might not need to cut, or you may even want to extend. For the purposes of this section we'll demonstrate with a passage featuring all of the above problem areas, so we can look at just how bold you can afford to be with your cuts:

'We can't go any further,' called the coachman. 'Here's where you alight, ma'am.'

Carlotta stepped lightly down from the carriage carrying her embroidered valise in her right hand. Instantly her black silk slippers sank into the thick mud, and she gave a cry, 'Oh!' Why hadn't she thought to spend some of the tortuously long carriage journey changing into more appropriate footwear for the rigours of countryside walking? Instead of sitting mutely whilst Deacon Bradbury had told his interminable anecdotes. What a simple fool she was; she was going to have to be stronger and bolder now that she was mistress of Camberly. And the first thing I'll do, she told herself firmly, will be to have this drive landscaped and properly gritted. Mud! It simply would not do. How would she welcome guests here if they had to pick their way through a swamp every time they wished to call?. Assuming, of course, that anyone would want to call. Her cheeks went hot at the memory of her foolish fantasies about endless dances and garden parties.

She realized that the tall, fair-haired gentleman she'd spotted from the window of the carriage was still standing silently, obviously waiting for her, holding his hand out to take her arm. She cleared her throat awkwardly and took a step forward, her shoes sticking in the mud, causing her to stumble and trip.

The fair-haired gentleman caught her arm. His eyes were cornflower blue, his jaw wide and generous, his face sunburnt and the hair that had first caught her eye curled down to his neckline in soft rings. He wore a faded velveteen jerkin the same colour as his eyes, with a gold brocade cravat poking delicately out of it and a heavy, ornate watch chain dangling from one pocket. His boots were of strong leather – no wrestling with the mud for him! – and altogether he seemed like a nobleman, but one dressed for countryside life.

She looked up into his face to see that he was giving her a reassuring smile. 'Let me take you to meet the servants,' he said.

They walked the rest of the drive in silence, and the carriage went on ahead. Carlotta saw that the servants were ranged on the broad steps at the front of the house, waiting to meet her.

Now, you may not want to cut *all* the adjectives from the above passage – it's fine to include a few to give the prose more colour – but let's remove as many as possible so we can see whether it makes a difference. Where there's an adverb, we'll substitute a stronger verb instead. There's a fair bit of repetition and recapping that can be removed completely, along with at least one paragraph where nothing's really happening. Overall, we need to have a think about the weight of the material – presumably this is an important character (perhaps a love interest) being introduced, so let's keep the focus on that, possibly extending those sentences a little, rather than including too much detail on peripheral stuff like mud:

> 'We can't go any further,' called the coachman. 'Here's where you alight, ma'am.'
>
> Carlotta stepped from the carriage carrying her valise. Her slippers sank into the mud, and she cried, 'Oh!' Why hadn't she spent some of the journey changing into better shoes? She was going to have to do something about this driveway before she could even think of entertaining here. Assuming, of course, that anyone would wish to call. Her cheeks went hot at the memory of her daydreams about dances and garden parties.
>
> The tall, fair-haired gentleman she'd spotted from the window of the carriage was holding out a hand. She cleared her throat and stumbled forward, her shoes sticking.
>
> He caught her arm, and she felt the strength beneath his faded velveteen jerkin. She looked up into his eyes to see that he was smiling. With his hair curling down his sunburnt cheek he looked like a farmhand, but his gold cravat and the watch chain poking from a pocket made her wonder.
>
> 'Let me take you to meet the servants,' he said.

As well as being ruthless with cuts here, we've added more detail to the 'meet cute' element of the scene, including a question mark over who this man is. This brings the romantic tension forwards and allows the scene to do some overarching pacing at the same time. We've left only those adjectives and elements of description that contribute something intriguing to this (*faded/velveteen/gold/sunburnt*). Carlotta's inner voice has been stripped right back, along with any recapping, but the gist of what's going through her mind remains the same.

This is perhaps a tricky example, because historical fiction can be wordier, lending itself to ornate description and slightly more convoluted phrasing – authors sometimes aim to replicate a historical flavour in their narrative style. But striving too hard to find an authentic voice can often lead into overwriting and ironically enough may result in more anachronisms and a less realistic tone. Here, we've tried to retain a slight sense of era simply in the way Carlotta's inner voice is phrased (*before she could even think of entertaining*) but left the prose simple and brisk.

If you're nervous about cutting, the golden rule is to **always save a copy of your work before you start.** You won't touch this version. If you like, think of it as your 'real' text and the one you're working on as more of an experiment. It's amazing how freeing this can be – and once you start cutting, and see how easy it is (and more importantly the life and vigour it brings to your prose) – you won't look back.

Tension troubleshooting

You'll probably notice that we've mentioned tension a LOT in this book. It's intrinsically bound up with every aspect of writing; it's probably true to say that creating tension is the key goal of fiction. That's not to say that every novel should be a nail-biting thriller or that every scene should feature characters in conflict – by 'tension', we simply mean the posing of questions or mysteries that aren't immediately answered, which translates to a page-turning quality – that 'gotta' factor that the reader should feel.

Because we've discussed this so much already we won't spend long on it here; instead, we'll do a quick summing-up of things you can check if you suspect your tension might be slack.

- **Are the stakes high enough?** Will something dreadful happen if your character fails to fulfil their goal or solve their problem? The results don't have to be catastrophic on a global scale (in fact, making the consequences too far reaching can diminish their personal importance to the protagonist) but they do have to matter to your main character.

- **Is your timescale tight?** Except in certain genres where it's expected (sagas for example) a story that straddles years, decades or centuries may struggle to sustain tension. The reason for this is logical – in a story that spans a big time period things always have time to resolve; the lovers might have lost touch *now*, but by this time next year they could be reunited. On the other hand, if our hero only has three hours to find a way off the space station before it explodes … the *ticking clock* is certainly a staple, but it's a useful one.

- **Are you making things hard for your main character?** Must they face their worst fear, or do something that challenges them physically or emotionally? Must they confront some deep, shameful part of themselves before they can progress? And **do the things that happen to them affect them, or do they brush them off too easily?** We worked with one author who inflicted a great deal of misery on her main character, but the story still lacked bite because the heroine was so blasé about everything that happened that we just couldn't take her – or her troubles – seriously.

- **Do you resolve the story's tensions too quickly?** As we saw from the Stephen King example above, good pacing relies on answering your story's questions – but not straight away. Let the reader's expectations build; their own imaginations go to work on the possibilities; let them wonder what the answers might hold. By the same token, if something terrible happens to your character – perhaps you leave one chapter on a cliffhanger, with the character about to be discovered somewhere they shouldn't be, for example – give us time to absorb this tension, and follow it through, rather than dissipating it straight away. There's nothing more disappointing than a great cliffhanger followed by a subsequent chapter that immediately punctures that tension – *but then the footsteps faded away. Phew! He was safe!*

- **Does each chapter contain at least one question or point of tension?** This might be as obvious as *who has Sonja received hate mail from?* Or as subtle as *what did Darren mean when he said, 'But you'd know all about that, wouldn't you?'* If you can't pick out a central point of tension in each scene or chapter then either find a way to inject this – make the scene work harder – or consider cutting it. Often, filler material of the sort that we've already discussed cutting or shortening won't contain tension because it's just marking time, and isn't actually needed.

- **Is there too much peripheral material surrounding this main point of tension?** Even in a scene containing a cracking plot point or a dazzlingly mysterious question, it's possible for our attention to wane. In some cases this may be because you've tried to extend the scene too far, spent too long writing yourself into it and haven't been able to decide how to conclude. As we've seen under pacing, above, some scenes do need weight, and time spent on them, but if you feel when you read through that the point of tension is being lost or sidelined, then this is a good time to wield your cutting knife.

- **Have you been in a rush to reveal your story's secrets?** Opening chapters tend to be a good indicator of what tension will be like in the remainder of the book, because the need to introduce characters and scenarios forces you to reveal what sort of a writer you are. If a first chapter contains a lot of telling or exposition – *Arty had come to live in Minnesota after the death of his wife from cancer three years previously. He still struggled with the grief, and he found it hard to make friends because of his fear of being hurt again* – then we can see you're a writer who lays everything out in the open. We've found out what makes Arty tick already, and there's not much motivation to read on.

- **Is too much of your tension manufactured?** Portentous authorial statements that hint at something terrible lurking around the corner; conflict that feels like purposeless bickering rather than progressing the plot; refusing to answer the questions that you've set up or deliberately withholding information from the reader: these can all be signs that you've tried too hard to introduce tension. Perhaps your natural sources of tension in the story need looking at again, or perhaps the tension is already present but you're not quite confident enough to let it speak for itself. Either way, manufactured tension tends to feel contrived, and can work against the *real* tensions in the story.

Feel the beat

We've tied a few disparate elements together in this chapter because they comprise a great toolkit for dealing with one specific area of prose: its heartbeat; its pulse; its rhythm. This is one of those areas that can feel frustrating and intangible – when writers or editors talk about the music or rhythm of writing, what do they mean? How can you hone your own rhythm? The aim is to take an abstract notion and turn it into manageable, quantifiable techniques.

Avoiding overwriting, pacing carefully, managing your exposition, being bold with cuts, and cranking up the tension – these are all guidelines which may be easy enough to understand in theory but harder to implement in your own work. The trick, as with editing in every area, is to start specific and gradually get broader. On your first read through of a scene, choose just one area to focus on – overwriting, perhaps – and make it your mission to pick out every instance you can find, even if you ultimately decide to leave some of them in. Or, if you're still playing around with ideas rather than writing a full novel, try writing an isolated scene specifically zeroing in on the pacing.

Once you've made each of these individual techniques your friend, they will start to come more naturally and you'll find that you're gradually able to unfocus a little, taking in the bigger picture as well as the fine detail. It's a question of becoming first consciously competent and then unconsciously competent; or, if you like, of becoming confident enough that you can switch off the parts of your brain you used to compose the music and just let yourself *feel* it. That process of feeling your way into your writing is something we'll go on to discuss in the next chapter.

8
Show not Tell

'Show not Tell' is often taught as a set of techniques and strictures: active vs passive writing; substituting strong verbs; removing adverbs. These comprise a useful toolbox, but they're not as important as getting into the Show not Tell State of Mind. This chapter will use Show not Tell as a guide to lead you through your prose, helping you sink deeper into your writing. By feeling your writing intensely yourself you'll transmit that emotion to the reader … and when you can make the reader feel, you've got them in the palm of your hand.

'Show, don't Tell' is probably something you've heard a lot as a new author; it's one of the most commonly used phrases in contemporary creative writing teaching. You might also have heard it described as **scene vs summary, active vs passive writing**, or **drama vs narrative**; which are all small parts of the whole. Because of the many different techniques associated with Show not Tell, and the way it connects with almost every aspect of your writing, it can be hard to get to grips with, and is often misunderstood.

At its simplest, the aim of showing is to bring the reader as close as possible to the action, allowing us to witness it firsthand and therefore delivering a more **involving** reading experience. Maybe that still sounds abstract, so let's first look at an example that incorporates some facets of Show not Tell:

Sarah walked slowly along the dark, creepy corridor. Suddenly she heard a sound that made her jump. It was terrifying, and she was sure that she was in danger. She turned quickly, but she couldn't see anything behind her. The darkness was completely impenetrable. There was a shuffling noise to her right, and she turned again, breathing fast, staring into the shadows. Just then, a light appeared, illuminating a kindly face in front of her. It was Stevens, the butler. She felt immediately relieved.

Compare this description of the same events:

Sarah edged along the corridor, one hand clutching at the air, the other clamped to her mouth. She heard a scuffle from behind and spun around, squinting into the gloom. There was no point – even if someone had been standing a foot away from her she couldn't have seen them. She swallowed, her throat pulsing with the hammering in her chest.

The sound came again – closer, now – and again she wheeled round, the blackness thick and cold against her cheek. Only the sound of her breathing. But there was something – surely, a stirring in the air, a presence, almost near enough to touch. She felt a scream fighting its way out; choked it back; groped behind her for the wall, the door, a way out – anything had to be better than this utter black and the nameless thing that even now was …

'Miss? Miss Sarah?'

A flame flickered into life, and out of its dim glow loomed a crinkled, shadow-cast face, its hollowed eyes glimmering at her. She gasped, the sound like a buzz-saw in the silence.

Then it gave her a crooked smile, and the breath trickled out of her.

Stevens, of course. What an idiot she was.

'What in devil's name are you doing blundering around in the dark, Miss?'

These two pieces of writing convey the same events, but they hopefully made you react differently. The first feels distanced and unengaging: the language is safe and boring, in spite of the fact that we're told explicitly how scary the scene is. Everything is laid out baldly, with no room for reader interpretation; our own imaginations go to sleep. This makes the reading experience very separate from us; we're outside it, rather than immersed in the scene. Hmm, we think, this is probably scary for Sarah. But we don't *feel scared*. By contrast, the second passage aims to convey that fear that Sarah is experiencing: it uses a number of devices associated with Show not Tell to make the hairs stand up on the reader's arms; to get them to feel the dankness of the air against their own skin, and share the crawling sense that Sarah isn't alone.

These devices can be broken down into literary principles. In particular, the second piece:

- uses **active sentence structures** (*she heard a scuffle*) as opposed to passive
- selects its vocabulary more carefully, **choosing the perfect word** (*a crinkled, shadow-cast face*) as opposed to settling for an easy short-hand description
- allows us to **make our own connections and interpretations** – it doesn't at any point use words like *fear, creepy* or *danger*
- **avoids adverbs**, replacing any weaker verb plus adverb constructions with a strong verb (*edged* instead of *walked slowly*)
- **avoids emotion words**, letting the atmosphere of the scene and the character's feelings come through in the action and description
- utilizes **specific details** – sounds, smells, physical sensations – instead of clichés or generalizations like *a sound, a light* or *a face*

- moves the action forward using **dialogue and incident** rather than narration (*it was Stevens the butler* is replaced by Stevens' own words, and some action)
- aims to **get inside the character's head** as much as possible, incorporating some inner voice (*Stevens, of course. What an idiot she was*)
- uses **figurative language** like **similes** and **metaphors** to create images that jolt to life (*like a buzz-saw; the breath trickled out of her*).

Looked at individually, each of these techniques is easy enough to understand and implement, and logically preferable because of the impact they have. In other words, it should be clear what to aim for, and why it's an effective choice for your writing. However, where many authors come unstuck is in an understanding of just how all-encompassing a concept this is.

You can probably see, even from the above, how many of the concepts are linked: **letting the reader make their own connections** and **avoiding emotion words**, for example, are two sides of the same coin. Similarly, **avoiding adverbs, using specific details**, and **choosing the perfect word**, are three different ways of looking at the same key point: a need for precision; the imperative not to 'settle' for the first choice. Because of this interconnection, Show not Tell as a whole is not as simple as running down a checklist of good practices. These techniques feed into each other and impact on one another, and getting one right might not necessarily mean you've nailed the whole process.

Therefore, Show not Tell may be best understood as a **writing mindset**, an overarching way of looking at *all of* your prose. That's not to say that you should always be showing – to convey factual information, summarize chunks of time, or keep the reader at a distance from the action for whatever reason, by all means tell. But to turn them on, terrify them, make them cry, make them laugh, you need to get into the showing mindset.

That mindset is about living, breathing and *feeling* as much of the action as possible. That's the overriding purpose of showing: to make your reader **experience the sensation** of a scene, whether that's the dynamic between two characters (having an argument, or falling in love), a specific emotion a character is feeling (like fear, or happiness) or a wider sense of the atmosphere and setting you're conveying (whether a location is vibrant, or calm, for example). If you *tell* us these things, we might understand what you're saying objectively but we won't experience it emotionally – taste the fear for ourselves, feel our own heart racing, or our skin tingling. If you *show*, then you're much more likely to transmit some of that real, sensory, experience to us. And that direct, electrifying connection is what makes for compelling fiction.

To help you get into the Show not Tell mindset, we will deal with it not by looking at the above techniques in isolation – there are plenty of resources out there which will tell you about active vs passive writing, or how to use figurative language, and mastering these techniques is important, but it won't necessarily help you become an expert at spotting or using Show not Tell in your own work. Instead, we want to use this concept as a lens through which we can study the various aspects of writing we've discussed in this book, tying them together and looking at them with this one key purpose in mind: drawing us right into the action; making us *feel*.

Show not Tell and characterization

Show not Tell is the life-blood of character. When we discussed characterization in Chapter 2, we used the example of meeting someone at a party who tells us how great they are, and how this might make us respond – as opposed to the way we'd feel if we witnessed their good qualities for ourselves. Characteristics we observe first hand feel real and memorable. It's like we're *getting to know* the character rather than simply reading about them:

Fran had always been someone Casey looked up to. She couldn't have told you why, exactly – only that Fran had some ineffable sense of wisdom and purpose, qualities that Casey knew she herself lacked. Spending time with Fran always felt calming, as though her soothing southern lilt, her gentleness, allowed Casey to temporarily shelve the million and one anxieties that she carried around with her every day.

This piece of writing already utilizes some of the techniques associated with showing. It's nicely inside Casey's head, giving us her voice and her feelings about her friend. However, as we touched on above, using Show not Tell techniques in isolation doesn't automatically mean you're showing. Here, Casey's inner voice is being used to tell. Look at the number of times we're told about characteristics and feelings: we have *looked up to … wisdom and purpose … calming … soothing … gentleness … anxieties*. As such, we aren't left with much work; we're not involved in the characterization in any way.

Consider a version of this that utilizes a brief scene, featuring **dialogue and incident**:

Casey slumped at the kitchen table, drumming her ink-stained fingers on the wood.

'Hey now, honey, it can't be that bad?' Fran tucked a straggle of hair behind Casey's ear, then eased into a chair opposite and reached for her hand. Her fingers were cool and dry. 'Can I help anyways?'

Casey looked into Fran's grey eyes, the lines around them deep and crinkled, and her shoulders relaxed. The knot in her throat eased enough for her to speak. 'I dunno, honestly. But maybe if anyone can, you can.'

Here, both the dynamic between the characters and the individual characterization comes across in the interactions – the specific details of gesture that show Fran's gentleness, and Casey's ink-stained fingers and straggly hair that speak of a less together persona. We avoid emotion words, and instead, Casey's anxieties are encapsulated in physical symptoms – the knot in her throat, her tense shoulders – and the scene manages to convey friendship and respect without ever explicitly mentioning these qualities. Because we've pieced the relationship together for ourselves, making our own connections and observations about what each of the friends brings to it, the scene carries a truth that is absent from the direct explanation of what's going on.

So, just as Show not Tell is a key tool when it comes to bringing your characters to life, it is equally important to Show the dynamic between characters, particularly when this is changing or shifting in some way. If two characters have come to a crisis in their relationship, have suddenly realized they have feelings for each other, or one has just discovered a secret about the other – these transitions need to be dramatized, rather than simply described:

> Finally the moment had come. Caro had been waiting for so long, and now he was admitting how he felt, she was unsure how to respond. Her heart was in her mouth; her palms damp; her knees trembled weakly. She had never felt this way about anyone.

Here, the outpouring of emotion we're subjected to is so sentimental that it simply doesn't feel believable. Though we do get some inner voice and some specific physical details, they're clichés – heart in mouth, weak knees – which do nothing to convey how this particular character, in this specific scenario, is experiencing the emotion. Despite the fact that we're inside Caro's head, it could be happening to anyone – her inner voice is a generalized authorial explanation of how someone in love might feel. Try not to offer trite, romantic over-simplifications; we want to experience the emotion in all its uniqueness and potency, and feel as though we're falling in love a little bit ourselves:

Caro slid the book back onto the shelf, and took down another, her eyes fixed on the page but seeing nothing; her fingers struggling to keep the volume from shaking. David stepped closer, laying a steady hand on her arm.

'Please,' he said. 'Look at me.'

'Shh,' came a brisk voice from the other side of the stack, then the librarian's shoes hush-hushed away across the carpet.

David lowered his voice, and said, 'Caro.'

She shivered at the sound of him speaking her name, and raised her eyes to his. What would she see there? A reflection of herself, or something else?

He was close, closer than she'd realized, and looking up to him brought her face near enough to feel his breath. He smelled faintly of candyfloss, and she remembered him telling her how much he'd loved sweets as a child. Now he looked down, his lashes a smudge of shadow on his cheek, and then he was gripping her hand, the back of her neck, and pulling her in to him, so that their mouths were a whisper apart.

'I love you,' he breathed into her. 'I love you.'

There it hung now in the air between them. And she couldn't find any words to say back to him. A step closer, not even that, and their lips would touch. Did she dare?

Again, we use **dialogue and incident** to bring the emotion to life; the scene is situated somewhere **specific**, which helps us to visualize it. We avoid explicitly mentioning the **emotions** that each character is feeling, though these come across no less clearly. We're **inside Caro's head** again, but here the inner voice feels truer and unique to her, encompassing some of her intimate knowledge about David, demonstrating the closeness of their relationship. There's some **figurative language**, too, giving the moment individuality. This is *Caro's experience* – only she could live it and describe it in this way.

This quality of uniqueness is at the heart of Show not Tell, and of writing generally; it's so important to create a world, and characters, that are yours, and that are fresh. There will be derivative elements in almost all writing, and indeed, as we discussed under genre, other authors feeding into your prose and influencing you is not always a bad thing. But it is by making an experience – be it a character, an incident, or an emotion – *new* to the reader, that you allow them to see it most clearly. This makes Show not Tell a key tool when it comes to using and manipulating **viewpoint**, a fictional device that's all about intimate, personal experience; we'll move on to talk about that next.

Show not Tell and viewpoint

When we discussed viewpoint in Chapter 3, we talked about getting inside the POV character's head to give us an intimate insight into them. If you look back at some of the examples from that chapter, keeping the key tenets of Show not Tell in mind, you'll notice that the process of bringing us closer to a character is in many ways a process of changing telling to showing.

In the scene featuring Nat in the bar, getting into a fight, the first passage contains lots of telling: *he was terrified … he took the offensive … he saw stars … he tried to collect himself.* We have some classic telling indicators here – emotion words and clichés;

summaries and generalizations instead of specific details. In the rewritten passage, we tried to get inside Nat's head, and many of the tools we used to do this were the tools of Show not Tell – specific physical details; choosing the perfect word to give us a better sense of Nat's own voice; use of figurative language.

The way these elements cross over is a great demonstration of the wider point we're making about Show not Tell – how interlinked it is with all aspects of your writing. But this is nowhere as true as it is with viewpoint: the two are so closely intertwined that if someone tells you your viewpoint isn't working, you can pretty much bet that you need to bring more Show not Tell into it somewhere. And the flip side: if you're told that telling is an issue in your prose, you'll probably need to do some work on viewpoint too. When marking up manuscripts, editors sometimes use the annotations POV and SNT, and the specific annotation POV/SNT when work is needed on both aspects simultaneously.

Because this is such an important technical relationship, we're going to look at examples that cover all the things we talked about under viewpoint: scene vs summary; head-hopping; inner voice; physicality; external impressions and authorial commentary.

Scene vs summary/inner voice

In many of the examples in Chapter 3, we rewrote passages to incorporate more action and interaction; taking the character out of their head and into the real world. In the example featuring Laura and Simon, we translated a passage that was entirely Laura's inner voice into a scene where the conflict between her and Simon was dramatized on the page rather than summarized via Laura's thought processes.

This can seem like a paradox for authors wrestling with Show not Tell and viewpoint: if you're told that a close use of viewpoint means **getting inside your character's head**, and simultaneously that successful showing means **getting inside your character's head**, why would you want to strip out inner voice?

This is why it's so important to think of Show not Tell not as a series of stylistic strictures, but more as an overarching mindset. Yes, inner voice is important, but some sorts of inner voice are better than others; inner voice that's part of a scene is invariably more involving than big chunks of introspection; and most importantly, inner voice that is being used to summarize important plot points, emotional developments, and moments of conflict, is one of the most insidious ways in which telling can creep into writing. *Inner voice is your friend, but you can't always trust it to do the right thing.*

Let's look at an example:

> And then ... he screwed his eyes shut as he remembered ... they'd fought. Oh yeah, they'd fought alright. The whole class must've seen it. So much for impressing Josh and Matty. God, it was embarrassing, and especially after he'd been giving it all that about how into him she was. The things she'd said ... He pulled the cover over his head. Maybe he could convince Mum he was sick today, just stay home and watch movies. But what was the point? He'd still have to face them tomorrow, or the day after. Why hadn't he just kept his big mouth shut?

The problem with this type of inner voice is that it's so nearly OK. It sounds authentic, there's direct action (*screwed up his eyes ... pulled the cover over his head*), it gives us character and relationship, and it does feature some conflict ... *almost*. And that's the key point – the conflict is there, but it's happened off-stage (the pluperfect 'had' construction is a common signifier that the action's taken place at one remove) and this reflective passage is being used to summarize it. We're not seeing it for ourselves; we're not *there*. It's *told*.

Compare this:

Matty leaned over and pinched one of his crisps, the frayed end of his tie dangling on the desk. 'So what happened after we left?'

Aaron almost told the truth – almost. But where had that ever got him? Oh yeah, we carried on playing Connect 4, and then her dad came and picked her up. Big whoop.

Instead, he grinned. 'Well, it got a LOT more interesting.'

Josh laughed, showing his white, even teeth. 'Interesting like…?'

Aaron groped the air in front of him, about where Chelle's boobs would've been if she'd been stood there. The other lads laughed.

'And what else?' Matty asked. The two of them were sat on his desk now, like they'd all been mates forever. A few other faces hovered near enough to earwig. A proper audience, just like at his old school.

'Well,' he began.

'Well what?' snapped a voice from behind him.

He shuffled round in his seat, knowing already who it would be, his neck burning. 'Chelle,' he said. 'What I meant was-'

'You'd make up a load of bull about what we done last night to make yourself look like the big man, yeah? And me sound like some kind of slag.' Her red hair was scraped back, and she had purple rings under her eyes. Even now, he found himself thinking that she looked like she'd been up all night, the state of her actually made his story more believable. Then he caught himself – and his cheeks flared as he wondered why she'd really had a sleepless night.

'No, I-'

'Whatever.' She jutted her chin at the three of them. 'You all think what you want to, I don't care. But him-' and here she crooked her little finger at Aaron. 'He knows the truth. And let's just say, there ain't that much to know.' She raised her eyebrows and smirked. Then, just in case they were in any doubt, she mouthed the word, 'tiny', then spun around and stalked from the classroom.

Here, the scene brings the conflict to life, drawing us right into the action. Aaron's inner voice is more immediate and intriguing – observations on what's going on in the present scene, and thoughts that are relevant to the action and/or prompted by it, which extend our understanding of what's going on in the scene. The musing on why Chelle might have been up all night potentially takes the plot off in a different direction and suggests other areas of tension to be explored. And the comments on *his old school* develop our understanding of Aaron's character, keeping him borderline sympathetic, in spite of his idiotic behaviour.

Because the inner voice is *not* being used to summarize action that we've missed, it's freed up to achieve its true literary purpose: it should not be a tool for exposition – it should be used to explore and develop character, and woven into an action scene it is able to do that because it no longer carries the burden of moving the narrative forwards. By **using** *dialogue and incident, instead of narration*, you are helping some of the other facets of Show not Tell to slot into place.

Physicality and external impressions

In Chapter 3, we talked about inhabiting the character, getting inside their skin as well as their mind to show what it literally, viscerally *feels like* to be them – seeing what they see, touching what they touch, hearing what they hear. To make this experience as unique as possible, you need precision and flair in your language. This means using lots of **specific detail, choosing the perfect word, active writing, avoiding adverbs** and employing **figurative language**.

This process of inhabiting a character is important throughout a novel, but particularly when the action involves a dramatic incident – something which might test the character physically, and cause them to experience extreme or extraordinary sensations. At this point, you need to exercise all your skills of description and imagination, putting yourself in the character's place and transmitting that in-body experience as vividly as possible:

> Ulrich splashed into the water and sank under the waves. It was freezing, and his arms and legs began to lose feeling almost immediately. He swam desperately to the surface and looked around. He could hear the shouts of other sailors, cries and struggles. The ship was sinking; everywhere his friends were drowning around him and there was nothing he could do. If he wasn't careful, he would drown too. He saw a spar floating nearby, and swum quickly towards it, clinging on as tight as he could as the waves crashed violently around him.

Again, this isn't a terrible piece of writing – there are some good verb choices like *clinging* and *crashed*, and we start to feel Ulrich's sensory experience with the line, *his arms and legs began to lose feeling*. However, note the number of adverbs – *quickly, immediately, as tight as he could, violently* – and the was/were sentence constructions – *it was freezing, the ship was sinking, his friends were drowning*. These summary phrases do little to convey the actual physical reality.

Consider a version which aims to be more specific:

Ulrich slammed into the waves, the breath hissing out of him – and then he was under, gagging, icy black foam flooding his throat. He clawed for the surface, his arms pulling against him, his legs dragging him back. He felt air on his face, and the roar of the sea rushed in, broken by screams.

'Save us!'

A hand grabbed for him, slippery as a fish, and instinctively he shook it off, kicking away from the grasping figure. As the waves dipped, he made out Laars, mouth gaping, blonde hair slicked to his ears, great arms chopping at the water like broken oars.

In this version, Ulrich's sensory experience is more fully realized: we have sounds, sights, physical sensations, and vivid writing – careful, apposite verb choices, primarily active constructions and some figurative language – so that the scene packs a visceral punch. We almost feel as though we're there with him.

At the same time, we've done more to convey his unique **external impressions**. Remember how, in the scene with Nat fighting in the bar, we used just one or two figures to give a more personalized sense of the crowd? Similarly, here, we've used just two of the other sailors to *suggest* the chaos around Ulrich – we don't need to state that there are other people in the water; the detail we paint in of Laars acts as a signifier for the wider picture, and is more effective and affecting, because he's someone who Ulrich knows personally.

Many authors think that Show not Tell involves more writing – adding wordage to extend the picture you've created – and this is sometimes the case, particularly when you need to make a full scene out of something you've previously only summarized. However, the above example demonstrates that Show not Tell allows you to do a lot with a little: if you choose your details with sufficient precision, the picture you create will be more vivid, but not necessarily longer.

Head-hopping and authorial commentary

Head-hopping tends to happen when an author hasn't decided on a POV, and as a result they flit between a few characters. Authorial commentary often goes hand in hand with head-hopping because without a clear POV for a scene there's an interpretative gap left which the author feels duty bound to fill:

> Sophie sank to her knees, her head almost touching the floor. She mustn't look up – she knew it was forbidden to gaze upon the queen until given permission – an offence punishable by death.
>
> Queen Elaine watched her subject coolly; she could almost see Sophie's shoulders shaking. Of course, what Sophie didn't know was that the punishment had never been enforced – the Queen was far too shrewd to go around executing her loyal subjects for what was usually an accident.
>
> The cold marble was beginning to make Sophie's knees ache. Just as she felt she could bear the suspense no longer she heard a voice. 'Get up, girl.'

The head-hopping here undermines suspense, since we can see that Sophie's not going to get in trouble even if she does breach etiquette. But it also leads to disorientation and confusion – how can the Queen know what Sophie is thinking, or the exact nature of Sophie's fears/anxieties? To clarify this point and firm up the reader's empathy with Sophie, we step in with authorial commentary (*What Sophie didn't know … the Queen was far too shrewd*).

Consider instead a scene that stays firmly rooted in Sophie's POV. What aspects of Show not Tell might we utilize? We'd need to be *inside Sophie's head* – although there's already inner voice here so that's not perhaps the key problem. We'd need **specific detail**, though with the *cold marble making Sophie's knees ache* we've already made a start in that direction. We're already progressing the action via **dialogue and incident**, so that doesn't need changing. The real issue here is that the head-hopping and authorial commentary has laid everything bare; there's nothing left for us to guess at. So let's try letting the reader **make their own connections and interpretations**:

Sophie sank to her knees, her head almost touching the floor. She mustn't look up – the rules were clear, and the punishment … she couldn't even let herself think about it.

In front of her the polished marble gleamed and glimmered in the candlelight. The light dancing across it seemed to draw her eyes upwards. No – she would not look. She pressed her forehead into the stone. A dull coldness spread through her.

To her left, a courtier cleared his throat, the sound echoing in the cavernous hall. From the dais above her came the rustle of taffeta, and soft footsteps descending. Then, two feet, clothed in gold brocade. White silk–clad ankles, the hem of a gown, and on up to a slim waist and a pale, pinched face… Sophie screwed her eyes shut, her chest tight, her palms slick on the stone. Surely it didn't count? It wasn't her fault!

Then a hand, light on her shoulder, and a voice, cool and distant. 'Get up, girl. Look at me. I shan't hurt you.'

In this rewrite we learn nothing about the Queen's view on the scene, except what we can guess at through her actions and dialogue. It sounds as though Sophie will be safe, but we don't have the same surety the previous authorial commentary gives us – and that little question mark is important. Sure, the Queen says she won't hurt Sophie, but we can't know whether she's speaking the truth. By remaining inside Sophie's POV, staying true to her immediate impressions and living her fears and uncertainty alongside her, the scene draws us in more suspensefully.

In general, the biggest problem with head-hopping prose is its lack of tension: when you're dealing with every character at once, scenes end up overloaded with emotional detail that leaves very little work for the reader. With no main point of empathy, the author must guide us as to what we should be feeling – effectively explaining away the tension in a scene. But when we share the POV character's experience more intimately, we experience the same emotions they do, and feel the tension naturally and organically.

Show not Tell and dialogue

Dialogue is a key tool for showing: it's what allows us to hear the characters directly as opposed to via reported speech or summary. And you'll remember that one of the key literary techniques associated with showing is *progression of the action via dialogue and incident rather than narration*. However, like the other tenets of Show not Tell, using speech doesn't automatically mean that you're writing in a *shown* way – it's perfectly possible to use it to *tell*, too.

In Chapter 6, we looked at what dialogue should achieve, and when it comes to applying Show not Tell to this area of your writing, it can be useful to go back to these rules of thumb, remembering that speech should be:

- **nuanced** – making use of subtext
- **specific** – individual to each character
- **contextual** – differing depending on what the characters are doing and who they're talking to
- **purposeful** – serving a function in terms of plot and character
- **active** – making use of action and drama rather than short-hand dialogue tags or adverbs.

You can quickly see here just how many of these attributes are also the markers of *showing*. And one of the main things that dialogue *shouldn't* do – be used as a tool for exposition – is essentially a direct exhortation not to use dialogue to *tell*.

Nuance, exposition and subtext

Good dialogue tends to leave a fair bit unsaid, skirting around subjects the characters might avoid discussing explicitly; it straddles a line between what the speech says and what the body language hints at beneath the surface (or what comes across in the character's thoughts); and it avoids stating outright things which both characters would be aware of. You're therefore aiming to *let the reader make their own connections and interpretations* (which includes **avoiding emotion words, avoiding exposition**, and **getting inside your character's head**). Look at an extract which breaks all these rules, and note how dry it feels:

> 'I'm so mad – I asked you not to tell anyone that I was pregnant,' Jane snapped. She was really angry now. 'I didn't want anyone to know until I had told the father. I'm not ready yet.'

'I know, and I'm sorry, I feel terrible,' Stacey said. 'It just slipped out when Tina asked why you weren't drinking. I couldn't think what to say.'

'I wish I hadn't told you. Now everyone's talking about me behind my back. I'm so embarrassed.'

This is potentially a fraught moment – two friends dealing with a difficult situation and the upset to their own relationship – but with everything spelled out the tension is lost. The dialogue and commentary tells us what each character is feeling – *embarrassed, angry, terrible* – generalizations which don't allow for any depth or complexity; and because it is being used to recap other scenarios (Jane telling Stacey her secret; the secret getting out; and the fact that other people are now gossiping) it doesn't feel realistic either. Both friends are already aware of these circumstances so talking about them explicitly feels contrived.

How might we address this and, by doing so, bring more tension to the dialogue, as well as a purpose that goes beyond merely restating the reasons for the conflict between them?

Stacey was chewing her thumb nail. 'I'm so sorry, I-'

'Don't,' said Jane. 'I don't want to hear it.' She looked over her shoulder towards the table where Tina and the other girls were now leaning in, whispering and wide-eyed behind their spritzers. Her neck prickled with heat. How was she ever going to rejoin them now? She might as well go home and stay there for the next – oh God, the next year, at least. Nausea bubbled in her gut, and she remembered that she hadn't eaten since breakfast – a bowl of Special K which she'd immediately chucked up.

'I wasn't thinking. I should've just poured you a glass at the same time as the rest of them.'

'Yeah, you should. Now I've got to come up with some massive lie about why I haven't told–' She stopped just in time. Because she wasn't ready to say his name yet – wasn't ready for anyone to know, let alone him.

Here, we haven't mentioned the words 'pregnant' or 'father', but the implications of the conversation are clear; and Jane's feelings – secretive, shameful – are all the more potent because the women avoid mentioning them outright. By making the reader draw in the blanks you help us to feel the surreptitiousness of the conversation alongside the characters. Note the inner voice and specific, physical detail we include, to hint at both the truth of what they're discussing, and Jane's feelings about it.

At the same time, the conversation feels more authentic because the characters don't spoon-feed each other information they already know – this underlines the intimacy of their relationship, which is a key source of tension in the scene. Where the first version felt simplistic, here we sense complex relationships at play and, perhaps most importantly, Jane's conflicted emotions about her pregnancy – the real reason she's angry here, not her friend's accidental betrayal.

Specificity and context

Great dialogue is both specific to whichever character you're portraying, and adaptable depending on the context. Note how, in the first example above, there's little to distinguish either character's speech because it's primarily being used to convey plot information; it reads like the author's pencilling in exposition. In the revised version, context and character plays a bigger part, with the two voices feeling distinct, moderating their language and behaviour because of where they are and what they're discussing.

Let's look at how Jane and Stacey's dialogue might shift if the context was different. Imagine they've gone back to their friends, having reached an uneasy truce. Stacey's trying to show moral support, and Jane's defensive and desperate to get out of there. Because this aspect of dialogue is all about the nitty gritty of each character's individual approach, we'll need to **choose the perfect word**, and use plenty of **specific detail**.

Jane hovered at the edge of the table while Stacey scrabbled around for her bag. It was like being back at school, arriving on the first day and not knowing anyone – except that these people had been her friends half her life.

Tina nudged the bag towards Stacey with a shiny purple fingernail, mouthing something at her that Jane couldn't make out.

'She's not feeling well,' said Stacey loudly. 'I'm taking her home.' God, did she have to make such a big deal out of it? The music pounded in Jane's head and her stomach heaved again. Oh no, not here.

'Poor love,' Tina said with a tight-lipped smile. 'She'd better go and get some rest.'

'I'll put her in a taxi and come and find you guys again, OK?' Stacey raised her eyebrows.

Jane'd had about enough of this. 'I am still here, you know. I'm knocked up, not deaf. I know you're all dying for me to leave so you can get on with bitching about me.'

Tina clapped a hand to her mouth, but Stacey broke into that wide smile that Jane knew so well, and gave her arm a quick squeeze.

'Oh, babes. Tell you what, I'm gonna come back with you and we can have a few glasses – I mean, watch a movie or something.' She bit her lip, and shook her head. 'I'm sorry – I can't seem to take my foot out of it tonight.' She put an arm around Jane's shoulders and steered her away, as Tina gaped like a guppy. 'You know this is killing her, don't you?' She grinned. 'Come on, let's get out of here.'

Here, the dialogue paints a different dynamic – Stacey is initially stiff and formal, putting up a front but still trying to placate the other women, and Jane is reticent, silent. Then, when Jane blurts out the bald truth, bursting the tension, it's as though Stacey is freed up to be more real, warm and forthright. Where Jane was on the offensive in the previous scene and Stacey on the back foot, here Stacey becomes the more dominant figure. Show not Tell helps build up that sense that the exchange is specific – not just to these characters, but to this precise situation.

Attribution and action

In Chapter 6, we looked at how supplementing dialogue attribution with action can make the dialogue feel more direct, letting the characters do the talking. This is also a process of replacing Telling with Showing; like excess exclamation marks or italics, complex or unnecessarily varied dialogue tags and adverbs can be a form of editorializing, as though you're stepping in to instruct us how to interpret the dialogue.

Let's use the same material again, but this time moving back in time to the scene where Stacey reveals Jane's secret:

'I got you an orange juice,' whispered Stacey. 'I wasn't sure…'

'It's fine, shh,' hissed Jane furiously. 'Tina's looking.'

'What's going on?' cooed Tina. 'Come on, no secrets on a girls' night, you know that. Sharesies.'

'I've been a bit sick-' began Jane tentatively, at the same time as Stacey cried defensively, 'Don't tell her!'

'Tell me what? Been sick – like – Oh my God,' Tina gasped. 'You're not …'

This dialogue is fairly sparky, and gets across the drama of Stacey putting her foot in it. However, the dialogue tags and adverbs feel forced, and don't leave much room for the reader to engage their own interpretative muscles. Like adverbs these attributive verbs are, essentially, another form of emotion word – a word that *tells* us how the characters are feeling. Let's try the scene using action instead:

'I got you an orange juice.' Stacey squeezed into the seat next to her. 'I wasn't sure…'

'It's fine, shh.' Jane cupped her hand around the glass. 'Tina's looking.'

'What's going on?' Tina's head snapped in their direction, raptor-quick. 'Come on, no secrets on a girls' night, you know that. Sharesies.'

'I've been a bit sick-' Jane's stomach curdled even as she said it. Please don't ask, please don't -

But she was too late. Stacey threw an arm around her. 'Don't tell her.'

'Tell me what? Been sick – like – Oh my God.' Tina's gaze flitted between them, taking in Jane's innocent-looking OJ, and her eyes went huge. 'You're not …'

Here, the accompanying action does the work; removing the too-obvious emotional signposting allows us to visualize the scene more clearly and feel some of the underlying emotion for ourselves.

Show not Tell and description

In Chapter 6, we talked about how to describe a scene using the POV character's impressions of it to make it personal and unique – by **staying inside your character's head**. We also discussed the importance of **choosing the perfect word, avoiding exposition**, and **using specific detail**. The one element we didn't cover under description was **passive vs active writing**, and that's what we will focus on here.

Dynamic description

It's a common misconception that using *was* or *were* in a sentence automatically means it's passive. In fact, the phrase 'passive writing' refers specifically to a sentence in which a thing or person being acted upon is introduced, followed by the action:

> *The ball was kicked by the boy* or simply *the ball was kicked.*

The effect of these constructions is a feeling of absence or imbalance – the real subject of the sentence, whoever is doing the kicking, is diminished or shunted out. Passive writing therefore tends to leave us with a hole where a character should be, and feels emotionally flat.

Use of the 'be' verb *can* be a signifier of passive writing, and if you're employing it frequently it's always worth checking that your constructions are as active as possible. However, overuse of this verb can also have a detrimental effect in its own right. Because passages of description are sometimes disassociated from action and dialogue, there can be a tendency to drift off into the continuous past; perhaps because we have fallen into the trap of looking 'back' at the description from a distance:

The autumn sun was low. Leaves were falling thickly, blown into damp, russet heaps at her feet. Above her the branches were picked out in clean lines across a sky that was a deep blue. The air was crisp; her breath was billowing out in soft clouds. Her hands were thrust into her pockets, and she was glad she'd chosen the fleece-lined jacket that morning.

As well as the passive constructions – *leaves were blown … branches were picked out … hands were thrust* – the sheer number of 'be' verbs creates a sluggish effect that makes the description feel lifeless in spite of the strong specific details it contains.

There are a couple of different ways of addressing this problem. Firstly, decide on the focus of the scene. Perhaps the description itself is important – it might be a piece of **infrastructure** demonstrating the changing of the seasons. The POV character's take on it might not be significant, and perhaps that's why the passive writing has crept in – you didn't need the character so you've subconsciously sidelined them. If that's the case, then consider removing the character altogether and making the description more active, by choosing stronger verbs and simple rather than continuous past tense constructions:

The afternoon sun glinted through branches that scored clean lines across the sky. Leaves swirled and clustered in russet heaps. Mist hung in the air.

This is brief now, and you might decide to add more detail, but equally you may not need it – the description that's left after the edit is sharper and more incisive. We've lost a lot of the adjectives and adverbs – they're simply not needed when your verbs are strong enough. As a piece of infrastructure or scene-setting this does exactly the job it's required to, without taking up too much space or letting us get bored or skim read.

Alternatively, you might decide that the character's presence in the scene *is* important: perhaps it's not just the passing of time that you want to capture, but the character's feelings about it. In that case, you would want to pull the character forward as the subject of each sentence:

> She hunched her shoulders against the chill and scuffed her feet through damp piles of leaves. Shoving her hands deeper into her pockets she glanced up, following the cloud of her breath into the treetops where branches scored stark lines against the cold blue sky.

Here, as well as reconfiguring our sentence structures actively rather than passively, our verb choices and adjectives are geared towards creating more of a mood, reflective of the character's take on it. So, we have *chill*, *hunched*, *scuffed*, *shoved*, *stark*, and *cold*; the atmosphere becomes intentionally melancholy, rather than being a simple, unnuanced depiction.

Active writing is one of the key principles of Show not Tell, but understanding its purpose is important. Active sentence structures primarily ensure **clarity and directness** – it's always obvious who's doing what, and action and description are easier to visualize. Because it's all about bringing the true subject of the sentence forwards, it allows you to foreground the **emotional driver**. And it also **cuts out excess wordage** (*the boy kicked the ball* is punchier than *the ball was kicked by the boy*) thereby ensuring precision in the prose. So, for a scene to be **vivid, emotional** and **precise**, active writing is useful.

Pass me the passive voice

Another misconception is that you should never write passively, but the passive voice does have a role. There may be times when you don't know, or you don't want the reader to know, who has performed an action. The passive voice can be used to help create an air of mystery:

> He eased the door of the safe open, heart thudding, and groped inside. Nothing. He stretched right to the back, but felt only the gritty metal of the safe's floor.
> The diamonds were gone.

Here, we don't know what has happened to the jewels, so the active voice isn't appropriate for the punchline. Imagine trying to rephrase this actively – *someone had taken the diamonds* feels clunky, and something like *the diamonds had disappeared* makes the diamonds seem to have performed the action, almost magically. *The diamonds were gone* makes it clear that the diamonds have been acted upon, whilst keeping the instigator of that action vague.

Or, maybe you want to place the reader in the position of a character who isn't precisely sure what's happening to them, evoking a sensation of passivity and helplessness:

> His feet were swept from under him, and he crashed to the floor, his jaw slamming into the concrete with a sickening crunch.

Notice the mixture of passive writing and active writing: *his feet were swept from under him* captures the unexpectedness of not knowing what's going on. Then we snap back into the character's physicality with *slamming into the concrete ... sickening crunch.*

Perhaps you need to be vague about the subject of the sentence, either because an action is being performed by multiple people or because the characters are evasive about who's performing it:

- *They decided that a vigil would be held that night.* (The vigil is what's important and an unspecified number of unnamed characters may be involved.)
- *'Your villages will be burned; your children enslaved,' said the high priest.* (The priest isn't planning to carry out the punishment himself, and leaving the perpetrator and detail unmentioned contributes to the menace in the threat.)

Or perhaps the subject–object is so extraordinary that we want to focus in on that:

- *This whole chapel was painted in just one day.*
- *Their bones have been buried here for thousands of years.*
- *The treasure was discovered by sailors in the fifteenth century.*

Here, it's not who did the painting, burying, or discovering that's important.

Finally, you might want to make a general, sweeping or all-encompassing statement that's applicable to everyone, rather than relating to a specific character:

- *Life as they knew it was destroyed in seconds.*
- *The rules had supposedly been set down to keep them all safe.*
- *The grain harvest was dependent on the spring showers.*

These actions have been performed by no one specific individual, but instead relate to god-like interventions or powers greater than the characters themselves. The passive voice highlights how everyone becomes equal, and equally helpless, in the face of forces outside their control.

So, whilst you would use the active voice when you want your description or infrastructure to be **vivid, emotional and precise**, if for any reason you need the action to be **vague, mysterious, generalized or distanced**, the passive voice may be the better choice – and though it is *telling* as opposed to *showing*, the telling serves a dramatic purpose.

Description as exposition

Description can be a useful tool to replace existing telling in your writing. Particularly when you're world-building, and often in the opening chapters of a novel, it can be tempting to sketch in details of the history and context, and this can often have a dry, distanced feel:

> Not so very long ago, witches had been burned right here in the village square; thieves and rapists tortured and hung. The laws were different now, not so strict, but Edward knew, just as everyone else knew, that harsh punishments were still meted out behind the closed gates of the castle.

The gruesome history – and menacing present – of Edward's world feels rather removed here. How could you use description instead, to bring these details searingly to life?

> In the dust of the village square hulked the gallows' rotten skeleton. It should've been pulled down six years ago, after the last public trial, but it'd been left, stained and creaking, as a reminder. Nothing hung from it now, though ravens and crows wheeled and cawed as though waiting for pickings. But Edward knew – they all knew – what it meant.
> 'We're still watching you.'

The same historical detail lives and breathes on the page – description takes the place of spoon-fed exposition, and creates an active moment that feels like part of the ongoing story.

Or:

> The rivers and canals formed part of a nationwide net-
> work that was used by spies, smugglers, thieves ... at
> night, the waterways would be alive with dark, mysteri-
> ous traffic − barges, skiffs and even rickety little row-
> ing boats punting quietly back and forth carrying who
> knew what.

This piece of expositional infrastructure is fine, but there's
more that could be done with the drama and tension it hints
at. Perhaps we could turn it into descriptive setting in a scene
featuring our protagonist?

> Glenny ducked under the dank arch of the aqueduct,
> her bare legs brushing past reeds and the prickly heads of
> bulrushes. From above her came a soft clanking, doubt-
> less from one of the barges that travelled the canals by
> night, all silky-silent and secret. Glenny wondered what
> this one was carrying. Moonshine, maybe, or gunpow-
> der. One day, she decided, she would ride the waterways
> herself.

This more immediate scene brings the secrecy and mystery
of the waterways to life via the impressions − and imagination −
of the protagonist, and feels more intriguing and involving as
a result.

Whether you're building infrastructure, setting the scene
or weaving ongoing detail into existing scenes, using active
writing and Show not Tell in your descriptions should help
make your descriptive passages lively, active and engaging − and
when description achieves these things it lingers in the mind
far longer, and more vividly.

Show not Tell and plot

So far, we've talked about Show not Tell as it applies to scene-by-scene and line-by-line elements of your writing – the fine detail of how you build convincing characters and create cracking prose. But it's also possible to apply this mindset to the over-arching aspects of your writing – structure, character arc, and cause and effect can all be positively shaped by Show not Tell.

However, where previously we've focused on changing the flavour of the writing – adapting and evolving the prose so that what appears on the page is more subtle and sophisticated – Show not Tell as it applies to plot is much more about **invisibility**. If you've ever found yourself reading a book or watching a film, and thinking, *oh, this is just the hero's darkest hour – everything will sort itself out soon*, you'll know how flat that can make you feel. A good story structure tends to be one that doesn't call attention to itself; that doesn't loudly announce its peaks and troughs, key moments and turning points. We need to know a story is heading in the right direction, without having our noses stuck in the map.

Showing the structure

This is very much about *letting the reader make their own connections*. Ideally, we should feel where we're at, but on an innate emotional level, rather than having each plot point spelled out. Imagine if your inciting event/main character's goal was signposted:

> Jack's world had fallen apart. Until he could prove he was innocent, his family would never take him back.

We would be clear about how life has changed for Jack, and what he needs to do to fix things, but this explicit exposition runs the risk of making your plotting feel formulaic and simplistic. If the scene in which your inciting incident takes place is sufficiently dramatic and compelling, there should be no need to alert us to what's going on:

> His mum's eyes were red and brimming. 'I just can't believe it,' she whispered.
>
> 'That's because it's not true!' Jack clenched his fists at his sides. 'I keep telling you, they–'
>
> His dad laid a heavy hand on Jack's shoulder. 'It's time to go, son. Can't you see your mum's had enough of these lies?'
>
> Jack stumbled back under the pressure, and his foot caught on the doormat. 'But where am I going to go?' He barely recognized the sound of his own voice. Over his dad's shoulder he saw Sal, half-way up the stairs, blue eyes wide, sucking a finger. It was one thing Mum and Dad thinking he'd – but little Sal, who never hurt anyone – he couldn't stand it. 'Please!'
>
> Now his dad was actually shoving Jack; he was over the lintel and on the step.
>
> 'Here.' Dad pressed a twenty into his hand. 'This'll tide you over.'
>
> 'But–'
>
> The door slammed shut, and Jack had to half-skip half-trip down the steps to stop himself falling. He looked towards the living room window and there was Uncle Al framed in the light, staring at him. And smiling. Why was he smiling?
>
> Al twitched the curtains closed, and the street was cloaked in darkness. Jack wanted to scream and rage, but his chest felt as though it had a vice around it.

> He sank to his heels on the pavement, fists buried in
> his eyes.

This scene shows us just as clearly how Jack's world has fallen
apart. But because it takes place dramatically, it feels like an
organic part of the story rather than a structural box that's been
ticked.

Or, imagine that you are at the point of bringing your character's emotional arc to a close, and you want to show how
they've changed and what they've learned. Authors are often
conscious of this need to the point where they include a line of
explanation, something like the following:

> Jack realized he'd grown up in the two months he'd
> been away. And yes, it'd been hard, learning that nobody
> was responsible for him except himself, but there'd been
> good things too – finding out that he was stronger than
> he'd thought, that he was capable of caring in a way he
> hadn't known was possible.

How could you show Jack's growth – both inner and outer –
in a way that *implies* it?

> Jack sank onto his bed, feeling the springs creak, just as
> they always had. He looked at the posters on his walls –
> a couple of BMX stunts; one of some Hollyoaks star in
> a pink bikini. Nothing had changed. Nothing.
>   He jumped to his feet; yanked open the cupboard
> door. He peeled off the hoodie and ripped jeans he'd
> virtually lived in for the last – how long had it been? –
> and flicked through clothes on their hangers. But the
> blue Superdry t-shirt he pulled on squeezed him around
> the neck and across the shoulders; in the end he had to

settle for a zip-up grey top that used to hang off him. He'd barely worn half these clothes, he realized, and now he never would. It was like the months he'd been away had just disappeared, had been stolen from him completely.

His throat was tight and aching, and he rubbed the back of his hand across his eyes. No, it wasn't fair, but what was the point in thinking that way? Better to look forward. Let's face it, he'd never needed all this stuff anyway. What he needed wasn't something you could buy.

What would Ella have done? Well, that was easy. He jogged downstairs to grab a bin-bag.

Mum sat at the kitchen table, her hands wrapped round a cup of tea. For a moment her face was blank, then she smiled at him. 'Throwing stuff away? Good, we can get you a whole new wardrobe if you like.'

'I'll probably donate it. But Mum, I don't need new clothes. In fact-' he squatted down next to her; took her hand in his. He swallowed. 'I'm sorry, but … I'm not sure I can stay.'

Here, we get an impression both of how much time has passed and how Jack has changed as a person. Interestingly, the resolution to this narrative arc comes as a surprise – presumably, Jack has spent the majority of the novel trying to prove his innocence and be accepted back by his family, and now he's got what he wanted he may end up abandoning it again. This twist, brought to life on the page, shows us how much Jack has grown. The plot has taught him new values and priorities, and he's realized that he can only move forward from the point the story has brought him to by making an even bigger change.

Cause and effect – the ultimate tool for a shown structure

If you're working to a plotting model there can sometimes be a tendency to signpost your plot points too heavily, as in the examples above. In some ways this is preferable to having a story that lacks structure – it's better to feel that we're being guided somewhere confidently than that the story is drifting. However, it can leave us too conscious of the story's underpinning mechanics, and if you can avoid this, your plot will feel smoother and more effortless.

If you're finding that your plotting has left you with a too-tight structure, with little room for creative freedom – perhaps you find yourself trudging between the story's tension peaks, marking time, writing filler, lacking organic bridging material – then it can help to go back to cause and effect. This is perhaps the most naturalistic approach there is because it relies simply on *following through a realistic set of consequences to everything that happens.* Literally, ask yourself, at the end of every scene, *and what would happen next?* You may find that this leads you a merry dance, and you decide not to include much of the material that the process throws up. But you should discover that whatever remains once you've stripped out any inessential scenes is germane, and feels absolutely true to the plot and characters.

Using the material above, let's imagine that you're trying to get from the inciting incident to tension peak one, *Jack discovers that Uncle Al is not who he says he is.* Your planned structure probably covers the big story moments, and mini tension peaks – maybe Jack breaking back into his parents' house to look for evidence; Jack hiding from the police; Jack realizing that Uncle Al has something to do with what's happening to him. But how are you going to move the story forwards from where the inciting incident has left you? *What would happen next?*

Alone, with only £20 in the world – what might Jack's next step be? The obvious choice might be a bed in a night shelter but Jack, reeling from the injustice of what's happening to him, would surely have other priorities. Perhaps he remembers that one of his friends at college has a dad in the police. He might turn up at hers, only for her to tell him that his picture is plastered all over the papers, and she doesn't want to get into trouble. If he wants help then he needs to change his appearance and get a false identity. She might take him to a shady character she knows through her dad who provides him with a fake ID – and comments on the fact that he recognizes Jack's (real) surname as the same name someone has recently chosen as their own false identity, which is what starts to alert Jack to Al's deception ...

Tracking the consequences – asking yourself *what happens next?* – can take you in some surprising directions and provide interim moments of excitement and drama in between your main tension peaks. If you keep your overall structure in mind, but let cause and effect guide you, the plot should feel as though it's developing organically in spite of the firm structure you have in place.

Using showing in a multi-layered structure

When you're attempting a more complex structure – for example, a narrative featuring several parallel story lines, or making use of flashbacks – it's easy for exposition to creep in. Particularly when you're dealing with characters' memories, it seems logical to slip into telling: summarizing brief recollections to drip-feed smaller parts of a bigger picture, gradually building up to a complete story-thread. Sometimes, this can work, if you have a light touch and are deft at weaving snippets of memory into a character's inner voice:

> She took a sip of coffee. He'd forgotten to add the sugar,
> and something about the unexpected bitterness jolted her
> back to that blistering day by the lake. To Sebastian, hold-
> ing out a slab of dark chocolate that slipped and melted
> in his fingers. To the silky water, and the goosebumps on
> her skin as he slid her under, one hand on her back …

When it comes to seeding in memories in this way, the key
is to keep them brief and pertinent, relevant to what's going on
in the present so that they don't appear out of nowhere, and not
so perfectly formed that they read unrealistically:

> As she waited for the bus, she suddenly remembered
> the day they'd sat by the lake together. Sebastian had
> been eating chocolate and he'd offered her some, dark,
> melting and bitter. She'd taken it from him but he'd
> grabbed her hand and held on. He'd sucked the choco-
> late from her fingers and she let him lead her into the
> water of the lake. She'd barely felt the cold, but still she
> had goosebumps on her skin at the feeling of the water
> and his fingers on her back.

This version contains identical information but without the
prompt of the coffee it feels out of the blue. In the first version
a few details were missing (as happens with memory) so it felt
sensual and impressionistic (again, as memory tends to be); in
the second version more is spelled out, so this feels less like a real
recollection and more like an opportunity to fill in backstory.

Backstory is often intrinsically dramatic or mysterious material, so summarizing it or presenting it as exposition is a missed
opportunity. How could you *show* the material, letting us be
more present? Could you use the sip of coffee as a segue and take
us back into a full flashback so the scene happens right in front of

us? Or, could you include the merest hint of this memory in the present-day scene, perhaps implying that it's something the POV character prefers not to think about, and instead turn the entire thread into a parallel narrative, perhaps from an omniscient or external point of view? Either way, see if you can use showing (in this instance, specifically **progressing the narrative via dialogue and incident**) to make the most of your material and keep every strand of your plot as immediate as possible.

Show not Tell and pacing

In Chapter 7, we learned that the term 'pacing' can refer to a couple of different things: firstly, the actual 'speed' at which scenes progress, and secondly the way you parcel out plot information to keep the reader's understanding and expectations building at a tantalizing rate.

When it comes to **drip-feeding plot information**, the role of Show not Tell is again to give the detail subtlety and invisibility; disguising plot developments and important bits of backstory by weaving them into ongoing action scenes. Rather than making it too obvious what's important and what's just background colour the weight and atmosphere of a scene imbues the detail with import – or not: some key bits of information might only become significant on second reading, or with the benefit of hindsight.

Imagine a scenario in which a young woman finds out after the death of her mother that there's a mystery around her birth. You could either state this explicitly (perhaps the truth is announced during the reading of the will); or, you could have the main character finding it out in a way that makes it clear there's something she doesn't know but leaves her with more to discover (she might find her birth certificate in the attic, with the names crossed out); or, you could start by weaving hints towards this truth into a scene that seems to be dealing with something else altogether:

Toni sat on the bottom step, watching the last of the guests leave, her head full of noise. These were the bits she hated, the in-between parts, where you couldn't hide in small talk but had to look people in the eye, hug them, give them something poignant to take away with them. Her brother was shaking Mac Davis' hand, making the old man's walnut face scrunch up into a grin. How was it that Miles had always found it so easy, whilst she, Toni, constantly seemed to say the wrong thing? She kicked the heel of her boot against the worn hall carpet and sighed.

A gentle hand on her arm brought her back to herself. It was – oh, what was her name, that biddy who'd shown up out of nowhere?

'Claire,' said the woman, as if reading her mind. 'And you're Antonia, of course. A beautiful name.'

'Mhmm,' agreed Toni. How were you supposed to respond to that? It wasn't as though she'd had anything to do with choosing her own name, after all.

'I just wanted to give you this,' said Claire. 'Your mother was such a special person.' She handed over a faded, crinkled scrap of paper, and Toni caught a glimpse of a black and white smiling face before stuffing it into her pocket. Not another picture of Mum. She didn't think she could bear it.

Claire was smiling sadly, that slightly pitying expression that Toni had got so used to in the last couple of weeks. Then she laid a hand on Toni's cheek, cupping her chin. She had to stop herself flinching at the touch – why was it strangers thought they could invade your personal space without asking? – and steeled herself for another, 'you look just like her' comment.

Instead, Claire said, 'You have your father's eyes.' Then she turned and headed for the door. Miles, just about to close it, opened his mouth to say goodbye but Claire brushed past him with the briefest of smiles.

Miles shrugged and shut the door behind her then turned back to Toni, eyebrows raised. 'Who was that?'

Toni's heart was fluttering; she couldn't speak.

Claire had known her father?

The scene initially seems to be about Toni's relationship with her brother, but ultimately steers her towards a number of mysteries, seeding future plot developments in a way that contributes to tension; it implies various things but confirms very little. The key tenet of Show not Tell you're utilizing is **letting the reader make their own connections** (though at the same time, you're also employing lots of other showing devices so that the scene is as dramatic and engaging as possible). Good overarching pacing is all about nuance and implication – building up your plot gradually, piece by piece, without waving a red flag every time something significant happens – and the Show not Tell mindset helps you remember that you don't need to hold your reader's hand through every plot development.

When we discussed pacing in relation to the **speed of the action**, we talked about whizzing through unimportant events, and slowing down for more exciting incidents. We looked at how to extend big moments into full scenes, **progressing the action via dialogue and incident rather than narration – using scene rather than summary**. We won't include further examples here, but you should now be able to see how many of the tools of showing these extended scenes make use of – **choosing the perfect word; avoiding adverbs; avoiding 'emotion' words; using specific details; getting inside your main character's head;** and **use of metaphor/simile (figurative language).**

The aspect of pacing we will focus on here is **speeding the story forward through less significant events,** because this is another area in which you will find telling useful. In addition to the elements we've already outlined that warrant briefer treatment (**inner voice, description, repetition, non-dramatic material** and **authorial indulgence**), there are going to be places where you may want to: flag up a change of scene or timescale; summarize a journey; pencil in prosaic backstory; mention a mealtime; gloss over a hello/goodbye; or let us know that your characters have gone to bed/woken up – but without giving these incidents much weight or space:

- *Winter was coming*
- *They greeted each other warmly*
- *After a back-breaking walk up the hill, they stopped to rest*
- *Dinner was over, and Sam was ready for bed*

Notice the *was/were* constructions, the adverbs, the emotion words … in these instances, it probably doesn't matter, since these are places we will naturally skim over anyway. That said, if you can find an equally brief, unassuming way of showing the same information, without tying yourself up in knots, there would be no harm in that:

- *The first frost lay crisp on the ground*
- *She grabbed him in a crushing hug*
- *At the top of the hill, Alison slumped to the ground. 'Enough!'*
- *Sam's belly was full and his eyes were drooping*

These revisions are still fairly told, and certainly not the most dazzling writing, but the slight injection of specific detail or character perspective makes them that tiny bit more interesting to read.

Using Show not Tell to pace your work is mainly a question of deciding how much weight to give to your material, both the surface action and to any underlying plotting or backstory that you plan to include. A good rule of thumb is that the more you show something, the more emotionally involving it will be (and therefore, the more it will linger, and the more import it will carry). If, instead, you want your pace to reflect the light or passing nature of the subject matter, then telling can help you deliberately keep things glib, and hold the reader at arm's length.

Show not Tell and overwriting

Depending on the type of overwriting you're prone to, Show not Tell can either help you avoid slipping into it … or exacerbate the problem. If you tend as a rule to write emotively, and you know that there are times when your prose slips into sentimentality, then certainly some of the tenets of Show not Tell can serve as useful reminders to keep excess emotion out of the writing and let the action speak for itself.

For instance, it's logical to assume that if you're writing a scene featuring high drama and strong feelings, then this might be reflected in the writing. However, laying on emotion too thickly can undermine the atmosphere you're trying to evoke:

> 'No!' Lara cried. 'I don't believe it!' She fell to her knees, tears pouring down her face. She felt as though her heart would burst.

Though there's not much actual telling here – and we have some physical detail and shown emotion – the moment still feels overwrought because the level of feeling you're trying to convey is just too high. The exclamation marks are a good indicator that you're hammering an emotion home too heavily. Imagine if you watched an actor on stage or screen dealing with grief by tearing at their hair or flinging themselves to the ground – the effect would be the same. So, although it may sound counter-intuitive, when you're writing scenes where something devastating is happening it can be best to keep the prose downbeat and understated. *Let the reader make their own connections – avoid emotion words:*

> 'No.' Lara's voice was a whisper. 'I don't ...' She pressed her fingers to her lips, shaking her head.

Here we're still showing using action and physical detail, but we've resisted the temptation to spoon-feed Lara's grief.

The flip side of Show not Tell in relation to overwriting is that the mandate to **choose the perfect word** and **make use of figurative writing** can lead you to strive too hard for freshness and inventiveness in the language. This is where overwriting can creep in with the best of intentions – you're basically doing the right thing with your prose, but overshooting the mark:

> His eyes slithered over her like writhing snakes. Her skin crept, the hairs prickling on the back of her neck and a chill zapping down her spine like icy water.

The two unusual verbs here – *slithered* and *zapping* – don't work for different reasons. We can't imagine eyes 'slithering' – eyes don't have movement or agency independent of whoever is doing the looking. And 'zapping' creates a mixed metaphor, since 'icy water' can't zap. In addition, we have two similes within a short space of time. One good image will carry more impact than several – and since neither of these images is particularly strong, it'd be better to cut both.

Looking at Show not Tell as it applies to overwriting is perhaps the best way of understanding why it's such a complex concept to master, because applying some of the techniques that are central to Show not Tell can simultaneously lead you into bad habits. Elsewhere, we've discussed why it can be better to stick to 'said' instead of employing lots of different attributive verbs – yet, Show not Tell lays out the importance of choosing the perfect verb, looking for something that is absolutely apposite for character and context. What makes striving for variation and freshness right in one circumstance, and wrong in another?

Show not Tell and the writer's instinct

There's no simple answer to the above question. It's partly a matter of accepted contemporary style – of understanding that some forms of writing are judged to be more elegant (which sometimes means more readable, and sometimes more invisible) than others. Self-editing is very much a case of learning and applying these rules and techniques; of checking that your writing 'works', against a measurable set of skills and disciplines.

However, honing the craft of writing involves not just learning the rules, but also becoming confident and sophisticated enough to know when and how to break them. This latter is the tricky one to get your head around, because it's not something that can be taught; it's about honing your writer's instinct, which involves time and practice. And this can take years – which isn't something most writers want to hear.

Making it your mission to master Show not Tell is a good start. It won't necessarily short-cut the process, but because it's a mindset as well as a set of rules, it can help you to switch off the part of your brain that's constantly telling you to edit, check, rein yourself in and do the right thing. If you know your writing techniques inside out, you've got your characters down perfectly, and you're working to a structure that you know is solid – but something's *still* not gelling, then it's possible you're over-thinking the whole process, in which case you may need to step back, breathe, and sink deeper into the Show not Tell mindset.

Writers often talk about inhabiting the 'alpha state' when they're at their most creative. This is a kind of dream-like consciousness where you may not be fully aware. Perhaps you've experienced this: you're doing something you're good at or familiar with, or that you enjoy – driving somewhere you've been many times before, playing or listening to a piece of music you know well, or reading a book that you find utterly absorbing – and you get to the end of whatever it is, and you can't remember doing it? It's very likely that you were in the alpha state during that time.

This can be a good place to be while you write – and sometimes when you self-edit – because it turns off the conscious, restrictive parts of your brain and unlocks the more imaginative, purely creative areas of your mind. If that sounds too abstract and airy-fairy, think of it this way instead: when you were a child, playing let's pretend, were you constantly thinking, *would this character do this? How would they sound? What do they look like?* No – for that moment you were that character, whether it was a lion, an alien, a princess or a robber. There was no conscious, laborious effort of imagination involved; you magically *became* someone or something else.

This state of pure imagination is the crux of Show not Tell: immersing yourself, and the reader, so deeply into the action and characterization that you embody what, and who, you're describing; experiencing the feelings that you're evoking as if they were your own. This process of immersion tends to work better for the original process of writing than it does for self-editing, but it can also help with editing when you've reached a stalemate: when you know something's not right but you're not sure what. If you're reading your work back in the alpha state and something jars you out of it, then there's a good chance that it's a passage you need to look at again.

Most of the tools you need for your writing journey are technical, identifiable, and clear-cut, and Show not Tell is a different beast – it's more emotional, abstract, and adaptable. If *telling* is a clear black marker pen, *showing* is a subtle, shifting palette of colours that allows you to be as bold or as impressionistic as you want.

If you can think yourself into this mindset and surrender yourself to the imaginative process in this way – whilst also employing the practical tools of the writing craft – then you're on your way to becoming both a technically skilled writer and an instinctual one. If you're technical as well as instinctual then you're capable of speaking to readers both intellectually and emotionally – grabbing them by the brain, heart, and guts all at once. And if you can achieve that magical combination, there's a good chance that you're on the road to publication.

Part II
Submitting your novel

9

How to submit your manuscript to the trade

Submitting too early is one of the biggest mistakes an author can make. In this chapter we'll help you decide whether your manuscript is ready to go out, and how to prepare yourself for submission, including some ways to keep control of the process so that you always know where you're at, and don't inadvertently breach publishing etiquette. Researching, tailoring and targeting your submission will help you avoid common pitfalls; preparing a dazzling package will ensure that when your work gets read it makes a brilliant first impression.

The first part of this book has equipped you with the editor's language and shown you how to self-edit your work into a polished and hopefully publishable manuscript. The second part will take you through a submissions approach that should land you on the agent's desk rather than the slush pile; give you the know-how to choose your agent and editor; and prepare you to be a professional writer.

We've edited and submitted numerous authors over the years and have had the privilege of seeing many of them get published with some hitting the bestseller lists. It's useful to know what it takes to deliver a book and to remain a published writer before you embark on this submission journey. However, it's also important to bear in mind that there is no set formula to getting yourself noticed.

An author's route is often circuitous, involving different forms of contact: a bald submission of 'here is my story, fingers crossed'; a speculative email; a meeting at a writer's conference; being short-listed in a competition; or approached by the trade... Whether they're going it alone, via a literary consultancy or an agent, or working directly with the publisher, the common denominator in success is the author's belief in their writing and their persistence, mixed with a sprinkling of luck, good timing and hard work.

Once the book is published its success may be easy to predict or completely unexpected. While there is a degree of uncertainty around how well a book will do once it's on the shelves what you *are* in control of is delivering the best book possible, in a professional manner.

US Insight

Although American agents will often undertake further edits of a manuscript, they are nonetheless looking for projects that feel completely polished. This means proof-read: a manuscript that has formatting or punctuation mistakes will automatically be rejected. And nothing kills interest faster than a book that works beautifully up to a certain point, then falls apart. An agent may feel less than confident in a writer's ability to revise, and wonder how they could have thought the book was ready to be seen. Don't submit your book thinking that unresolved problems will 'be sorted out when it's edited'. Those problems need to be fixed before you send it out.

Just as editors at the big US publishers are under pressure to move books through the publishing process more quickly, agents are experiencing some of that same pressure. These agents are seeing more submissions than ever.

The good news is that some of them are taking on more authors than ever as well. However, they have less time to devote to developing an individual author through one-to-one editing and workshopping. More agents are sending authors back to a professional outside editor before they will sign them up. If your manuscript isn't fully mapped out and finalized, be prepared to be asked to do more work before the agent will consider signing you. Even if an agent signs you, be prepared to do another round of edits. But American agents – like American editors – ideally would love to see a manuscript that needs next to no fresh work to get behind, sell, and publish.

Be sure you're ready

First, check that the manuscript is in a highly polished first draft shape to allow, if need be, for further editorial input and the agent or editor to contribute their vision. The trick is to know when to stop self-editing; tying up a manuscript too perfectly can have a deadening effect and encourage resistance to further feedback. You want to present a manuscript that invites positive brainstorming (not so big a challenge that it puts an agent off), and has room to accommodate the publisher's creative insight and knowledge of what's feasible.

For instance, a publisher may love your story and style but have a word count range they need to stick to. If yours is 30,000 words over what is practical to publish you'll need to do some cutting. This may involve taking out a character, merging some plot threads, or even trimming a set number of words per chapter. If the bones of the story are solid, then revision of this nature should improve what you have, rather than unravelling its core.

To check that your manuscript is in a polished and submittable state, print it out and have a read through aloud – and on screen again. If nothing jars and you're enjoying yourself and gripped then you're on the right track. Get informed readers or a literary consultancy to give you feedback: if the reaction is all round positive and you've taken it as far as you can on your own then it's ready.

US Insight

Virtually all agents will be reading your submission digitally but we do read and experience text differently from platform to platform. If your book is published, it will exist electronically as well as in a physical edition. Seeing your book laid out as though it is already an e-book on a device (rather than on a computer screen) can help you catch continuity issues, grammatical mistakes, and the like. It will also help you review the pacing. On the other hand, reading it on paper can help you experience your own book in an organic and holistic way. Reading in both formats back-to-back is even better, as you will see it through both lenses. Try to read each edition through in one long sitting.

Why work with an agent – and why not?

We strongly advocate getting an agent prior to a publisher as they usually earn more than their 10–15 per cent commission when negotiating a deal and they safeguard your relationship with your editor. They get to wrangle over your jacket cover while you remain the easy-to-work-with author. However, you don't necessarily need one and in some instances you may even be more attractive to a publisher *without* an agent. Perhaps you are just what they are looking for and the fit is wonderful without any third-party involvement. They may also be hoping for a better deal without the agent's know-how, so be as informed as you can. The Society of Authors have trained lawyers who will check a contract for you if you don't have an agent to do so.

If you're not having any luck in securing an agent and are finding the process frustrating then do try submitting direct to a publisher. While most publishers have an official policy of not accepting unsolicited manuscripts (those submitted by the author and not by an agent) and recommend that you approach an agent first, if you've done your research you may have an inroad to an editor that you can exploit. And because unsolicited manuscripts have been discouraged for many years their desks are perhaps clearer than they once were. We know plenty of authors who've gone direct to an editor or secured a contract unagented. If one type of door is consistently closed and you're confident in your bestseller-to-be then perhaps try a different door.

We also know that the majority of authors who have effective agents are delighted with their arrangement, and many have a life-long relationship through the ups and downs. You don't need a best friend, but you do need someone you can work with well and who believes in you. This is why in the first instance you will want to do some research – not only to make your submission attention grabbing, but also to reach out to the right agent for you.

(We'll refer from now on to submitting to agents but if you're submitting directly to publishers just replace the word *agent* for *editor*.)

US Insight

American agents and publishers are always on the lookout for new and unique voices that can sell into many territories. They want to know that there is a viable market for your work. That said, don't write to a current trend – these change quickly. Write the book that you are passionate about and believe in. Even if your book does fit into a current (or recently past) trend, try to outwit the confines of that niche. Staying fresh and ahead of what is already saturating the marketplace will help you get your book sold.

Do write the whole book! Increasingly, American agents need to see the whole project. They are looking to see if the author has really worked all the way through. Non-fiction is one exception to this: you can certainly write the entire manuscript, but traditional non-fiction (such as history, biography, self-help, etc.) can sell from a high-level proposal. (A good non-fiction proposal will include an overview of the entire project, the introduction, an annotated table of contents, a sample chapter, and a marketing section.) The exception to this is memoir: most agents and publishers regard memoir as working in the marketplace more like fiction, and will want to see the entire manuscript.

Do your research and tailor your submission

This is the fun bit! Scour trade books that list agents and publishers; read blogs and articles; refer to books in a similar genre to yours or books that you admire in general; and note who the agent/publisher is so you can make a wish list. Creating an excel sheet is a good idea, including names, contact details, and why you intend to submit to them (you'll add to this once you begin submitting). You_may have read an interview or seen a tweet calling out for a particular genre or saying that they like cats – and you have a cat book. You may have met an agent at a writers' conference, or entered a competition where they were the judge. There are numerous ways to build up a profile without being *too familiar* about it (occasionally agents can get spooked).

However you choose to do it, a key factor in getting your submission noticed by the agent in question is to make your letter as personal as possible. A submissions reader is much more likely to pass on a letter that starts: 'I met you at the Romantic Novelists' Association Winter Party and you kindly asked to see some opening material of my Regency saga', or 'I read in *Writing Magazine* that you've just set up your agency and are looking for historical novels', or 'I see on your website that you represent my favourite romantic fiction writer (name of author) so I'm hoping that my Regency saga will appeal'.

In your research, take particular note of: editors who have just set up as agents; junior agents who are building up a list; or a recently formed agency or imprint – they will all be looking for new authors. While senior agents have a good reputation for a reason, they may only be taking on a few authors a year.

US Insight

Like agents everywhere, American agents are overwhelmed with submissions. Some can get several hundred a day in digital form, as well as traditional hardcopy submissions. Authors should look closely at the agent's website and see what will be the usual waiting period for new queries – it's not unusual for an agent to take three months to respond to a query and pages. Then comes the hard part – the patient waiting!

Almost all American publishers won't look at unagented manuscripts. (That's the official line, although of course there are always exceptions.) The good news is that there are more new agents in the US market than ever before. Really investigate who's doing what, and submit to agents that seem like they'd be a good match for you. For American agents, the more targeted your submission is, the better. Given the volume of projects that they see daily, ensuring that your submission aligns with that agent's key interests is vital. For example, one agent may occasionally take on a fantasy novel, but if they only represent a couple of best-sellers in that category, you are much better off submitting to an agent who represents fantasy as a specific interest.

Most agents will take on a project outside their own general area of interest and expertise – if it is an unusual project that is unusually strong. But by and large, you want to find an agent who is fully immersed in your category. They will know the editors who work with your kind of book, and they themselves will have the expertise to edit your book to the marketplace. Additionally, an agent who really knows your genre can help you develop your career as a whole. They will be able to think strategically about your development as an author, and be your partner in your success.

The cover letter

Your primary objective is to provide a quick, efficient reference for the agent to see who you are and what you're submitting. Keep it to one page if you can, with your address, phone number and email. Personalize your letter with a reason why you're submitting to them, as discussed, and list the title, word count, genre, and age range (if it's children's).

Then you'll need a paragraph blurb or book description and a paragraph of biography in the first person including anything that is writer related or quirky, or perhaps whatever inspired you to write the book. If you have an online presence or you're a speaker who commands an audience and sales then this is useful to know. You may want to mention other books within the market and say why your book is pertinent or different, especially for non-fiction. However, avoid saying your book is better or will be a bestseller!

You should say if you've been published before, listing the book and publisher; or if you've been represented (you don't need to name the agent). There are plenty of good reasons for leaving a previous agent – for example, changing genre into an area that the agent doesn't represent, or just the parting of ways. You can afford to be vague at this point; if they're interested you'll have an opportunity later to fill in the gaps. If it wasn't that amicable it's best to retain a degree of professionalism: be factual, say you've moved on and are excited about the next leg of your writer journey. Keep any venting – however justified – for your friends and family.

Finish the letter by stating if you've submitted to more than one agent – transparency is appreciated. You don't need to list other agents by name but do say that you'll let the recipient of the letter know of any developments. If it's on exclusive submission – perhaps they contacted you and requested the manuscript – then you might ask for a date to check back in. Finally, thank them and triple-check for typos before sending. We recommend a follow-up after six to eight weeks if you've not heard anything, and we'll cover this in more detail further on.

US Insight

American agents are more likely to respond to a sharply written and short query. It shouldn't be cutesy or use emojis, but it can reflect your writing style. Think of this blurb as flap copy for your eventual book, or as very short marketing copy: it should tease the reader while revealing enough about the book to hold their attention. It needs to sell the book to the agent, or it won't get read. It should tell the agent why they want to read your book, without saying that outright.

Any writing credentials or any competitions you've won should be included upfront, as that will spur the agent to keep reading. Tell the agent that you have looked at their site and list, and feel that your project matches their interests. Always include the word count. Say who you feel your readers are, and where your book fits in your genre. But – and this is a big but – don't compare your novel to whatever the biggest and bestselling book of the moment is, nor to a classic. Agents see this as both lazy and self-aggrandizing and you may end up with an automatic form rejection. Surprise them by comparing your book to one that performed well and is well known, but demonstrates that you are immersed in your genre. Your comparison titles should accurately reflect the marketplace.

If you have been working in a writers' group and there are members who have landed an agent or publisher, or if you have friends who have been published, see if you can get a one- to two-sentence blurb from one of them and include it in your submission. It's important that the person doing this is recognizable in the industry. It doesn't need to be a best-selling author; someone notable, or who has been successfully published and reviewed is fine.

American agents are seeing more submissions accompanied by this kind of blurb, and it is very effective. If you are lucky enough to have good contacts, their endorsement can really help you get over the transom.

However tempting it may be, try not to blanket submit. The less personalized the submission the more generic it will appear, as if you're hoping that someone – anyone – will bite, and therefore are not so confident about your book. Also, getting feedback from a selected few in stages is really useful. If there's something you agree with, you can revise accordingly before making another round of submissions.

If your submission is turned down then it's unlikely you'll be able to resubmit at a later date, even if it's been revised extensively. Some authors change their name to disguise the work but agents tend not to forget a concept or style of writing and usually keep records. A targeted approach makes the handling of the submissions process – who you've submitted to, who's responded, and what they've said – more manageable.

US Insight

There are agents who specifically say that they will not look at multiple submissions. If you have your heart set on that agent, try them first, and tell them that you are following their guidelines on exclusive submission. But say that, since they have it exclusively, you will look to hear from them within a few weeks before going out to other agents. That exclusivity should create a sense of priority for the agent. This will be true if your agent does an exclusive publisher submission down the line as well.

Submission letter example 1

From: author, address, phone number, email

To Agent at Agency sent by post or email (date)

Dear Margaret Grange,

You kindly gave me a one-to-one at the SCBWI conference and offered to look at the opening chapters for my 11+ novel, CHANGE OF HEART (40,000 words).

Tabitha is that girl who everyone wants to be friends with: perfect hair, gorgeous smile, great clothes, and brains to boot. But friendship with Tabitha comes at a price: if you abide by her rules all will be well; if you don't she'll take you apart. But why has she set her sights on the dowdy Joanna? Has Tabitha seen the *real* Joanna, or is she just another pawn in one of her games? When Joanna gives Tabitha a taste of her own medicine, her perfect veneer begins to crack. But now Joanna's got a glimpse of power, will she be able to stop?

I am a mother of four children, now all at school except one, and I write around the edges. I find that when time is precious I'm organized and get more done! Prior to being a mum I worked in IT managing a large team so I'm used to deadlines and juggling workloads. I am now writing book two, another 11+ social issues, and have completed 15,000 words so far.

Thank you so much for meeting me and asking to see more material and I will keep my fingers crossed that you love it. Since we met I got shortlisted for the Emerging Writers Award and have submitted to three other agents who expressed interest. I will of course let you know of any developments.

Warm wishes,

Georgina Gordon

Submission letter example 2

Dear Andrew Bolton,

I found your name on a creative writing workshop that you're speaking at (the one in Bath) and noted your quest for memoirs. Your reputation for being one of the best non-fiction agents is also impressive.

According to your guidelines I'm submitting by email the first three chapters of my proposal for DEATH ON A KITCHEN TABLE. I grew up in a chaotic and romantic household with animals wandering in and out of the kitchen and tons of siblings. My father was a coroner and over breakfast – often with a chicken or two pecking at the crumbs on the table – my parents would log who had died overnight along with heartfelt stories about that person and their life. This led to a fascination with celebrating characters: their foibles, their achievements, their families, their pets, and the impact they had on their community or the world at large.

I am a professional paraglider but my hobby is facilitating a website that allows people to write a mini memoir/vlog that captures the essence of who they are. There is also a special section for their pets. I set this up two years ago and now have 7000 members, with a significant Facebook and Twitter following, and have collated some of the stories (with their or their family's permission if it's posthumous) into this part memoir, part anthology, part celebration of life. To give you a taste: there's a former spy, a sheep farmer who has never left the island he grew up on, a philanthropist, a lepidopterist who fostered over 40 children...

As this is my first foray into submitting I have only approached your good self. However, I wonder if I may follow this up in a few weeks' time to see if it appeals? Thank you so much for your time and consideration.

Best,

John Green

Submission letter example 3

Dear Lydia Gold,

I believe we met a number of years ago when I was published by Penguin (THE SHAFT and HIDE). I had an agent back then but life took over and I hung up my writing boots, as it were, and moved to Spain. I have since returned to the UK with my family and alongside my job as a game designer I have penned a new thriller called THE LINE (80,000 words).

Revered tech guru, Bill Constance, launches a revolutionary data implant that allows those who can afford it to have immediate access-to-all information. It acts like a computer encyclopedia inside your brain: you can speak Cantonese at will; receive up-to-the-second world news; there's even a memory retriever for people you've met before (very useful at ambassador parties). When the dark elite – the real world-supremacists – take an interest in Bill's invention he's elevated beyond his dreams. But as the AI chip takes on a personality of its own the world has to come together to overthrow the forces threatening mankind and restore the balance.

As this is set in the UK and US two other agents in both territories received the same material yesterday and one has kindly requested to meet me. I wouldn't want anyone to feel rushed into making a decision so I've set a response date for three weeks' time. I do hope that's OK and of course I will let you know of any further developments.

Thank you so much for your time and I really hope you like it.

Best,

S. A. Appleton

These should give you a flavour of what a cover letter might look like and what you might include in various different circumstances. If you're unsure about writing a salesy blurb (they're tricky to get right) try a simpler, more factual paragraph description:

> THE LINE is a story about Bill Constance, a tech guru, who launches a revolutionary implant that allows the user access to all information past and present. As the AI implants take on a life of their own it becomes apparent that humanity is threatened. Bill has the key to reset the world-balance, but who can he trust and will he be in time?

As the above examples hopefully demonstrate, you don't need to have had previous success or impressive credentials, or be exotic or unusual. In fact, trying too hard to be different can work against you. If this is your first book and you enjoy walks in the park and can't resist hot chocolate with marshmallows then say so – this will give a warm impression of you. Equally if you want to keep things crisp, have a look at some biographies of published writers which are often perfunctory: where they were born, where they're based, whether this is their first book and if they're penning the next.

In summary, agents want to be able to see quickly what you are submitting. They will be looking for: a reason why you've chosen them; a high concept (something they've not seen before) or a twist on a familiar genre; a snapshot of who you are; any relevant writer history; and an idea of how many other agents they're up against. Your objective is to get them reading your writing as soon as possible, as it will be the style and voice that will clinch their interest.

Formatting your work

If your manuscript looks clean and industry formatted this will speak volumes – and it's easy to get right. General rules are: submit it unbound (with elastic bands but no page ties); use a recognized font and size (Times New Roman, size 12 or 14); and double-space your work with clean margins all around. If your manuscript is on the long side it can be tempting to decrease the font and spacing to squeeze the book into a more manageable size, but editors have an innate rhythm of reading and if they're turning the page more slowly than they're used to they may think pacing is an issue; in addition, they might want to use the margins for marking-up. Most submissions are by email these days, so saving money on postage and printing is not such an issue as it used to be. We know a number of agents, however, who like hard copies. Follow their guidelines, whatever those may be, including on whether printing on both sides of the paper is acceptable.

US Insight

On this side of the pond, virtually all agents will require an electronic submission. If you are able, try to use the most up-to-date software: you do not want the agent to encounter any technological hurdles in reading your manuscript. Some agents will ask that you submit your pages in Word Doc (rather than as a PDF) as that often transfers best to a reading device or tablet.

Formatting is very important with an electronic submission. You want to make sure that your manuscript looks clean and adheres to traditional and professional formatting. Stick to a clear 12-point font, use either 1.5 or

---

double spacing, and always number the pages. Try email-
ing yourself the full submission first. Open it up and make
sure the layout is OK and looks the way you want it to
look. Your synopsis can be the first page of your manuscript, or attached as a separate document. The agent's
website might have specifics on that. Otherwise, do it
whichever way is most efficient for you.

At the start of each new chapter (or scene) the first paragraph
should be left justified. Each subsequent paragraph should then
be one tab indented with no space (hard return) in between
paragraphs. When a new character speaks this should also be on
a separate line and indented. It's helpful to have a header with
your name and the title of the book in a smaller font size on
each page in case your manuscript gets separated – and finally
it's imperative to number those pages!

Every manuscript needs a **title page:**

BY
KATHRYN PRICE
HELEN CORNER-BRYANT

On Editing

*How to edit your novel the
professional way*

Please contact:

Cornerstones Literary Consultancy

Contact Helen@cornerstones.co.uk or
tel: 01308 897374

www.cornerstones.co.uk and
www.cornerstonesUS.com

An example of **page layout:**

On Editing/Corner-Bryant

(header – font 8, abbreviated title and author name it)

Chapter One

(centred, size font 16, Times New Roman and bold)

Where the Two Rivers Meet

She pressed into her horse's neck and drove her legs into his sides feeling him quicken, his hooves thundering and scattering stones as they rounded the corner.

'Come on, querido, just a little faster.'

'Go on boy, you can do it.' She closed her eyes and of a saddle under her. His body swerved as if on the angle of a pin and she squeezed everything in tight as darkness blanked out the light and branches cracked into her hair. A second later she allowed herself to glance up ignoring the burning in her scalp; as he slowed to a trot his ears pricked, his neck slick with sweat.

(Times New Roman, font 12, double-spaced, 1.5 to 2 inch margins, paginated)

The synopsis

You're not alone if you feel anxious at the prospect of writing a synopsis. But there are ways to make it straightforward and it's always better to include one in your submission – even if the agent prefers not to read them. When we're considering a manuscript to submit to agents, we prefer to read it blind and only refer to the synopsis if there seems to be one plot hole too many or the character's going in the wrong direction. The synopsis is useful to see if the author has a hold on the story and if there's a satisfying shape to it – a gripping beginning, a meaty middle and a twisty conclusion. And yes, we want to know exactly how the story ends. This is not a teaser blurb but more a practical, structural reference sheet.

There are many views on what a synopsis should be, but for submitting purposes we favour focusing on your main character and plot and only mentioning minor characters or subplots if they have a direct impact on moving the story forward. A synopsis can have its own shape, and does not have to follow the story sequentially. It should generally be a page long, single-spaced and in the present tense. It's best to signpost that it's a SYNOPSIS and list the title, author name, word length and genre.

If you're working from the three-act graph discussed in Chapter 4, you can pin the plot from the graph into the synopsis. In this way you can be sure that your synopsis provides a clear demonstration of the story's strong underlying structure:

Paragraph 1: Act 1: set-up (including internal conflict)
Paragraph 2: Inciting event
Paragraphs 3–5: Act 2: around three main turning points/mini-climaxes of the story (including character arc) and high point
Paragraph 6: Rug-pulling and darkest moment
Paragraph 7: Act 3: climax

Paragraph 8: Resolution, with a focus on how the character(s) have changed

Once you have the essential elements in place you can play around with the sequence. For instance, half the book may be set-up; in your thriller you might open with part of the climax and then jump back in time; the high point may come after the low point and so on.

Similarly, a synopsis can serve as a diagnostic tool if you measure it against the graph. If something isn't working, try to pick out the main points on the graph from your synopsis to check that there's a clear inciting incident, that your character is consistently driving the story forwards, and your plot has enough tension peaks.

US Insight

Your synopsis should convey the narrative arc, highlight the main problem and developments within the plot, reveal the main characters, and show how the story concludes. You need to communicate that the book is realistic and makes sense, whilst providing a strong and lively summary of your plot. Using active voice and third person in your synopsis will help to demonstrate your skills.

In the case of your synopsis, less is always more! Choose each word with care and really hone it down to be as concise and sharp as possible. You are not telling the whole story – you are writing a fascinating summary; one that is designed to intrigue. Don't include value judgements or describe the book as though you are reviewing it. An agent will be turned off if you editorialize about your own work. And if your synopsis seems confusing to you, then it will be even more confusing to a prospective agent. Being clear and convincing is key.

An example of a **synopsis**:

SYNOPSIS

THE FAIRY WARRIOR by Hattie Blythe, fantasy, lower
middle grade, 15,000 words.

Rosie, an 11-year-old orphan fairy, has always wanted
someone to love and be loved by, for it is lore that no fairy
should be alone. With her parents dead in mysterious
circumstances – legend has it they were slain by dragons,
ancient enemies of the fairies, now all disappeared – she
finds salvation in the king's palace where she's favoured
for her courage and fighting skills. It becomes apparent
that the king has her in mind for a bigger challenge, one
that could save their world. He believes that an ancient
prophecy, which says that the dragons will awaken to
wreak their revenge, is about to come true.

But Rosie has a secret, and she knows that it's only a
matter of time before the king realizes her dark heart:
she has always understood the language of dragons, their
whispers reaching across the plains in her half sleep.

Now Fairyland is crumbling and their powers are waning because someone is leaking fairy dust and the jewels
that adorned the sacred tomb are disappearing. When the
Ruby – the heart of their magic and protection – is taken,
Rosie, accompanied by her archer friend Harry, is sent
into the winterland to retrieve it. With Harry by her side
Rosie overcomes many obstacles: a river of snakes, the
forest of lies, and the riddle maze, until eventually she is
led into a trap by a dragon shapeshifter.

Rosie is kept prisoner in a pit of mist, and instead
of rescuing her Harry leaves her to die. She must face
the possibility that he has been obstructing her quest

all along, and may even be responsible for the death of Fairyland. Harry escapes via a magic tunnel in a trail of flame and Rosie calls out to him in dragon language. He falters but doesn't look back.

To her surprise, Rosie is helped by the shapeshifter. After hearing her speak in the dragon tongue he now believes she is the saviour who can free them from the evil dragon queen, who has imprisoned them all for a thousand moons. Once upon a time, fairies and dragons lived peacefully alongside one another. Will Rosie be the one to restore this ancient friendship?

Accepting that her knowledge of dragons is a gift and not a curse, Rosie agrees to help. She intends to slay the dragon queen, but in her last breath the queen begs for-giveness and holds out the Ruby. Rosie is about to spare her, when the queen laughs at how Rosie's parents died protecting their fairy child, the one who would suppos-edly come to destroy her one day … and now Rosie has failed. With all her might, Rosie slams the dragon queen into a cave of ice where she will be trapped for eternity.

Returning to Fairyland, Rosie hands back the Ruby but does not share the King's triumph. She's realized Harry was the one person she truly cared for, and now she has to live with his betrayal. When she tracks him down in the 'banished world' – for no fairy with a dark heart is allowed through the gates of truth – he too begs her forgiveness. He is in fact her brother, snatched by the dragon queen and sent back to Fairyland as her spy. In order to protect Rosie he had to look as if he was following the queen's orders. It was he who alerted the shapeshifter, and whispered victory into the dragon queen's ears to lower her guard.

Now that order has been restored he is free to live by Rosie's side. Together they watch the celebration of peace as dragons and fairies rake the skies with rays of rainbows and sparks. Rosie takes his hand and smiles.

In this example we have spent longer outlining the emotional conflict in the set-up and climax, and less time with the mid-section – in fantasy fiction, phrases like *the forest of lies* and *riddle maze* can be used to summarize a wealth of exciting material. Rosie's external quest is simple enough – to defeat the dragon and restore peace to the kingdom – but her main emotional conflict, and the centre of the story, is finding a home and a family and discovering the truth about her past and her parents. With a more externally plot-driven story – such as you might find in crime fiction or thrillers – you'll probably spend less time on the set-up and emotional arc (*he has been a lone wolf since his wife left him, driven by work and a sense of justice*) and more time on the plot in the mid-section to climax, as that will be where the main drama unfolds. For literary fiction, you may want to foreground the themes and emotional arcs. For women's commercial your synopsis will need to establish an aspirational heroine with a deep emotional fear or goal (love, finding oneself, overcoming adversity) and set up some believable conflict and convincing heroes. A sci-fi synopsis might need at least a paragraph on world-building, and may also foreground thematic concerns like a current fear (such as nature failing) or an extrapolation of humanity's future. For historical fiction, we need to see authenticity, and conflict filled characters whose emotional and plot arcs interweave closely. For any story there should be a driving emotional fear or goal with strong characters and a well-paced, carefully structured plot.

For stories with multiple characters, shifting viewpoints and lots of mini plot arcs, try to find the one character who is more central than others to give a sense of focus to the synopsis. Foreground the main spine or overarching shape of the story, rather than trying to cover every separate plot thread in detail. You might need to spend some time on set-up and establishing individual goals and aims, but ensure links between the characters are clear, and focus on how the action of the story brings them together.

Have a look at the following as an example of dealing with multiple characters and more than one POV:

SYNOPSIS

REUNION by Thomas Watson, thriller, 80,000 words

Lisa's always had the perfect life: she's beautiful, easy going and popular. However, inwardly she's been plagued by self-doubt since her mother left her when she was a child. Her boyfriend Peter, a lawyer, is her rock – but unbeknown to her he has a drug problem he's only just managing to keep a lid on. When an old friend from uni, Nancy, contacts them to say she's just inherited a large estate and would love to host a reunion, it seems like a good opportunity to escape their problems for a while. When they arrive they're delighted to see that the final guest is Michael, who used to be the joker of their group but has now turned his life around.

The first night sees the group cutting loose and rediscovering their friendship. In a drunken heart to heart, Lisa tells Nancy about her mother – the first person apart from Peter who she's ever told – and Nancy suggests that when the weekend is over maybe the two of them can do some research and try to find her. But as the night progresses, tensions bubble to the surface; Nancy flaunts her new wealth and, high as a kite, Peter flirts outrageously with her. Michael tries to play peacemaker, but when Lisa runs off into the night and doesn't come back they all realize things have gone too far. They contact the police but no help arrives: the sudden snowfall has cut them off. As the group turns in on itself their secrets emerge: how Peter is nearly bankrupt; how Michael used to be in love with Lisa and wrote her a letter declaring his feelings, which never arrived; how Nancy has always been jealous of Lisa.

When Peter and Nancy disappear off into a bedroom, Michael goes in search of Lisa and finds her huddled in an abandoned outbuilding. Michael's not sure whether to tell her about Peter, but she's in complete denial about him, so certain that he loves her; in the end Michael decides to protect her from the truth. He coaxes her back to the house, but when they return they find Nancy unconscious and Peter dead. It looks like a sex game gone wrong, and Lisa breaks down. Nancy awakes, groggy, claiming she can't remember what happened. But Lisa doesn't believe her and by the time the police and ambulance finally arrive she's hysterical, accusing Nancy of betraying her trust and trying to sabotage her life. Nancy is arrested and charged with manslaughter.

One year later, Nancy is in prison but appealing her sentence, and Michael and Lisa are rebuilding their lives – together. On a sailing holiday she tells him she's pregnant. He's ecstatic and they are both full of hope for the future. As they sit watching the sunset from the prow of the boat, Michael confesses that part of him is glad about what happened, since it brought them together. Peter didn't deserve her. Sleepily, Lisa agrees; she always knew what Peter was really like, but didn't want to let herself believe it.

In the following days, Lisa starts to realize that something has changed between them. Michael becomes
secretive, controlling, asking suspicious questions about
her relationship with Peter. She reflects on his words:
Peter didn't deserve you. Is it possible that Michael had
something to do with what happened to Peter? Lisa
begins to fear for her safety and for that of her unborn
child. Things come to a head when Michael accuses
her of being cynical and manipulative; he says he thinks
she'll be a terrible mother and he's never going to be
able to trust her with their child. He seems to have gone
crazy, making insane accusations and becoming aggres-
sive; even accusing her of killing Peter herself. In a terrifying cat and mouse climax Lisa manages to overcome
him and he falls overboard.

Returning home alone, Lisa decides that if even
Michael, who seemed so solid, couldn't be trusted, then
the only person she can rely on is herself. She will raise
the baby alone; be the devoted mother that she never
had. Time passes and she finds peace as a mother, but
she still dwells on the past, and she knows she needs
to lay the ghosts of what happened that night to rest.
Going through her chest of memories she pulls out the
love letter from Michael – the one he thought she'd
never received. Poor Michael: she'd thought he would
provide for her in the way that Peter no longer could,
and he'd been so easy to trick. But once he stopped
believing her there was no way she could let him live.

As she looks upon her sleeping child the door-
bell rings. Two uniformed police are waiting outside
together with her long lost mother – contacted by
Nancy – to take care of Lisa's daughter.

Because this plot will feature both Michael's POV and Lisa's (who'll be an unreliable narrator) we've opted to keep the POV in the synopsis fairly general so that we don't have to get into the potentially quite complicated mechanics of the story. This also allows us to foreground the external action and tension (so important in a thriller) without getting bogged down by emotional complexities.

In summary

You've done your research and have your agent profile sheet and contact details to hand; you've polished your cover letter and synopsis and formatted your opening pages. Now you're ready to submit. This may be by phone initially (it's worth checking the agent is still at the agency or if there is someone else more appropriate to submit to), or by email. If you're sending your material by post and want it returned, don't forget the stamped jiffy bag with stamps rather than the dated sticker the post office will try to give you.

Once the material has gone out to four to six agents, do a follow-up a few weeks later to check they received your material, and expect to hear something in six to eight weeks. If you don't hear back after three months, send a note to thank them for their time and say you assume you're free to submit elsewhere. A common complaint from agents is that an author's neglected to tell them they've been signed up, especially if the agent has spent time on a manuscript, so do be mindful of etiquette. The majority of agents are super-efficient and respectful of an author's time and will try their hardest to get a response to you as soon as they can.

Lastly, keep a record of everyone you've sent your material to, including the date and type of response – and it's a good idea to keep this list to hand. An author once told us that she received a phone call from an interested agent. However, she didn't immediately recall which agency she worked for and there ensued a rather muddled conversation. All the while in the background was her 90-year-old (deaf) mother wanting to know who was on the phone and how her cup of tea was coming along. As *cup of tea* is a phrase often used when an agent does or doesn't like a manuscript it ended up being a comedy of errors. The author was so embarrassed that she put down the phone and never followed it up. When you receive that wonderful phone call, email or letter of interest you want to be able to refer to your updated profile submissions sheet and know exactly who you're dealing with and what stage you're at with them. The next step is to see how the agent wants to progress things, and we'll talk about that in the next chapter.

US Insight

It's a good idea to blind-copy yourself on every submission and communication you have with an agency or publisher. No matter what might happen to your hard drive, everything is saved in the cloud. It's also useful to create a Gmail account just for your publishing emails and communications so that you have an easy one-stop place for all your letters and documents; this is a great way to keep a secondary record of when you sent out what. And of course, create the most usable and friendly database that works for you. The important thing is to keep track: it can take dozens of submissions to land an agent and it can be a lot of detail to manage. But remember: you only need one person to fall in love with your work and represent you, so don't give up!

10
Working with your agent and publisher

Rejection is a part of the process, but that doesn't mean you have to like it! However, you **can** learn from it, and in this chapter we'll help you spot the difference between stock responses and personal feedback that you can use. When you finally secure your agent, will you know what to ask them and how to work with them? Will you know how to deal with feedback in a way that's professional and proactive? With the tools you've learned in this book you should be able to approach the final stages in the publishing process with confidence: working together with your agent and publisher to ensure your book makes a splash, and takes you one step closer to realizing your dreams.

Dealing with rejections

By now your submission should be polished and glittering and ready to go. However, rejections are an inevitable part of the process and knowing how to manage them can make a big difference to whether you succeed or fail. While it may feel self-defeating to begin your submission process by considering rejection, it's linked into feedback and all about making your submission/story stronger as a result. It is also the thing that most authors fear when submitting, so if you tackle it head on it should set you up for a positive experience all round.

Most authors who go on to get published will have experienced at least one rejection, unless they're very lucky, and while it can dampen things initially, there may be some gems glinting in the dust that you can put to good use. The first step is to learn to distinguish between them. If there is **no feedback and they are generic turn downs** – 'liked the story but not for us' – then it could mean something or nothing. Either the firewall is strong and it's not getting to the agent you submitted to; or it really is just not right for them, and they don't need to say why; or there is something not working that you can't see.

You won't be able to glean any specifics if it's a generic turn down, and this is when you might come to a literary consultancy to get it checked, or go to an informed beta reader who knows the market thus saving time in the long run. It may need drastic revision but have huge potential in which case you could go back at a later date and resubmit, especially if you have a respected party's endorsement (but you will need to be transparent with the agency about the fact that they've seen it before). Or you may decide that the idea is good but not exceptional and move on to your next book. Your first novel needs to fly; and we discuss the reasons for this further on.

US Insight

There are some stock phrases that American agents use, like 'too quiet', or 'I didn't fall in love'. These don't necessarily mean that there's anything fundamentally wrong with the book: it is simply the language that agents use when a book isn't right for them. Agents will always want to represent sure-fire winners that don't require a lot of positioning in the marketplace, but much of what they take chances on is guided by their personal taste. Just as not every book is for every reader, every submission is not for every agent. So don't let these kinds of phrases put you

---

off, but use that rejection to dig deeper into which agents might love the kind of book you are writing. And regardless of response, always send a thank you note back to the agent for their time – you never know what will happen with your next project, and goodwill is always returned.

If the turn down **refers to specifics in the story** (*I found Marla too unsympathetic*) then you know it's been read and considered. If there is feedback on how to improve your manuscript then do take this on board and see if it resonates. Most agents are fantastic editors and know the market inside out, and any feedback they offer should be treated like gold dust. However, some agents are more sales-orientated or don't have the time to provide involved feedback; and sometimes a reason for turning down a manuscript or the direction that they advise you to take may not be the right solution for you. But even this kind of feedback can be useful.

For instance, perhaps one agent says they don't like your opening and that you should start the story somewhere else; and another agent says it starts in the right place but you need to build up the tension. The feedback seems contradictory, but at the same time you do have a niggling feeling that something's not right. Who should you believe? In this instance they're essentially saying the same thing: your opening isn't working. How you rectify that will be down to your intuition and know-how, and what feels right for your story. If feedback really isn't gelling, then it may be subjective, in which case you can probably continue submitting the same version. The important thing is to brainstorm any feedback and check it from all angles.

US Insight

It can be especially discouraging when writers receive a lot of rejections that qualify as a *near miss*. This is really the third and most positive form of rejection: it offers up some strong praise of your manuscript, but says that in the end something didn't quite come together or work for the agent. If you have received a handful of these kinds of rejections, stop submitting and evaluate what you are hearing.

Sort through all the responses and see what really resonates with you. It's always tempting to start revising based on every piece of feedback you get, but you need to make sure that your revisions are holistic. Consider every suggestion in a thoughtful and measured way so that you are remaining true to your book. Don't undertake drastic revisions based on one rejection letter.

On the other hand, if you receive a number of rejections all mentioning the same issue, then you know that you need to think again. Is there a common theme to the feedback? Are all the agents citing the pacing? Or a particular piece of the plot? Is the setting too familiar or too unrealistic? Really analyse the comments you are getting. This may be the time to make revisions.

Finally, trust your instincts if you are getting advice that seems wildly off the mark: what one agent doesn't love, another might adore.

Follow-up contact

Remember, an agent's first responsibility is to their published (fee-paying) clients and anything additional such as considering new authors will be dealt with in their own time. That said, they do what they do because they're driven to discover emerging talent, so keep that in mind if you're feeling impatient or discouraged.

If you don't hear from an agent after a month or so it may be time for a follow-up that will hopefully nudge them to move your submission to the top of the pile:

> 'I hope you don't mind my checking in but I wondered if you've had a chance to consider my novel, LOVE ME TRUE? I am due to go on holiday for two weeks and won't have access to my emails. It would be wonderful if you contacted me but awful if it took me weeks to get back to you! However, I don't mean to rush you if you need more time.'

Or if you've had some interest, out of courtesy you need to let the other agents know:

> 'I'm not sure if you've had a chance to consider my thriller, KNOCK, KNOCK – I'm sure you're extremely busy so I apologize for checking in again so soon. However, I thought I'd let you know that I've had a request for the full manuscript in case that changes things for you. I will of course let you know of any developments.'

Or:

> 'I sent my proposal THE BUTTERFLY EFFECT OF THE TRUTH ON POLITICS AND SOCIETY some weeks ago and I'm due to come up to London next week to meet with some interested parties. Would it be appropriate if we had a quick cup of coffee? Or I would be happy to book in a more convenient date if that's not feasible. In case you don't have the submission to hand I'm a chief government advisor on how world events and

politics affect society and how one voice can gather force with upswelling ramifications. Your agency has come highly recommended to me so I'd be delighted to explore this further. Of course if it's not for you please do let me know, and thank you for your kind consideration.'

Be prepared for two responses to other agent interest. Either the first agent will step back and let the interested agent take the lead. They may even suggest that you get back in touch if nothing comes of it. Or, it may spur them on to remain in the running. Either way you're keeping them informed and being polite, and it may have positive repercussions. But don't deliberately create a fervour if there is no substance to it as this could backfire.

If at any stage in the process you receive a note expressing interest and wanting to read more material, or asking to meet, then this is a fantastic step forward.

The agent meeting

This is a sign that the agent is very interested in your writing and wants to see if you can work well together and whether you have a similar vision. In most cases you'll already have a sense of who they are and how they operate from referring to their website and list of authors, but do refresh your memory before you meet. An internet search should highlight articles, interviews, chats in writer forums; you may have spoken to them at a festival or conference or know about them via word of mouth. If you're in contact you'll have a sense of their mannerisms: are they brisk and efficient; warm and creative; do they offer revision suggestions (or not)?

This is also an opportunity for the agent to wax lyrical about what they love about your story, and to suggest revision if needed, and here they will be gauging your reaction to check if you're open to ideas. Some agents will have specific points to raise and others might be more speculative.

You should have the confidence by now to get to the root of an issue and suggest ways to fix any problems. Remember it is your story: only you will know what feels comfortable and achievable – and you are the one who will need to deliver. If your mind goes blank and you're finding it stressful, try not to worry. Note everything down; perhaps summarize what the agent is proposing at the end of the meeting and if you're still unsure say you'll get back to them with a plan once you've given it some proper thought. The main thing is to keep a cool head, be yourself, and not be dazzled by the interest. Do you admire this agent and feel you could work with them and their agency? If you've enjoyed brainstorming with them, there's a good chance you'll mesh well together.

US Insight

The agent meeting is very much like a first date: you will be feeling the agent out to get a sense of their personality, energy, and style, and the agent will be doing the same with you. That first meeting can be intimidating, so try to go in feeling calm and focused. If you can, schedule the meeting at a time that you know you are at your best. Be prepared to ask specific questions about how the agent works, but also to talk about how you might build your platform and promote yourself.

If revisions are proposed and you do a bit of live brainstorming, try not to get into a debate. The agent will be trying to find the best solution for your book and the market. Remember the two opposing agent responses about building up or changing the beginning of a story? A similar approach can work when you're considering implementing agent feedback that you're not quite sure about:

> 'I can see how you might want me to build up the beginning and it's obviously not currently working. What if I started with Chapter Two when she arrives at the house and took out Chapter One which is mainly backstory? That should throw the reader into the drama of the argument and then I could seed in backstory and her dilemma as this chapter unfolds?'

Whether they agree with your solution or not, they will be reassured that you're a confident self-editor and have a handle on your story. Arriving at the right solution during the meeting isn't really the important thing: it's whether you're receptive to feedback and how you handle the editing process.

An interested agent will also want to sell in the agency and to give you an idea of who they intend to submit to if you agree to sign up. If they hand you a contract, take it away with you and sign/return it once you've had a proper read through. Remember the Society of Authors are helpful if you have any queries or concerns.

What to look for in an agent

There are many lovely and effective agents out there who know the business, have great contacts and understand the publishing cycle. You will also have done your research at the beginning and should already have a sense of the agency's reputation and the agent's credentials. There are boutique agencies and large agencies, some longstanding and some new start-ups, and all offer a unique selling point.

Most agencies are members of the Authors' Agents' Association which offers a standard of working practice; members will have an asterisk alongside their listing in the *Writers' & Artists' Yearbook*. If they're not a member it doesn't mean they're not effective or above board – one of the criteria is a certain turn-over over of a period of five years; perhaps this agent has been a publisher for many years and has just set up.

US Insight

Have a real conversation about the industry rather than a formalized question and answer session. Ask the agent what they read for pleasure, and share what you read. Find out what publishers they like to work with and why. Often, the more general the conversation, the more specific a sense of their personality and style you'll get.

The agent–author relationship is a complex one. On one hand, it is a professional relationship in which YOU are the client and the agent works for you. They only earn money if they successfully represent you. But it is also very personal. Authors and agents can become close and know a great deal about each other's lives. Many authors and agents – and authors and editors – develop deep friendships. Publishing is highly social and a lot of business happens through personal relationships. The fact is, agents like to work with authors they like. It makes the tough and daunting process of getting published more congenial and human.

Some agents forge more intimate relationships than others, and you should find a balance that works for you. Some authors only talk with their agents about

---

the business of their books, while other authors play poker with their agents every week. Find the agent that fits your comfort zone and that you can trust. You will be relying on that agent to not just sell your work, but represent you as an author and help your career grow. Ideally, you want an agent who understands that they are not representing 'books' but authors. It's a subtle but important difference.

It comes down to what type of person you can work with and who you want representing you. Feel your way and don't (necessarily) jump at the first offer of representation – unless the spark is there. If an agent doesn't respond to your emails and takes months to get back to you; if they're inconsistent or constantly too busy; they haven't produced anything on your behalf for a long time; or they come across as bullish, or gushy one moment and dismissive the next, then you may decide to walk the other way. (If you're in a contract already and decide you want to change, then there is an etiquette for separating yourself from them. More on this later.)

For now, you're in your initial agent meeting and there are a few things you'll want to be clear about upfront.

Rights and responsibilities

Agency agreements can vary widely from agency to agency. However, the standard UK agent's commission rate is between 10 and 15 per cent. Foreign rights that have been retained by the agent is usually 20 per cent to reflect the sub-agent's fee. Your agent will have an idea of which rights they'll want to keep and which ones they'll negotiate with the publisher depending on who has the better contacts and which party can optimize the book's potential. They won't necessarily know this until they get publisher interest.

Most agents retain dramatic (film and TV) rights. If your book is optioned it may take one and a half to three years to be turned into a film and this can be renegotiated. Many books that are optioned don't make it to production stage but if yours does it will be turned into a script which you may not have control over.

US Insight

The above is generally true of American agent rates as well. It's not unheard of for some new agents to ask for a 20 per cent commission on ALL domestic rights across the board and 25 per cent on overseas and film and performance, but 15 per cent domestic and 20 per cent overseas and co-agented material remains the standard.

What extra costs does the agency expect you to cover – postage and photocopying of the manuscript is usual, but are there any hidden costs? What is their notice period and general Terms of Business? What services will they provide as an agent? Will they give you detailed ongoing editorial support or offer only broad advice and expect you to know how to self-edit? Some agents are great salesmen and good negotiators but not so hands on editorially; some are strong in both areas. If your manuscript requires more editorial input than they are able to provide then it's your responsibility to bring it up to a publishable standard. Some agents will split the costs with the author for any external editorial input but this is rare.

Avoid agents who charge a fee upfront. While it's not against the law to be an agent and charge for editorial input – after all, they will receive ongoing payment in their commission further down the line – it's an AAA guideline. In essence they should be making money for you.

US Insight

Some agency agreements will cover any and all projects that you have. Others will list the specific book you are currently working on with them, with an extension clause that will continue to the next book unless you terminate the contract. Be aware that once an agent sells your book, they are the agent for that book in perpetuity, which will include new editions or subsidiary rights to the book – even years later. This is why it is imperative that you never work with an agent on a handshake agreement. Many American agents did still work on 'gentlemen's handshakes' until about a decade ago, but now, written agreements have become the norm. You need a signed and executed agency agreement that outlines all the terms and responsibilities.

Read your agency agreement through carefully, but keep in mind that you may not have a great deal of negotiating room. Publishing has its own rules and culture – some of it quite arcane! There are industry standards that will be reflected in an agency agreement – these are often specific to publishing and no other industry. You can get a sense of what is normative, ethical and professional from a little research online. In the US, the AAR (Association of Authors' Representatives) and the Author's Guild are both excellent resources.

Ask how the agent likes their authors to work with them. This is a courtesy question: while you won't be the type of author who calls them out of hours in a constant state of emotional flux, chasing for answers, or being too demanding (they'll most likely find a way to drop you if that's the case) it shows that you're aware of the author/agent mode of conduct.

Find out which publisher(s) they have in mind to approach. They may not have a definitive list for this meeting but they should have an idea once the contract is signed. Discuss how to build on your career: writing articles and blogs; visiting schools (if you're a children's writer); attending festivals; getting an idea of which awards your book might be suitable for. You'll also want to brainstorm book two and so on.

Think about what you're able to deliver in terms of your writing schedule. It may be that your work or family commitments will only allow one book every two years; or you know you're able to deliver two books a year; or you've always had a desire to write historical fiction at some point even though women's commercial is the genre that you're likely to stick to for a number of years. You may not know your intended direction yet but if you have an idea then it's best to express it sooner rather than later.

One of our authors, after a long and successful career in writing for children, decided she wanted to write a life-style memoir. She'd just changed agents and didn't know if the new agent handled both, but a quick google search confirmed that she did. If her agent hadn't been equipped to do both she might have made an exception, especially if children's was to remain the dominant genre. But if she had decided to focus solely on non-fiction for the next number of years then she might have had to change agents again.

What if you're not signed up?

Your meeting with the agent doesn't necessarily mean they'll be offering a contract. They may be interested in your story or you, but have significant revision suggestions. Before they sign you up they may want to know you can deliver a manuscript that they can sell – and it might take months or years before this happens. The fact that they've invested in you and are in it for the long haul speaks volumes and any reluctance to commit is probably less about them hedging their bets and more about managing expectations on both sides.

The agent may suggest a different direction for you to go in, especially if they think you have promise but this isn't the right book to launch you. This can feel frustrating, especially after all your hard work, but a weak first book can damage your writing career while an exceptional one can smooth your path for many years to come. Once you've made a name for yourself this first book may end up coming out as book three or four.

If you've not signed a contract you are free to go elsewhere – but if the agent continues to work editorially with you it's only fair to keep them informed of any developments. They will undoubtedly be hoping that their input thus far will curry good favour and loyalty. If you like what you see and you can imagine them facing down a line of publishers; if you think they will stand by your side when the going gets tough, then you've probably found a great match and it's worth keeping the relationship ticking over even if they're not ready to sign you up yet.

US Insight

It's important at this stage to make sure that you are on the same editorial page with any prospective agent. If an agent asks for substantial and transformative changes to your manuscript, really examine your feelings about this and be certain that you are comfortable doing what is requested – particularly if there's no guaranteed offer of representation on the table. The agent should presumably have experience in the kind of book you are writing and this editorial and market knowledge is valuable.

You'll want to think about your ability to execute the requested revisions, and you might not be able to decide that on the spot during the meeting. It is always acceptable to tell an agent that you need to digest things before you start revising. The most important thing is that you trust what you are hearing, and trust the messenger. Although it's possible an agent will do some editorial work with you and still bow out of representing you, you need to feel that your work and effort is leading in a positive direction.

If the agent is interested in you and your work, but the book in hand isn't right for some reason, be open to starting a new project for this agent. You can always keep shopping the one you have while working on something fresh for that particular agent, but if your current project doesn't land with someone, you will already be working towards something solid down the line.

Next, you'll need to deliver something that the agent is excited and confident to submit and this may take some time. Meanwhile, avoid sending lots of queries and piecemeal chapters along the way unless they have specifically asked for them. If it's a new novel that they've requested then produce a rough synopsis and first chapter to ensure you're on the right track. They'll want to know you can deliver the full story, so get on with writing but perhaps offer to send the first 50 pages when they're complete.

Though it might be tempting to use your interested agent as a sounding board, do avoid sending several ideas and opening chapters or even the full manuscript of each one: this will be daunting and time consuming. Be confident enough to present your best idea but have a back-up. If you're really unsure and believe all seven are fantastic, perhaps come to a literary consultancy to preserve your relationship with the agent: they may even be relieved to have a third pair of hands to brainstorm options. We often work in tandem with the agent to enable an author to produce the best work to launch their career.

If you take their suggestions but go elsewhere anyway – perhaps you didn't get a good feeling for the match – then that's your prerogative. But be aware of etiquette: always thank an agent for their time and be clear about how things have been left. Tact and diplomacy go a long way in publishing and you never know when a passing relationship will come back around in a helpful way.

Getting an offer

An agent's role is to get the best deal for you, be it in monetary terms OR where the fit has the most potential. Your agent may urge you to go with a publisher who offers less money but where you have a rapport with the editor, or their marketing plans are innovative, foreign rights reputation impressive and so on.

US Insight

The agent should always be working in your best interests. This can give rise to occasional tensions. If, for example, you get two offers, one slightly lower but from a smaller and more boutique house, there may be very strong reasons to take that offer over the higher one. It is generally going to be in the agent's best interest to push for you to

---

accept the highest offer; after all, that will be how they earn the highest possible commission. But a good agent will talk you through all aspects of every offer, and if possible, arrange for you to meet with all the publishers so that you can figure out what feels right. You may want to work with a particular editor, or with a particular imprint. A thoughtful agent will guide you through the process, putting you first.

Your book may have such a high concept and be so beautifully written that your agent thinks it has the potential to go to auction. When this happens your agent will submit to some choice publishers with a date for a response. The publisher who offers the best all round deal (they won't know who they're up against) gets the book: this is not the time to have a rethink and go for a publisher who offers less because you like them more. If the agent sets up the auction well and it creates an industry buzz then it can bring in high advances – money that the publisher gives you in exchange for the licence to publish your book (you always retain the copyright). However, the flip side is if no publisher makes an offer or the money is less than it might have been had the agent submitted exclusively or with less fanfare.

If a publisher/s is interested they will most likely want to meet you. The publisher may have already made their offer or is yet to do so. Either way it's all proving positive, and a wonderful position to be in after all your hard work. Similarly to the agent meeting, they'll want to know you share a vision for your book and that you are open to revision if need be. You may brainstorm editorial changes, the title, book positioning; they'll take you through the publishing schedule and potential marketing plans. It will also be a chance to talk about your career, including new ideas (especially if the deal is for two books) and they may even want to see a synopsis and sample chapter for the next one.

If the interested party is an editor they may need to take your book to the weekly acquisitions meeting and make a case for why the publisher should make an offer. We've known many books to get to this stage only for the passionate editor to be denied by sales or marketing. It's a crushing blow, but the editor loved your book enough to champion it, which is some consolation.

However, if the editor or publisher has the go-ahead they will work out a projection of unit cost per book and how many copies they think will sell in hardback, paperback and trade paperback; along with many other factors such as marketing spend. It's a bit of a guessing game and there are no guarantees; until a book is published no one quite knows how well it will sell. But the offer will be based on this algorithm and the publisher's vision and intent.

On receiving their offer your agent may negotiate for a higher advance; an escalating royalty rate if your book sells over a certain amount of copies; a higher percentage on certain rights and so forth. This process may frazzle your nerves but as with any negotiation it usually comes down to what feels fair and achievable for both parties.

US Insight

Your publishing contract will have delivery dates and out-side publishing dates in it, but there is another contract date you should ask your agent to try and negotiate. This is an editing window date. It can be hard to get into a contract, but is worth asking for. This is a clause that says that once you have turned in your complete manuscript, you must hear something from the editor within a given

---

time period. The specifics may vary from publishing house to house, and from agent to agent, but 90 days is average. This doesn't necessarily mean that you will receive edits in that time, but that your editor must at least read your manuscript and give you some early response to it.

If there is more than one offer on the table it could turn into a bidding war which should clear the way to make an informed decision. You may end up going with a publisher who offers less but the editor is incisive and you like working with them. Or there's an indie publisher in the running with a more exciting marketing plan and a track record in their books winning awards. Perhaps one of the big four wants your book as a lead title and entices you with a fantastic advance and it's all bells and whistles. We've known publishers to send a wooing hamper of items that appeared in the book; present the author with a miniature fairy book alongside cupcakes based on the characters; or set up a crime scene with the book cordoned off outside the publisher's entrance. It can be flattering and fun and your agent will be there guiding you.

Money matters

Putting the dazzle to one side, bear in mind that a large advance is ideally recouped in sales after the publisher's costs. If your book does not 'earn out' or recoup this money (quite common) the publisher will see it as a loss. This could make things difficult down the line if they're looking to make their list more efficient and deciding which titles to remainder (revert the rights back to the author which frees you up to go elsewhere). Or it may not: all publishers are aware of the profit and loss potential of a book and it's not always down to money. If you're a debut writer who hasn't earned out on book one or two they may see you as a long term investment that will eventually reap rewards when it comes to book three and so on.

As a writer you will have been working for no pay so far, so an idea of when you might receive your monies is all-important. If you accept the publisher's offer the advance is usually paid in thirds: one third on signature of the contract, one third on delivery of the manuscript and a third on publication. We would advise against spending every penny before delivering the manuscript: in rare cases the author may have to pay back the advance if the manuscript is substantially different to what the publisher was expecting. If it was bought on a proposal, perhaps the finished manuscript isn't up to standard or the genre/focus has changed. Remember you need to keep to the contracted word length and deliver the manuscript on time as these things can mess with the publishing schedule.

If there's been a breakdown in the relationship this can go both ways. If the publisher folds there will be T&Cs so double check these; you may be entitled to keep the advance. But if you're at fault for whatever reason you might well need to pay it back. However, most publishers will have a degree of flexibility and be understanding – especially if life gets in the way of the delivery date, for instance – and won't demand repayment. But it will be down to their discretion, so be considerate and professional and take your obligations seriously.

Delivering the manuscript

Once you have your contract you'll be kept busy delivering book one and seeing it through the publishing process whilst also working on book two (even if the contract is for one book only). Working to contract is a different experience to writing a book in your own time, pre-agent/publisher. There are high expectations and pressures and you'll want to dedicate yourself to it as a career for a number of years, even if it's alongside your day job. We often ask our authors if they're ready for this level of commitment. If they're unsure then we advise them to hold off submitting or acquiring an agent or publisher. You have to feel confident you can deliver what's expected of you.

US Insight

It's important to keep your agent informed of your progress, and if you are hitting any obstacles along the way – personal or professional. If something is going on in your life that is going to affect your ability to meet a deadline, or manage something the publisher is requesting, let the agent know as soon as you possibly can so that they can navigate this with the publisher on your behalf. This is why trust and a strong working relationship is so crucial. Things happen in life that we cannot control and your agent should have your back.

The agent will also run interference between you and your editor if you encounter some editorial issue or problem with your book. No editorial issue should be insurmountable, even if it feels that way at the time. Your agent will try to find a productive solution, and be your buffer if things get tense. Sometimes, they will need to find a workable middle ground, so be open-minded should editing conflicts arise. Look to your agent to weigh in and help!

It's also worth cultivating a strong and collegial relationship with the agent's assistant. Regardless of how hands-on
an agent is, you will be communicating through their assistant at least some of the time. Just as the agent is a gatekeeper
for the publisher, the agent's assistant is the gatekeeper to
the agent. These assistants are generally run off their feet, so
exercise tact and patience. I've seen more than one assistant
go on to become a full agent representing authors, or an
acquiring editor at a big publisher. Take the time to get
to know that assistant and build a good relationship with
them. It will benefit you in the long and short term.

Switching agents

Unfortunately, having an agent doesn't automatically lead to a
deal. Your agent may not have the right contacts – you won't
know this for sure but you'll have an idea when you view
their list of publishers and begin to see the responses. Maybe
they were full of enthusiasm when they first took you on but
have lost some of their energy and passion along the way and
are no longer the best champion for you or the book. There
could be a more practical reason – perhaps the agent's stepping back, or near retirement; or you've switched into a genre
that the agent doesn't represent. Or perhaps they are fantastic,
with a long list of successes, but no publisher is biting because
the manuscript is too experimental or it's the wrong time for
the market. If it's this latter reason then it may be prudent to
hold off switching.

Whatever the reason, if you feel it's time for a change and/
or the relationship has broken down then there's an etiquette
to the separation. We usually advise that you talk things through
with the agent first, and meet if possible to check that you

are both doing everything possible to advance your career. You may just need reassurance that the agent remains committed to you and you might come away feeling enthused again.

If after the meeting you're still certain that you need to part company then you should write and give notice. It can be phrased respectfully and doesn't need to be awkward or acrimonious; they may already have an idea that change is afoot. If you've been published, bear in mind that they will keep receiving royalties for any book they've represented and sold on your behalf. Even if you've not been published you'll likely need to produce something new for your next agent to sell.

You may have a new agent lined up or not; there are two schools of thought on this. Some prefer you to make a clean break before approaching them and some are open to a confidential chat before you decide to leave your existing agent. Explain your concerns with the current situation – perhaps your book has been submitted to 27 publishers. Of course, the new agent may not be able to do anything additional and advise that you remain with your reputable agent. But if they can see areas for change or envisage a new approach, or you're an author they've long admired, they may express keen interest. You won't really know what the agent's preference or mode of conduct is and it's a case of dipping your toe or getting independent advice.

Either way, don't do anything hasty. We passed one author through to a highly respected agent who's known for getting great deals. She is also known for being rather intimidating but we felt the author would grow into her as her career progressed. After the first few books were sold the author still felt her agent was unapproachable and was inclined to switch. We had a long talk and she stuck it out, though we were poised to help as she's lovely and talented; and the agent is, after all, working *for* the author. Years down the line their partnership has become more balanced as the author has needed less hand-holding and her career is steady.

What may at first seem impossible for a fledgling author can turn out to be more than OK, especially if the deals are coming in.

However, if no deals are forthcoming, your relationship has soured, or it's amicable but stale, then switching can be beneficial and give your writing and self-esteem a boost. Whatever the reason, make sure you get this in writing and that the break is official.

US Insight

If you are making a break with an agent, always ask for a full copy of your file as part of your 'divorce' agreement. Your new agent may need to see all of it in order for them to work effectively on your behalf. Even though your new agent didn't represent your previous work(s), they usually undertake the management of any new issues that crop up with them, even though they will not receive commission. This is something that your new agent can communicate with your previous agent on as things move forward. Your former agent will most likely be comfortable with this, and they should be professional in their stewardship of the books you had with them, as they will still be receiving commissions on anything they sold on your behalf.

The publishing process

One of our authors, Katherine Langrish, once described her agent as *her* angel – someone who looks after *her* interests – and her editor as the *book's* guardian angel: someone who looks after the publishing house first, and the author second. We think that sums it up rather beautifully.

Your agent has secured your deal, you've delivered your manuscript, and your editor will be your main point of contact from now on, although your agent will remain in the wings to handle anything that needs liaising over. In terms of preparing your manuscript for publication you'll be working closely with your editor and the publisher.

The book will go into the publishing wheel: a jacket is designed, an Advance Information sheet will be put together to give out to booksellers displaying jacket, blurb and buying information including the publication date. There may be point of sale material (posters etc.) for booksellers; advertising campaigns; author tours; articles; and interviews set up – especially if it's a lead title. Readying a book for publication can happen swiftly if events demand it (a celebrity dies, or world events take a turn, for instance) but the usual length of time is about a year.

US Insight

When the process is underway, it is easy for the publisher to forget to keep the agent in the loop. And of course, your agent may not need to be copied into every single editorial back-and-forth or included in every conversation: once you are well and truly involved in the publishing process, there will be many emails from many people and departments. Take it upon yourself to keep your agent up to date on anything important.

Your manuscript will be structurally edited by your editor and line edited (page by page mark ups) but hopefully you will have delivered a relatively clean manuscript and not much revision will be required. It will then be copyedited and you'll receive a list of queries and amendments to accept or decline. A copyeditor's job is complex: they keep a track of your characters and watch for consistency of names, appearance and continuity; they also fact-check. It's your job to ensure that all the facts are correct, but if a date in your historical novel jars, for instance, the copyeditor may flag it up as something that needs double-checking. Their main job is to edit for syntax and flow and they will also have an in-house style guide to follow.

Then it's the proofreading stage. You will be sent a type-set proof to check alongside your editor and it may even get proofed again by the publisher. It's really too late to change your mind about something major, rearrange the structure in any way or delete or add to passages. You are mainly checking for typographical errors and you should only make a sugges-tion for a change if it's essential. Anything beyond 10 to 15 per cent of changes you may need to pay for! Around this time your publisher may send out uncorrected bound proofs to sub-agents for foreign rights sales, and also to reviewers. And by this point you should be giving serious thought to publicity.

Publicity

There is usually only a budget for lead titles, so much of the publicity will come down to you. Social media – Twitter, Face-book and so on – is a great way to garner interest and build a following. Make sure you have a website as well – Wordpress is easy to use and looks professional. Visit your local bookshop(s), as most like to support authors in their area; the same applies to local radio and newspapers. Contact any organization related to your subject matter or yourself to spread the word, and con-sider approaching specialist magazines in case they wish to do an interview. It's useful to have a promotional business card that you can physically hand out or email over – with the jacket cover, blurb and information on how to contact you or the publisher. This is also cheaper than sending a copy of the book.

US Insight

Even with a large publisher, much of the responsibility for marketing and publicity will still land on the author. And in the US, the writer's platform is king. If you already have a big platform, then you will be much more likely to get an agent's attention, and your agent will be more likely to interest a publisher. Before you even submit, try to build up your following in any way you can. Blog, connect to writers' groups, and join organizations. Use every connection available to you to increase your profile. And that always means social media.

You will need to get comfortable with whatever platform you are working with. It isn't useful for an author to have an outdated blog, or a Facebook page with posts that are more than a few weeks old. And Twitter only really works if you can master the form. Follow lots of authors in your category and hopefully they will start following you in turn. Tweet in a way which is both relevant and interesting, so people will retweet you.

Know your readership, and what type of social media platform they're most likely to use and relate to. For example, if you are writing middle grade fiction your actual readers are too young to be on Facebook. It might a good way for you to connect to their parents and teachers, however, so create posts that are intended for them, rather than for the readers themselves. To reach middle grade readers, Instagram might be a better fit. Here, writers and readers create and build their audiences through 'bookstagram' accounts, where authors can add images and illustrations to pull in their audience. Advertising is starting to gain some traction on Instagram as well, and it's worth exploring if it is an effective advertising platform for your book.

Customize your posts and profile to each platform. There is no one-size-fits-all, so adapt each format to work for you. It is important to stay current, and post frequently – even short posts or photos keep your social media profile updated and active. Keep your output positive and pertinent to your audience. Engage with your readers. They want to know about you as well as your books, so share as much as is appropriate and comfortable for you. (That said, don't be afraid to maintain your privacy. Your online persona should relate to your publishing career whilst feeling balanced and sane for you!) Social media trends – what's in and what isn't – shift rapidly so remember to remain informed and move with the times.

It's a good idea to liaise with the marketing and publicity department in case they can forward any copies of your books or help out in any way. If you're doing a talk at a writer's festival or visiting a school – both of which you should be paid to do by the organizing parties – publicity can arrange for copies to be sent in advance. You may have an innovative idea to promote your book (again, liaise with publicity). For instance, one author who'd written a mountain climbing thriller left a wheelbarrow of books at the bottom of a mountain for climbers to take home with them. At the end of the day all the copies had been taken. If you're giving books away, why not slip a card inside requesting that anyone who reads it writes a review on Amazon? Urging readers to leave a review is all-important, particularly for such an influential behemoth as Amazon where any book that hits a certain amount of five stars alerts their promotional algorithm.

US Insight

We talk a great deal about 'discoverability' in publishing – the way that readers find out about a new author, or a new book from an established author. With the disappearance of many independent bookstores in the US and the rise of on-line book buying, discoverability is trickier than ever to achieve. Fewer people are able or likely to wander into a neighborhood bookstore and simply browse, picking up something that looks interesting that they might not have known about otherwise. Brainstorm ways to build word-of-mouth for your book. From friends to your college alumni magazine, there is no avenue too small to pursue when trying to spread a buzz!

The book launch and reviews

Every author should celebrate their publication day with a book launch. It's a rite of passage that is great to acknowledge, not only for you but for your friends and family. However, book launches hosted and paid for by the publisher tend to be for big-profile authors only, especially if it's likely to create media attention and reviews. If you end up organizing your own the publisher may or may not put some money towards it. It doesn't have to be expensive – it can be in a local bar or bookshop, providing your own drinks and food – and the publicist, editor and agent may still attend. Even for lead title authors this is often the preferred route.

If yours is a lead title, prepare for (but don't expect) a show-stopping bonanza of a themed party to reflect your book. You never know, your publisher might sweep you off your feet! They may also have organized an author tour with radio, press, and TV interviews which will tie in with your publication date.

For book reviews, publicity will send out copies to the appropriate press. If you receive wonderful quote(s) these may go on the front cover or inside flaps. If you get a bad review, while the immediate and understandable response is to chuck it in the bin, you might decide to fish it out again and put it to good use. One author we know was lucky enough to have a debut title that went into the top ten bestselling charts, which was great, of course. However, a couple of reviews expressed disappointment in the pace, particularly in the mid-section. For book two he was determined not to have a repeat of this and it ended up being a much stronger book as a result.

Book sales and performance

Your publication day is hugely exciting and we recommend marking it by touring bookshops and getting a friend to promote you shamelessly. Draw up a list of any bookshops that don't have it on their shelves or system, and pass this on to sales in case it's useful. However, don't harangue the publisher: chain bookstores have a central buying office and they may have decided for whatever reason not to buy your book, despite the publisher pushing it at the time. An independent bookshop can make that decision, however, and they may like the sound of your book and order it in. They may ask you to sign copies or to hold a book signing event. Advertising this in advance is important as you want people to turn up! But do bring some friends or family as it can be daunting on your own. And don't forget to let publicity know.

What makes a bestseller?

In the UK there are about 150,000–200,000 new and revised books published each year in physical and electronic formats.

Sales are charted by Nielsen Bookscan and by electronic point of sale (EPoS) and the size of these may depend on when your book is published. If it's during a time when not many are being released then it could soar into the top lists with less competition. If it's a traditionally busy period such as Christmas or Mother's Day, or summer reads, and your book is themed accordingly then it may have a better chance than others – but possibly less of a shelf life once that period is over. Sales vary according to season, which genre is in vogue, and various other factors.

What is considered a healthy performance also varies dramatically. There are numerous considerations: the ratio of number of copies sold in hardback versus trade paperback, mass market paperback and e-books; and whether you hit a particular bestseller list. There's the size of the print run versus returns and the net (actual) number of copies sold, which you'll see in your royalty statement. Expectations will differ depending on author and publisher.

Smaller print runs are the norm because they're less risky. For instance, a hardback print run for a non-fiction title may only be 5,000 copies and a mass market paperback may be between 10,000 and 40,000, but a celebrity or proven bestseller writer will have much larger print runs. It may be less or more and these will be decided by your publisher in accordance with the advance offered in the first place.

It's often a bit of a punt and it's best not to get too hung up on it. If the accounting more or less evens out the publisher will be pleased; if it surpasses expectation they'll be delighted; and if it sells poorly it may not matter: hopefully, they're in it for the long term. A bookseller/central buyer might be less forgiving: they will refer to sales for book one when considering stocking book two, but again you can't really control or predict this. However, when you're tirelessly promoting your book it's worth remembering that every sale helps.

Many factors can influence a book's performance. Word of mouth is one of the most effective tools, but positive reviews, '3 for 2' Waterstones promotions, awards and prizes, and a recommendation from a high-profile book club such as Richard & Judy, can all catapult your book into the stars. Many of these factors are out of your control. But if you've written the best book you can and chosen your agent and publisher wisely you'll have a great head start.

And finally...

You're hopefully well on your way to becoming a professional writer; perhaps a bestseller-in-the-making, a published writer looking to relaunch, or an editor now equipped to give a writer the strongest start. By learning to listen to your instincts and brainstorm solutions that marry both your creative and critical sides, your writing should evolve into something powerful and magical. Keep your vision in mind, rewrite the best book you possibly can, and the rest should follow.

If you're a writer yet to realize your dreams, remember that success isn't always about getting published. If you're finding this a pressure – perhaps with a book that doesn't seem to be going anywhere – take some time out to remind yourself why you write and rediscover the joy of it. If you're following your inspiration, and writing the book that you would want to read then not only is this a reward in itself but it should naturally take you in exciting directions.

We hope this book will contribute in some way to your writer's journey, inspire you to succeed, and help you navigate publication and beyond. We'd love to hear your stories - you can find us here: www.cornerstones.co.uk – check out our beach, office dog and come and write with us!

Bibliography

Banks, Iain M. *Use of Weapons* (Macdonald & Co, 1990)

Brontë, Emily *Wuthering Heights* (first published 1884)

Brown, Dan *The Da Vinci Code* (Bantam Press, 2003)

Child, Lee *Killing Floor* (Bantam Books, 1998)

Christie, Agatha *Murder on the Orient Express* (first published 1934)

Collins, Suzanne *The Hunger Games* (Scholastic, 2008)

Donoghue, Emma *Room* (Picador, 2011)

Faber, Michel *The Crimson Petal and the White* (Canongate Books, 2002)

Fielding, Helen *Bridget Jones's Diary* (Picador, 1996)

Fitzgerald, F. Scott *The Great Gatsby* (first published 1925)

Flynn, Gillian *Gone Girl* (Hachette UK, 2012)

Grant, Michael *Gone* (HarperCollins Books, 2008)

Hawkins, Paula *The Girl on the Train* (Doubleday, 2015)

Hoban, Russell *Riddley Walker* (Jonathan Cape, 1980)

Irving, John *A Prayer for Owen Meany* (William Morrow and Company, 1989)

King, Stephen *Misery* (Viking Press, 1987)

King, Stephen *The Stand* (Anchor Books, 1978)

Mantel, Hilary *Wolf Hall* (Fourth Estate, 2009)

Mitchell, David *Cloud Atlas* (Sceptre, 2004)

Nabokov, Vladimir *Lolita* (first published 1955)

Ness, Patrick *The Knife of Never Letting Go* (Walker Books, 2008)

Nicholls, David *One Day* (HarperCollins, 2009)

Nicholls, David *Us* (HarperCollins, 2014)

Noon, Jeff *Vurt* (Ringpull Press, 1993)

Palahniuk, Chuck *Fight Club* (Norton and Company, 1996)

Power, Kevin *The Yellow Birds* (Sceptre, 2012)

Pullman, Philip *His Dark Materials* trilogy (Scholastic, 1995)

Townsend, Sue *The Secret Diary of Adrian Mole, Aged 13 3/4* (Methuen, 1982)

Twain, Mark *Adventures of Huckleberry Finn* (first published 1885)

Watson, S.J. *Before I Go To Sleep* (Doubleday, 2011)

Index

Cornerstones
Literary
Consultancy

'Cornerstones' wealth of experience was invaluable and
my trust in their guidance has paid off. Helen quickly
matched me with a top agent and I'm now working on
book two. Thank you Cornerstones!'
Gay Marris

'Cornerstones struck a perfect balance between
encouragement and detailed criticism. Their help was
invaluable.'
**Jake Woodhouse, After the Silence,
Sunday Times Bestseller**

Structural editing, copyediting and proofreading

Scouts for leading literary agents

Listed by The Society of Authors

Cornerstones
+44 (0) 1308 897374
www.cornerstones.co.uk
www.cornerstonesUS.com